Jose Maria Sison:
At Home in the World

Portrait of a Revolutionary

The well-purposed exile continues
To fight for his motherland
Against those who banished him,
The unwelcomed exploiters of his people,
And is certain that he is at home
In his own country and the world.

— FROM **SOMETIMES, THE HEART YEARNS FOR MANGOES**
BY JOSE MARIA SISON

Jose Maria Sison:
At Home in the World

Portrait of a Revolutionary

Conversations with

Ninotchka Rosca

Open Hand Publishing, LLC
Greensboro, North Carolina
www.openhand.com

ISBN 0-940880-70-9 (hardcover); ISBN 0-940880-72-5 (paperback)

Open Hand Publishing, LLC
P.O. Box 20207
Greensboro, NC 27420
336-292-8585
e-mail: info@openhand.com
www.openhand.com

Book and Cover Design: The Roberts Group

Library of Congress Cataloging-in-Publication Data

Sison, Jose Maria, 1939-
Jose Maria Sison : at home in the world : portrait of a revolutionary / conversations with Ninotchka Rosca.--1st. ed.
p. cm.
Includes index.
ISBN 0-940880-70-9 (hardcover) -- ISBN 0-940880-72-5 (pbk.)
1. Philippines--Politics and government--1973-1086. 2. Philippines--Politics and government--1986- 3. Communism--Philippines--History. 4. Sison, Jose Maria, 1939---Interviews. 5. Communists--Philippines--Interviews. I. Rosca, Ninotchka. II. Title.

DS686.5.S4386 2004
959.904'6'092--dc22 2004049200

FIRST EDITION 2004
Printed in USA

CONTENTS

Publisher's Note vi

Preface of the Authors ix

Introduction: A Biographical Sketch 1

Chapter One
A Dangerous Existence 39
Poem: The Guerrilla Is Like A Poet 73

Chapter Two
Against One Regime After Another 75
Poem: The Bladed Poem 103

Chapter Three
Rectification and Rebuilding 105
Poem: The Forest Is Still Enchanted 141

Chapter Four
The Global Situation and Revolutionary Internationalism 143
Poem: The Giant Oak 179

Chapter Five
Trends and Prospects 181
Poem: Sometimes, the Heart Yearns for Mangoes 215

Postscript: Revolution Versus Terrorism 217

Appendix One
Sympathy for the Victims and Condemnation of Terrorism 243

Appendix Two
The Sison Way 247

Index 253

PUBLISHER'S NOTE

It is our mission to publish books that promote positive social change as well as respect and understanding among all people. This effort has become all the more important in the post 9-11 period. In this context we are proud to present *Jose Maria Sison: At Home in the World—Portrait of a Revolutionary*, one of the first two books in our new anti-imperialism series.

Our other new book, *Imperial Washington*, is actually a reprint of the 1922 book by the first United States Senator from the state of South Dakota, Richard F. Pettigrew. Pettigrew's frontier life and principled view opposing the new course of empire which the United States had embarked upon (a view shared by the beloved Mark Twain) make it clear that anti-imperialism is as "American as apple pie".

By contrast the book in your hands is as contemporary as today's headlines. *Jose Maria Sison: At Home in the World—Portrait of a Revolutionary* is an impressive collaboration between Professor Sison, arguably the most important Filipino revolutionary leader of the twentieth century and himself an award-winning poet, and Ninotchka Rosca, an internationally acclaimed journalist and novelist who has won numerous awards, including the American Book Award.

In May 2001, when I signed the contract to do this book with Ms. Rosca and Professor Sison, I was quite excited for Open Hand Publishing, LLC as well as our readers. Open Hand would have the opportunity to present a thought-provoking political biography/autobiography. The U.S. reader, in particular, would get a rare glimpse into the life, the motivation and the thinking of a revolutionary leader of a significant national liberation struggle aimed at achieving freedom from the "embrace" of our own United States government.

With the events of September 11th, several months later, and especially the Bush Administration's declaration, in its aftermath, of a state of perpetual war abroad and dramatic developments toward martial law at home, a book which presents the real flesh and blood "other side" is all the more timely and important.

This situation was underscored further, on August 9, 2002 when the U.S. State Department designated the Communist Party of the Philippines (CPP) and the New People's Army (NPA) as "foreign terrorist organizations"; and a few days later, on August 12th, the U.S. Treasury Department ordered the freezing of the assets of the CPP and NPA as well as those of Jose Maria Sison. The very next day, the Dutch government issued the so-called Sanction Regulation Against Terrorism 2002 III, freezing the joint bank account of Professor Sison and his wife Julie de Lima. Meanwhile, Philippine President Gloria Macapagal-Arroyo, in coordination with the U.S. government, designated these same forces as "terrorist", despite the fact that Professor Sison has no charges pending against him of any kind in his homeland and the fact that the terrorism charge has no legal basis or standing in the Philippines at all.

The views of Jose Maria Sison on terrorism in general and on the horrific events of September 11, 2001, in particular, are clearly outlined in his September 18, 2001 Press Statement issued only one week after the September 11th events and printed in the back of this volume as Appendix A.

The tremendous affection which most Filipinos continue to have for "Joma" Sison is reflected in the fact that even leading members of the Philippine government have refused to join President Macapagal-Arroyo and the Bush Administration in condemning Jose Maria Sison as a terrorist. Philippine Vice President Teofisto Guingona has staunchly insisted, despite their great political differences, that Mr. Sison is a true Filipino patriot. Senate Majority Leader, Loren Legarda, arguably the most popular woman politician in the Philippines, has stated, "...no one can doubt the integrity of their patriotism or the depth of their commitment to help bring about a more just and more human society. I look to the day Joma and the others can finally come home to our collective embrace." The compelling magazine article, "The Sison Way", written by Ms. Rosca as she was working on this book, provides insight into why even his Filipino adversaries respect and admire Jose Maria Sison. It is presented as Appendix B at the end of this volume.

The book is structured so as to take advantage of the literary strengths of the authors. Ninotchka Rosca provides a dramatic biographical sketch of Mr. Sison to open the book. Photos then lead to the first of five chapters and a postscript each of which contains about forty questions from Ms. Rosca as she probes the thinking of Jose Maria Sison about his life and times. Each chapter is preceded by photos and is followed by a poem written by Mr. Sison, an award-winning poet. The photos and poetry hopefully add a profoundly different aesthetic dimension to the topic covered in the chapter. We hope that the way that the book is structured helps the reader to put a human face to this veteran revolutionary leader.

The horrific events of September 11th and their aftermath have no doubt prolonged the process of producing this book. For our part, Open Hand's Board of Directors revisited the question of whether to go forward with the project in the face of the curtailment of civil liberties in the USA and the "terrorist" designation of Jose Maria Sison abroad. Of course, except for this publisher's note, the opinions expressed herein are those of the authors. Nevertheless, we at Open Hand Publishing, LLC concluded that the issue of "free speech", which involves the need for the people to be armed with knowledge, makes this book even more significant for the future of humanity than the original conception. We have attempted to accurately present the authors' ideas.

Finally, it is our hope that this book presents authentic information with which the reader can make an intelligent determination about whether Jose Maria Sison is the "terrorist" that the Bush Administration has designated or the "liberation fighter" that the authors clearly believe him to be.

RICHARD A. KORITZ
Open Hand Publishing, LLC
April 2004

PREFACE OF THE AUTHORS

We, interviewee and interviewer, started work on this book in June 2001 and wished to put it out on time before May 1, 2002. But other kinds of work kept pressing on us and intervening.

The delay in finishing the book has been beneficial. The time gained allowed us to enrich the book, with questions and answers pertaining to the "terrorist" listing initiated by the US and carried on further by the Dutch government and the European Council against the subject of this book.

We have been able to connect the book with the full implications and consequences of the bankrupt "free market" globalization, the 9/11 events and the crisis of the US and world capitalist system. We are glad to relate the life story and role of the interviewee to a challenging world of sharpening crisis, growing fascism, imperialist wars of aggression, popular protests and revolutionary resistance.

We are most thankful to Richard Koritz of Open Hand Publishing LLC, for giving important suggestions, for being so patient with us and allowing us to go beyond one deadline after another. We admire his wisdom and courage in having this book published despite the threats posed by the USA PATRIOT Act and the atmosphere generated by the factors of fascism and war.

We thank Julie de Lima-Sison, Ruth de Leon and other friends who helped in critiquing, editing and proofreading the manuscript. We are especially indebted to Ms. De Lima-Sison for collecting, selecting and arranging the photographs and maps. We also feel indebted to all friends who were in our company during periods of work and assisted us in so many ways. The interviewer is particularly grateful to her New York friends whose support extended even to the level of the day's quiet needs, a meal or two during times of work on the manuscript.

We are confident that this book will be informative, edifying and enjoyable to readers in various parts of the world. This book is not simply about the struggle of the interviewee, his organizations or his people. It is about the struggle of the proletariat and oppressed peoples and nations for national liberation and socialism against imperialism and all reaction.

JOSE MARIA SISON
NINOTCHKA ROSCA
December 1, 2003

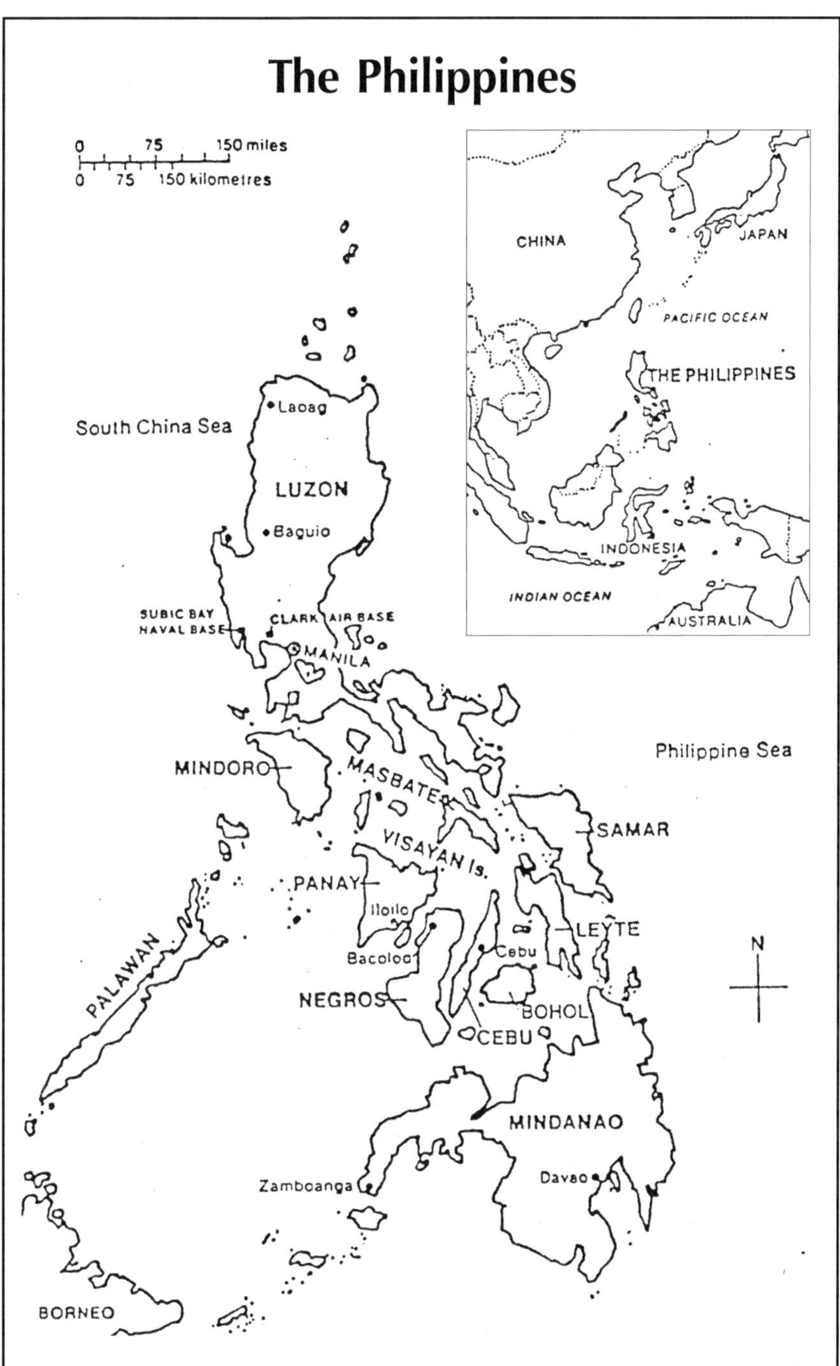

The Philippines
0 75 150 miles
0 75 150 kilometres
CHINA
JAPAN
PACIFIC OCEAN
THE PHILIPPINES
INDONESIA
INDIAN OCEAN
AUSTRALIA
South China Sea
Laoag
LUZON
Baguio
SUBIC BAY
NAVAL BASE
CLARK AIR BASE
MANILA
Philippine Sea
MINDORO
MASBATE
SAMAR
VISAYAN Is.
PANAY
Iloilo
LEYTE
Bacolod
Cebu
N
PALAWAN
NEGROS
BOHOL
CEBU
MINDANAO
Zamboanga
Davao
BORNEO

Drawing depicts US troops in Samar killing Filipinos over ten years old in obedience to the order of US general Jacob Smith. (US Library of Congress archives)

Filipinos massacred by US troops during the Filipino-American war that started on February 4, 1899. (US Library of Congress archives)

INTRODUCTION: A BIOGRAPHICAL SKETCH

A Revolutionary Is Not A Terrorist

Fourteen points sum up the life of Jose Maria Sison in his complaint to the European Court of Justice demanding the removal of his name from the list of terrorists issued by the Council of the European Union. But no phrase in the 34-paged document indicates who or what Professor Sison is more than the demand that the Council of the European Union and Commission of the European Communities not only remove his name and person from the list but also pay him damages.

It is rare for people from poor and powerless countries to take on powerful governments. To the delighted exclamation of Filipinos the world over, Jose Maria Sison is proving to be the exception. The demand for damages is a valuation of one's honor and reputation. A revolutionary is not a terrorist.

At the crux of this court action lies a deceptive maneuver by the Philippine government to coerce the revolutionary National Democratic Front to accept a virtual surrender or risk a direct confrontation with the US. Taking advantage of the United States' need to have allies post-September 11, the Philippine government sought to have its domestic rivals included in the US "war on terrorism." Obviously in accordance with an agreement between Bush and President Gloria Macapagal-Arroyo reached during the latter's state visit to the US in November 2001, US Secretary of State Colin Powell announced on August 9, 2002, shortly after his visit to Manila, the designation of the Communist Party of the Philippines/New Peoples Army a foreign terrorist organization. The US Treasury Department Office of Foreign Assets Control subsequently added Sison, Jose Maria (a.k.a. Liwanag, Armando), together with the CPP/NPA, to its list of

"Specially Designated Nationals and Blocked Persons".

Professor Sison has admitted to having been Amado Guerrero, former CPP chair. But, in his application to the European Court he points out that "the CPP Constitution requires that the Chairman be present in the Philippines in order to lead the central organs and the entire CPP on a daily basis."

Ironically, even as Professor Sison, the CPP and the NPA continue to be classified as "terrorists," the administration of President Macapagal-Arroyo has begun to re-open peace negotiations with the National Democratic Front of the Philippines (NDFP). The latter includes both the CPP and the NPA, and Professor Sison is the chief NDFP political consultant. Should the negotiations go through as planned in February, 2004, Professor Sison will sit at the table with representatives of a government which had lobbied for his inclusion in the "terrorists" list—as he had done many times before; as he did in 2001, when the Philippine government unilaterally "recessed" the peace talks.

The summer of 2001 most likely exemplified the rhythm of existence in Europe for exiled Filipino revolutionaries led by Jose Maria Sison: frenetic activity punctuating days of ennui and quiet study; interaction within and among a severely restricted social circle juxtaposed against a world-spanning political concern.

It began with the founding congress of the International League of Peoples' Struggles (ILPS) the weekend of May 24th. Some 400 men and women from 232 mass organizations from 40 countries descended on the hotel Landgoed in Almen, an amiable Dutch village of foliage-shrouded brick buildings breathing cold in the weak sunlight, where only 200 participants were expected. Despite the disintegration of well-laid registration plans, the ILPS founding congress was a resounding success, auguring well for the political center designed to bring together people engaged in the struggle for national and social liberation.

Not surprising, roughly 28% of the delegates were of Philippine origin, though not all residents of that country and some a generation or even two removed from it. They came, both in the knowledge that, while joining anything Professor Sison led could be disruptive of normal existence, with him there was always something new to learn. The day the first plenary opened at Hansehof Hall in the small city of Zutphen, those who flew 17 hours from Manila, Philippines sat in the lobby like exhausted dark herons, suitcases, bags and backpacks arranged in neat nests about their feet.

Barely two weeks later, Sison and his community were traveling via plane, train, ferry and bus to Oslo, Norway, for the second round of peace talks between the National Democratic Front of the Philippines (NDFP) and the new Philippine government of Gloria Macapagal-Arroyo. The peace talks had gone on for 15 years, through three Philippine presidents. Some 38 folders of documents, each four inches thick, on shelves in the NDFP Utrecht (the Netherlands) office, catalogued the process. The first round that April 2001 had gone off without incident, agreements reached painlessly; it seemed that, with a president and a panel who'd grown up with the revolution's generations, a measure of peace could be achieved with minimum compromise.

But hardly had this round of talks begun when the government panel declared a unilateral recess. The excuse was the death of a notorious former Marcos military torturer, via gunfire from the New People's Army (NPA), the CPP's armed organization.

The respite afforded by the recess of the peace talks was broken by the death of Antonio Zumel, honorary chairperson of the NDFP. Summer was ending in an unbearable mood. Zumel succumbed to a variety of longstanding disorders a few days after his 69th birthday. A former president of the National Press Club of the Philippines, he had gone underground when the late Ferdinand E. Marcos declared martial law in 1972. Nearly 30 years later, his friends, colleagues and comrades honored his life and contributions to the Philippine revolution at a quiet service in the country of his exile. Among those who rose to pay him tribute was Jose Maria Sison, himself a writer and revolutionary, who had been perhaps the most significant influence on Zumel's life. In the middle of a sentence, Sison abruptly stopped, gave an awkward smile and left the podium. A hundred people witnessed this with mixed emotions; Sison was not one known to lose composure or fortitude, no matter the occasion. A subtle adjustment took place, altering people's idea and image of the founding chairman of the Communist Party of the Philippines (CPP).

Jose Maria Sison had set the tenor of political discourse and led the struggle in the archipelago since the age of 20. Belief and trust in him were created by nine years of legal mass struggles (1959-1968), eight years underground (late 1969-1977), nine years in prison (1977-1986), undergoing torture, including eighteen months with one arm and one leg shackled to the frame of a steel bed, and now more than a decade in exile (1987-2001) in a country whose language, to Filipinos, is always only on the verge of comprehension.

To his own peers, he remains the measure of a generation's greatness and the standard by which commitment and service to the people are gauged. To the young, his writings provide a comprehensive view of Philippine history and a viable analysis of the perennial crisis afflicting the country. In common parlance, he taught his people to ask questions, indeed what questions to ask, and gave them explanations as to *why we are the way we are, who's responsible for the way we are, what should we be if we are not to be the way we are and how should we go about becoming different*. For 40 years, the answers have remained steadfast. More importantly, Professor Sison himself has remained steadfast to the vision he helped craft. In a country and nation where there are no absolutes, where a jerry-rigged existence often dictates that one sell today what one held most precious yesterday—from land to women—such constancy is precious.

About Jose Maria Sison

Listed by American political science professor Robert Gorham in *A Bibliographical Dictionary of Marxism (London: Publishing Ltd., 1986)*, as among the most important 210 Marxists since the publication of the 1848 *Communist Manifesto*, Jose Maria Sison has based his leadership on changing the way people look at the world, look at themselves and their relationship to that world. He has done this and does it through his writings, both poetry and political analyses; and through the way his own life has been lived: in the organizing of, and in leading and guiding, every significant Filipino activist group, as well as the entire revolutionary movement itself.

Of his writings, the most influential are *Struggle for National Democracy* (1964), *Philippine Society and Revolution* (1971), *Our Urgent Tasks* (1974), and *Specific Characteristics of Our People's War* (1976), the last three under his *nom de guerre* Amado Guerrero. In the last decade, his ideas comprised the cornerstones of the CPP's Second Great Rectification Movement (1990-1992), as embodied in *Re-affirm Our Basic Principles and Rectify Errors* (published in *Rebolusyon*, 1992 January-March). His poetry, recognized regionally through a Southeast Asian WRITE Award conferred by the King of Thailand, serves both as model and encouragement among young Filipino writers to immerse themselves in Philippine revolutionary literary traditions.

But it's in the thousands and thousands of Filipinos and Filipinas, working collectively in mass organizations which Professor Sison himself characterizes as world-class, and which political observers the world over accept as the strongest and most unique feature of the Philippine revolutionary movement where his legacy lies most tellingly. From the small Student Cultural Association of the University of the Philippines (SCAUP) founded in 1959, to the *Kabataang Makabayan* (KM—Patriotic Youth) founded in 1964, to Bagong Alyansang Makabayan (BAYAN—New Patriotic Alliance) founded in 1985, to the National Democratic Front (NDFP) itself, founded in 1973, each Sison-inspired and motivated organization represents an advance in political thought, strategy and achievement. Every single one played a major role in the political development of the people of the archipelago.

Professor Jose Maria Sison is popularly referred to as Ka Joma (*ka* for *kasama,* comrade), JMS, Joema, Joe, Mahoma, or, if one were a close friend, Marya (Filipino pronunciation of Maria).The joke is that one can tell when a person began his/her involvement in the movement by which moniker he/she uses for Professor Sison. Strangely enough, if one used his formal name, it had to be complete: Jose Maria Sison. Few felt that Jose alone sufficed to identify such a unique individual.

Underground and in the countryside, Joma would be the *propesor* (professor), the peasants linking him to the honorable tradition of *guro* (teacher, from the Sanskit guru). Ironically, in the last decade, Western Europe would also know him by the title professor. By whatever name, however, Ka Joma seemed the most unlikely and yet the likeliest to revive a moribund Communist Party, and ignite a revolution impossible to smother, never mind that four Philippine presidents tried and a fifth is now trying. He seems to embody the Marxist thesis that individuals *become* in accordance with the needs of the times; on the other hand, his life leads one to conclude that how the times unfold also depends on the character of the very individual that responds to those needs.

Jose Maria Sison was born on February 8, 1939, of a clan of landlords in Cabugao, Ilocos Sur, in a region where the only extant Luzon epic, *Biag ti Lam-ang,* about an Ilocano warrior, survived the combined assault of 400 years of Spanish colonialism and Christianity. He grew up and acquired consciousness in the Ilocos region and the city of Manila, at a time when

US neo-colonialism appeared permanently rooted in the archipelago, all rebellion pacified, all protest quelled, and all questioning stifled.

The 1950s rebellion waged by the *Hukbong Mapagpalaya ng Bayan* (People's Liberation Army), contemptuously called the Huks by reactionary forces led by U.S. advisers, had been crushed decisively, its main units decimated, scattered or reduced to small roving bands. Practically the entire Political Bureau and the Central Committee of the CPP itself had been captured and imprisoned. US control of the archipelago was so tight that an American CIA colonel could get away with slapping a disobedient Philippine president; CIA-connected Filipino military officers could threaten another hapless Philippine president who instituted import and currency controls or deigned to even breathe a foreign policy slightly divergent from that of the so-called "Free World."

US domination of the islands was visible in the presence of Clark Air Base and Subic Naval Base, the largest American overseas military bases. Parenthetically, one of the 22 sites reserved for US bases was a Sison property in the seaside barrio of Salomague in Ka Joma's hometown. The Philippines was also a source of recruits and skilled personnel for the US military. Even the state university ran classes at Clark. To this day, Filipino recruits of the US military are not required to change their citizenship, so certain are the former colonial masters of the colonized's loyalty.

Long before he began organizing at the University of the Philippines, there were indications that Ka Joma wouldn't be the usual run of rich family scion. Sons of wealthy families have their lives mapped out for them. Jose Maria Sison was no exception. By his father's plans, he was supposed to train in journalism, enter law school, go to Harvard for graduate studies, return and marry the daughter of a rich family, enter politics and perhaps become president. In such a tried and tested clan manner would the family's economic and social position be preserved and expanded. He was supposed to become what current Philippine activists call a *trapo* (Filipino portmanteau for traditional politician, also Tagalog for dustcloth).

The Sisons trace their origins to a 16th century trading ship captain from Fujien Province, China, but the first Filipino Sison was registered in the 18th century in Lingayen, Pangasinan, as a Sangley mestizo (Chinese-Malay), in peculiar racist practice of Spanish colonial rule. A Sison moved to Vigan, Ilocos Sur in 1810 and married into a Spanish-Malay clan. Over the ensuing years, the Sisons would wend their way through the contradictions of the times, now serving the colonial government, now joining in local and national anti-colonial movements. Professor Sison's grandfather, Don Gorgonio Sison, was Cabugao's last *gobernadorcillo* (little governor) under Spanish colonialism, municipal president under the Philippine revolutionary government and first town mayor under US colonialism. On the other hand, Don Gorgonio's father-in-law, Don Leandro Serrano, and his sons had also been arrested, imprisoned and tortured, first by Spanish officers for complicity in Asia's first anti-colonial revolution in 1896 and then by US occupation forces in 1898, who also shipped them to exile.

That revolution and reaction should run as intertwined themes in generation after generation in the Philippines is no surprise. The country has been in one firefight after another, people surviving and prevailing the best way they can, ever since the Spaniards stumbled upon the islands in 1521. Most members of the Filipino intelligentsia can lay claim to such a contradictory legacy. Few, however, synthesize both history and life experience to create a relevant political philosophy. Still fewer merge words with actions. When they do, they bring together so many strands of the archipelago's life that the result is simply *grand*.

Contrary to the standard practice of wealthy families, the boy Sison was not sent to a private Catholic school and instead attended public school for his elementary education. This brought him into close contact with the children of the poor. How significant this was to the formation of his worldview was evident in a rich-poor love story he wrote in Grade Three, which was published in the Ilocano magazine *Bannawag*. The story didn't have the usual happy ending, indicating that even at a young age, class conciliation was not in Sison's experiential and intellectual realm.

At age 12, he was sent to Manila for high school education at the Jesuit Ateneo de Manila. He had difficulty adjusting to the school's religious demands. Suspected of leading his classmates in a protest against a Jesuit teacher, he was given an honorable dismissal at the end of his second year, despite his standing as an honors student. His parents transferred him to the Dominican friar-run Letran. Here as in Ateneo, he did well in academics but got low grades in religion. By graduation, he had decided on two things: to enroll at the secular University of the Philippines and to finish his four-year course in three years.

He was not, however, entering the university as a *tabula rasa*. At Letran, he had encountered the writings of Marx and Engels, ironically in an anti-communist book; he had listened to his father's expressed admiration for Don Claro M. Recto, the lone senator to question Philippine-US relations;

and he had heard Huk stories from his barber, who was a sympathizer of the communist-led rebellion.

The Times of a Radical

The decade of the 1950s opened with a declaration of armed struggle by the *Partido Komunista ng Pilipinas* (PKP—Communist Party of the Philippines), wielding the *Hukbong Mapagpalaya ng Bayan* (HMB—People's Liberation Army), in an ill-conceived plan to seize state power in two years. That the CPP had been practically coerced into such a move, shortly after World War II and US grant of independence to the country, by the re-imposition of US and landlord control, did not blur the fact that the revolutionary forces were not prepared for the banner of "all-out armed struggle" that the party unfolded. The defeat of armed struggle plunged the archipelago into a decade of revolutionary ebb.

The PKP was first established on November 7, 1930 by Crisanto Evangelista, a trade union leader. Although the archipelago had struggled for nearly 400 years, first against Spanish colonialism, then against US colonialism, averaging nearly one uprising every two years, the fire of resistance leaping from region to region, island to island, the PKP's founding was the first effort towards a comprehensive analysis of the country's history and conditions. It marked the first time a comprehensive vision was put forward towards the creation of a self-contained nation. Henceforth the adversarial language would be Marxist and class a demarcation of one's place within the country's alignment of forces.

That the archipelago had over 7,000 islands and 150 languages, hence an equal number of ethno-linguistic communities, served Spanish, American and other invaders well. By pitting one tribe against another, the Spaniards were able to maintain control with only a minuscule armed force. Spanish colonial authority relied on subjective control exercised by Spanish friars and priests, through Inquisition-type Catholicism. The natives, called *indios*, were also maintained at the uneducated and subsistence level, burdened by taxes, tributes and conscript labor. It was only the opening of the Suez Canal in 1869 which enabled a small *mestizo* (Malay-Chinese-Spanish mixed blood) stratum of *indio* society to engage in trade and thereby appropriate surplus wealth. From this would come the *ilustrados* who first posited the idea of nationhood. But it would take a self-educated worker, the great Andres Bonifacio, to match action to words. He established the *Katipunan ng Kataas-taasan at Kagalang-galangang Anak ng Bayan* (Society of the Highest, Most Respected Children of the People), a secret revolutionary organization which would be known as the *Katipunan*.

Bonifacio and the *Katipunan* launched the first Philippine national liberation struggle in 1896. But at its height, he was murdered by a faction led by a Letran-educated former *gobernadorcillo* Emilio Aguinaldo. The latter compromised the revolution, accepted a truce with the Spaniards, and exiled himself and other leaders to Hong Kong. When he returned to the archipelago, he hitched a ride on a US warship. The Spanish-American War had broken out on the other side of the globe. The Aquinaldo leadership would proclaim and inaugurate the first Philippine Republic on June 12, 1898, under a constitution that stated categorically that the archipelago would forge its nationhood under the protection of the United States.

When the latter refused, after Spanish surrender, to recognize the Republic of the Philippines, the Philippine-American War broke out on February 4, 1899. Although pacifying the islands required deployment of half of the US Armed Forces and lasted more than a decade, this war would be minimized as the Philippine Insurgency, its revolutionary leaders called insurgents and bandits. Nearly one-tenth of the Philippine population died in this war. One-eighth of the population of Luzon, where Manila is located, perished as a result of the US military onslaught.

The Philippines was an American colony when the Communist Party of the Philippines was born. The PKP was primarily a worker's organization, operating in the city of Manila. It led a checkered existence, now legal, now illegal, based on the whims and needs of the American colonial authorities. Only a year old, it was outlawed, the pretext being the violence that ensued when police attacked a workers' rally in Manila on May 1, 1931. In 1932, Evangelista and other PKP leaders were convicted of sedition and sentenced to internal exile. In the same year, the *Partido Sosyalista ng Pilipinas* (PSP—Socialist Party of the Philippines) independently came into existence as a peasant movement in the Central Luzon countryside.

Faced by surging fascism overseas, the Philippine commonwealth government, still under US colonial authority, legalized the PKP in 1937, hoping to use its members as cannon fodder in the looming world war. This paved the way for the PKP and PSP to merge in 1938, creating the worker-peasant alliance much desired by Marxist parties. But war was already on the horizon and Japan attacked the Philippines in December 1941, soon after the Pearl Harbor bombing. Within a year, the Japanese Imperial

Army was dominant over the archipelago, with American forces and collaborators either captured or in retreat to Australia. The Japanese decimated the first-line leadership of the merged PKP-PSP in February 1942. For the rest of its short history, the PKP-PSP would be led by two sets of brothers: the Lava and Taruc brothers.

On March 29, 1942, the new leadership formed the *Hukbong Bayan Laban sa Hapon* (Hukbalahap—People's Army Against Japan). The call was to resist the invaders and their collaborators. The main base was at the foot of an isolated mountain, Mount Arayat, rising like a clenched fist out of the Central Plains of Luzon. Symbolism notwithstanding, the base was easily overrun, first by 10,000 Japanese troops.

One by-product of the struggle against the Japanese invaders was the establishment of peasant power and peasant control over lands abandoned by landlords who had fled either to the urban areas or overseas with the US Armed Forces. With the return of the US military in October 1944, the landlords reclaimed both land and tenants. Despite this, the PKP opted for legal participation in what was supposed to be a fully independent Philippines. But while the US was willing to relinquish administration of the country, it was not willing to relinquish economic control. A New York-based organization of American businessmen with investments in the archipelago demanded and got parity rights— i.e., equal rights as Filipinos in the exploitation of the country's natural resources. This required a constitutional amendment, which in turn required divesting members of the Democratic Alliance, a broad front political party of nationalists and revolutionaries, of their seats in the Philippine Congress.

The banning of the elected congressmen was accompanied by concerted attacks on trade unions, peasant associations and other organizations deemed influenced by the PKP. Arrests, imprisonment and assassinations were par for the course. In 1950, when all avenues for accommodation seemed closed, the PKP called for armed struggle. The Hukbalahap became *Hukbong Mapagpalaya ng Bayan* or People's Liberation Army.

To bridge the gap between city and countryside, the PKP created a strange structure—a Political Bureau-In headed by Jose Lava, and a Political Bureau-Out, headed by his brother Jesus. The city-based Politburo-In was captured easily while the countryside-based Politburo-Out became immersed in a factional strife with two Taruc brothers, who had entered the PKP through the merger with the socialist party. Luis Taruc was commander-in-chief of the HMB and his brother Peregrino was in the Education Department of the PKP.

After the debacle of the armed struggle, Jesus Lava, as leader of the PKP, issued several policy decisions which further eroded PKP strength. Among these was the policy decision in 1955 to liquidate the people's army and convert it into an "organizational brigade." Another was the "single-file policy" of 1957, which reduced contact among party cadres to a one-on-one basis, thereby destroying the collective essence of party life. When the decade ended, the PKP was practically non-existent and non-operational, its reputation a matter of reminiscence among aging men and women. Into this fallow political state entered Jose Maria Sison, fresh from having organized the largest protest rally of university students in nearly three decades. He was then also a neophyte staff researcher and writer of the trade union movement.

A Self-Created Marxist

Joma was 20 years old when he graduated from the University of the Philippines, earning his four-year English degree in three, majoring in journalism and creative writing, in accordance with the first part of his father's plan. He obtained a teaching fellowship while working on his masters. But he had been organizing informal study groups, having at last found some Marxist books in the university library, reading Marx, Engels, Mao Zedong, and some articles on the 1950s Huk rebellion. In 1959, he forged his first organization, the Student Cultural Association of the Philippines (SCAUP), a parody of the UP Student Catholic Action (UPSCA). The Catholic Church maintained vigilant control over the secular university, through faculty members who were lay clerics, through UPSCA and via an American Jesuit priest assigned to the UP Catholic Chapel.

In 1961, verbal denunciations of the university, done largely by the religious and by military intelligence—for allegedly harboring communists and atheists—crystallized into a witch hunt by the Congressional Committee on Anti-Filipino Activities (CAFA). Among those targeted were faculty members of the Philosophy Department, then dominated by logical positivists and agnostics. Anti-communist hysteria was so intense and CIA psy-war operations so successful that doubting the existence of a white god was equated to being **against** everything Filipino.

The SCAUP, under the guidance of Jose Maria Sison, shaped an alliance of university organizations against the congressional hearings. It mounted a rally of 5,000 students and faculty before Congress, overrunning the hearings and halting it permanently, preventing a McCarthyite wave from destroying a government guarantee of academic freedom. SCAUP gained prestige and became a premier campus organization.

On the heels of this success, Jose Maria Sison criticized the curriculum of the English Department for its heavily pro-Christian choice of readings, and demanded the inclusion of radical writers. His teaching contract was not renewed, even though he was close to finishing his masters. Bad news certainly, for the young Sison had met Julieta de Lima, a young woman of dark and petite comeliness from Bicol Province. She had finished her degree in library science and was working as a university cataloguer when she agreed to marry Sison.

Because she was and is exceedingly self-effacing, Ms. De Lima was and is easy to underestimate. But she was by Sison's side when the organizing began. The marriage having lasted four decades, all indications point to her remaining there to the end. Ms. De Lima, like her husband, would go underground, be captured, be imprisoned and like him, carry a substantial amount of government reward money on her head, among only a handful of Filipinas to be so honored.

In the early '60s, however, with one child and another on the way, losing one's employment was real hardship. The Sisons had to relinquish cheap faculty housing and share a relative's house. Despite the children, Julieta de Lima Sison became the family's breadwinner, her salary augmented with a supply of produce from the Sison farmlands. Joma looked for employment but a challenged ruling system was both unforgiving and relentless. An intelligence dossier materialized at every prospective employer's elbow. Even a brief stint at a private agricultural university ended when the university administration deemed him responsible for strikes in another enterprise of the owner. Overseas graduate school was no longer an option. The American Embassy in Manila had blacklisted Sison since 1961, a ban that persists to the present. Punishment, rather than co-optation, was authority's preferred response to any challenge.

For the wielders of power in the Philippines, discontent was never the result of conditions but rather the work of instigators and agitators. In this manner, those in power held themselves not responsible, even though 70% of the population lived in unspeakable poverty, 20th century technology represented in the rural areas only by sodas and cigarettes, three stones still serving for a stove. Objectively speaking, there was no reason then as now for the poverty, the country being the world's fifth largest gold producer and having nearly all mineral resources for industrial development, with land so fertile practically anything, even tulips, grew, with seas a blue garden of seaweed, fish and crustaceans. Yet, to this time, one meal a day was common among the poor, whose numbers increased exponentially with the passing of time, among a population where nearly 50% were minors.

Where a society was held together by institutionalized violence and pillage, intelligence and skills mattered little. Only the National Association of Trade Unions, opened its doors to the young Sison, the way to mainstream society being decisively blocked. While doing union work, he obtained a grant to study Indonesian language and literature. He still speaks Bahasa Indonesia. On a ferry ride to Norway in 2001, hearing from a tourist that she had just been to Bali, Sison asked if she spoke the language—which occasioned much laughter among the young Filipinos accompanying him. They thought it was a bizarre pick-up line.

Indonesia, southern neighbor of the Philippines, was a mecca for Southeast Asian intellectuals in the 1950s and early 1960s. Under the leadership of Sukarno, the Indonesians had driven out the Dutch and established their own state and nation. It had the largest communist party, the *Partai Komunist Indonesia* (PKI—Communist Party of Indonesia), outside the socialist bloc. Here, Jose Maria Sison learned more about national liberation struggles and Marxism, making friends with PKI leaders and members. On his return to the Philippines, he was stopped at the airport, his books and papers seized by Intelligence. Among them would be his draft master's thesis on the Filipino novelist, Nick Joaquin. This was one degree he would not finish.

Before leaving for Indonesia, however, Sison had received a message from Jesus Lava, still hiding in Manila, asking for a meeting. A year passed before the request could be acted on. Lava assigned a nephew of his and the young Sison, already a self-made Marxist, to form an Executive Committee. In early 1963, then, Sison found himself in a committee of five: two Lavas, one close Lava friend, a union leader and himself. Jesus Lava hovered in the background as PKP secretary-general. Sison would be designated secretary for youth.

The Organizer

Two events in mid-decade would turn out to be life-altering decisions for Jose Maria Sison. First, with a charter membership of around 80, he led the founding of *Kabataang Makabayan* (KM—Patriotic Youth), a political center for young men and women, irrespective of class. Having joined the faculty of the Lyceum of the Philippines, he had a rich terrain for recruitment and organizing. Second, he proposed to the PKP that a summing up and critique of Party history and experience were in order.

This was 1964. One Ferdinand Edralin Marcos, senate president from Ilocos Norte, switched political parties to bag the presidential candidacy. Marcos exhibited the same strategic thinking that Jose Maria Sison had, the difference being that the former thought in centrifugal terms—of himself first, his family, his friends. Marcos had a reputation for being brilliant, topping the bar exams, and buying war medals after WWII to establish his claim to being the war's most decorated hero. In actuality, his family collaborated with the Japanese invaders. In the creation of a personal mythology, Marcos would have no equal.

The KM gave Marcos's candidacy critical support, because of a campaign promise to keep the Philippines out of the Vietnam War, which had become an American war. His predecessor, Diosdado Macapagal, father of current Philippine President Gloria Macapagal-Arroyo, had imposed decontrol measures, reversing his own predecessor's policy of protecting the fledgling Philippine economy from transnational corporations. It was a futile attempt to curry favor with the US and the International Monetary Fund/World Bank.

Macapagal's four-year-term had been uneasy at best, with constant rumors of an impending *coup d'etat.* A degree of cosmetic nationalism—changing independence day from the US-mandated July 4th to June 12th, the founding of the first Philippine Republic; a friendship with Sukarno ; and a vision of an alliance among Malaysia, the Philippines and Indonesia—had earned him the displeasure of the United States.

Sukarno lost power in 1965, in a bloodbath still remembered by one Balinese writer as rivers so clogged with bodies not an inch of water surface could be seen. The PKI, largest party in Southeast Asia, disappeared almost overnight. The freewheeling air of radicalism was replaced by such stultifying control that when I visited Indonesia, nearly 30 years later, students would be asking if they could inquire of the government if they could ask for a permit to picket.

With Indonesia quiescent, a newer—and yet older—hotspot in Southeast Asia drew the region's attention: Vietnam. Because the Philippines hosted the US's largest overseas military bases, it was merely a matter of time before the country was drawn into the war. Most Filipinos did not realize that through the CIA, Filipinos were already working with the US to defeat a national liberation movement. One even drafted the constitution of South Vietnam; others were in Cambodia and Laos. Operation Brotherhood of the Philippine Jaycees was all over Indochina.

True to his character, Marcos did an immediate turn-about upon winning the elections. He sent a Philippine military contingent, the Philippine Civic Action Group or PhilCAG under Lt. Col. Fidel V. Ramos, to build the infrastructure for a mechanized war. This brought the KM and SCAUP into direct confrontation with the Marcos government.

Mindful perhaps of appearing like Vietnam's French colonizers, the US presented the war as a fight against communism and hastily built a pseudo-alliance with its client-states. The first summit was hosted by the Philippines and Marcos, who received the accolade from President Lyndon B. Johnson of being "America's right arm in Asia." On the eve of the summit, in October 1966, Jose Maria Sison led a picket in front of the Manila Hotel. The police promptly routed the picketers, arresting and jailing Sison and friends for a few hours.

The following day, on October 24th, UP students led a march by 5,000 students. The police dispersed the demonstrators by wielding truncheons, breaking heads open, stepping on the fallen. Thus was born the October 24th Movement, under the leadership of then Student Council President Voltaire Garcia, a law student. He would become a delegate to the Constitutional Convention, be arrested and imprisoned by Marcos in 1972, the stress of which would lead to his early death. He was among the first members of the NDFP's Preparatory Commission.

This brutal dispersal was repeated again and again, as students took to the streets in ever increasing numbers. KM membership grew to thousands. At its second national congress in 1967, three years after its founding, it could elect representatives from every city and every region to its national council. In a polyglot country, the KM created what had been deemed impossible: a language of common concepts, ideas and conclusions, the language of a single vision rising out of the fractured history and disparate islands of the archipelago.

At the University of the Philippines, the SCAUP, the UP branch of the KM and various left groups started the drive to capture the Student Council and the university student newspaper, the *Philippine Collegian.* SCAUP led the first walk-out of College of Arts and Sciences students and organized a lecture series on socialism. The Student Council inaugurated projects like the Nationalist Corps, sending students to rural areas to study, learn and work alongside peasants. What had been discussion groups of ten or a dozen students mushroomed to wall-to-wall teach-ins, students meeting in hallways, on the lawns, in building lobbies.

Through the KM, dissent hit the university belt, a district in downtown Manila where five huge universities were located with tens of thousands of students. A KM branch operated in every single one.

While the war in Vietnam was the initial focus of the discontent, questions about American involvement in that country led inevitably to questions about US presence in the Philippines. When an American GI shot and killed a boy scavenging in the garbage dump of Clark Air Base, when his superiors gave the boy's parents tins of sardines and a sack of rice in recompense, the debates exploded into pickets and rallies, and sheer disgust with the military bases.

Marcos contributed his own self-indulgence and corruption to the general disaffection with government. Having the national costume, the *barong*, re-designed by Pierre Cardin was the least of it. Through sweetheart deals with Antilles-registered companies, actually owned by him and his friends and relations, government money was steadily privately expropriated. The lifestyle the Marcoses created, supposedly along the lines of the Kennedys' Camelot, had aspects incomprehensible to Filipinos. When Imelda Marcos's retinue hied off to Switzerland for rejuvenation shots concocted from duck embryos, the expense was doubly scandalous to Filipinos who ate duck eggs with embryos washed down by beer. Imelda's construction fever was also starting—nice excuse for the heavy borrowing that the Marcos government did with the IMF/WB. From a few hundred millions of dollars at the start of Marcos's term, the foreign debt began its agonizing climb to billions of dollars. By his fall in 1986, the Philippines was the only Asian country among Latin American countries in the list of top borrowers of the IMF/WB.

Marcos also unmoored the currency from its government mandated dollar-rate exchange. People watched in dismay as the peso sank seven to the dollar, twelve to the dollar, gasoline prices sky-rocketing, power costs rising, savings shriveling and even food itself becoming an impossible luxury.

Pride went alongside the currency fall. The "second only to Japan" rank of the Philippine standard-of-living in the post-WWII period turned out to be a delusion. Nothing made sense anymore. The search for answers, for new directions, became imperative, then urgent, among the young. Suddenly, they wanted to check out imperialism's old boogey, the People's Republic of China, never mind that the Philippines had no diplomatic relations with that country. Suddenly, everyone was reading Marx, Engels, Lenin and Mao. Into this seething cauldron, Jose Maria Sison's *Struggle for National Democracy* dropped, a book which gave name to the essence of the vision the young were looking for. Instantly, it was map and guide to the student activist.

Underneath the success, all was not well within the PKP, where Jose Maria Sison, hemmed in by the Lavas, strove to create a modicum of organization. Jesus Lava had surrendered in 1964 to the Macapagal administration, leaving his inexperienced relatives, all with comfortable city lives, in charge of the PKP. Still, Sison tried to forge a revolutionary party out of the material handed to him. He submitted a draft summing-up of PKP history under the three Lava brothers (1942-1964.) A Lava nephew objected, proposed presenting his own summing-up, never did and instead began trying to isolate Sison. He was also quarreling with a cousin over party leadership. Sison realized that the PKP was in an incorrigible mess. In April, 1967, he organized a new provisional political bureau with members drawn from trade unions, a peasant organization and the youth movement.

The following year, he led the re-establishment of the Communist Party of the Philippines and three months later, the formation of the *Bagong Hukbong Bayan* (NPA—New People's Army). He went underground, ending his legal existence as Jose Maria Sison. He left behind, in the urban areas, hundreds of thousands of students singing about the NPA, how the people's warriors were on their way to the city from the countryside; they sang as they walked out of classrooms, into the streets, to gather in front of Congress, of the Presidential Palace, of every erring institution, to demand accountability and responsibility of the landlord-dominated government.

As if to celebrate Sison's new level of commitment, the First Quarter Storm broke out in 1970—three months of daily demonstrations, growing into weekly protest rallies each massing from 50,000 to 100,000 young men and women. Organizations were metastasizing all over the archipelago, new ones sprouting, including the MAKIBAKA, an all-women group which promptly picketed the ubiquitous beauty contests in Manila.

The trigger to all this was the brutal dispersal by gunfire, not truncheons, of demonstrators at a Marcos State of the Nation speech before

Congress on January 25th. For three months non-stop, young men and women ran the gantlet of riot police and gunfire, to affirm their commitment to national democracy. It was fitting accolade to the full-grown revolutionary Jose Maria Sison had become. He was 30 years old.

A Petite Summing Up

The first ten years of Jose Maria Sison's growth and practice as a Marxist and revolutionary endowed the Philippine Left with characteristics which remain to this day. The 1961 overrunning of the congressional witch hunt of the University of the Philippines was the first time a mass assembly brought government functions to a halt. Multiplied a thousand times over, it would translate itself into People Power, strong enough to overthrow two presidents, though not, as he himself would warn, an entire political system.

Years later, as the entire Soviet bloc fell and the Berlin Wall disappeared, an American writer would remark to me that it was the Philippines that started all of it and no one remembered anymore. There was no way for me to explain the irony of her comment.

The vital role that youth organizations—growing from Sison's tiny SCAUP in 1959 to the KM in 1964 to the Movement for a Democratic Philippines (MDP) in 1970—played in the country's near-instant politicization meant that the young would always have a special place in the Left. As Sison himself would say, a movement without many young people was in trouble. By the time he went underground, the KM was 20,000 strong; it was also center and core of interlocking alliances, both formal and informal, of student and youth organizations. At its full strength in the 1970-1972 period, the youth movement could mobilize up to 150,000 for demonstrations and rallies in Manila alone. More than this, it was the young who read, wrote, debated and discussed, who went to factories and fields to organize, ignoring danger and difficulties, all on a matter of principle.

Because he was himself a voracious reader and prodigious writer, Sison conferred a tradition of scholarship to radical Filipinos. As in no other place in the world had a movement been as well documented, organizations churning out statements, flyers, press releases, etc., at the first hint of an issue or controversy. For a while, every organization had a vision-mission-goal document, plus a welter of explicatory materials. Where books were a luxury and where the tradition was oral, this was a new and intense thing. The educational materials created clarity of politics and political intent, where hitherto obscurantism had prevailed.

Because he was a poet, Sison also bequeathed to the open mass movement a tradition of culture-making. The KM had its own cultural arm, starting as a Cultural Bureau eventually metamorphosing into the *Panday Sining* (Art Smithy). All basic organizations, especially those of workers, peasants, women and the youth, would have their own cultural groups. Writers and artists also self-organized to help the national democratic movement. Not only did some of the country's leading writers and artists arise out of or belong to the national democratic movement; the drive to know one's self historically created the artistic impulse to integrate modern content with traditional art forms and music.

The draft political report Sison submitted to the PKP had a sub-text: errors and shortcomings were sources of lessons. Pride, ego and "face" were not to stop any revolutionary from learning those lessons, in the interest of advancing the movement. To date, assessment and evaluation, small and large summing-ups, remain integral to the activist life, as strengths and weaknesses are identified and methodologies refined.

The involvement of Julieta de Lima in all of his undertakings no doubt inspired the idea of women's formal involvement in politics, political movements and the revolution. The KM had its women's bureau, designed to recruit and train women for activism and leadership. This was both new and yet a continuance of tradition. The Philippines had a women's political party long before anyone else.The *babaylan* (local priestesses) led the first resistance against Spanish colonialism and Christianity. By formally acknowledging the critical value of women to a political movement, indeed to a revolutionary movement, Sison paved the way for increasing numbers of Filipinas to engage in the making of politics. The KM Women's Bureau is generally acknowledged as ancestress of both the underground MAKIBAKA (*Malayang Kilusan ng Bagong Kababaihan*—Free Movement of New Womanhood) and GABRIELA, the largest and most militant open women's alliance in the archipelago. The Philippines now is reputed to have the strongest women's movement in Southeast Asia.

By giving up a life of comfort, by electing to go underground, by involving himself not only in leading but also immersing himself in revolutionary armed struggle, Sison hammered home the ideal of praxis: *as you say life should be lived, so should your own life be lived.* His life and work exemplified the unity of theory and practice. Armchair or cappuccino political theorists have not been held in any kind of respect in the Philippines ever since.

By his life as well, Sison made vivid the truth that even as circumstances forged a person, so could a person forge circumstances. Among a people well trained in fatalism, one of whose constant phrases was *bahala na* (it's up to god), this lesson was profound.

Embryonic though these characteristics might have been when Sison went underground, they were salient features of the Philippine national democratic movement. They helped the movement weather four decades of repression and suppression.

In the Storm's Eye

On December 26, 1968, Amado Guerrero (beloved warrior) led some 70 men and women in the re-establishment of the Communist Party of the Philippines. He was elected chairman of its Central Committee. The following year, on March 29th, the New People's Army was founded, with 65 fighters led by Commander Dante, *nom de guerre* of Bernabe Buscayno, a guerrilla leader of a remnant band from the HMB (Huk).

The two dates were a virtual code. By holding its re-establishment on the birthday of Mao Zedong, the new CPP signaled a turning away from the Soviet party line, denouncing it as revisionist and as a betrayal of Lenin and Stalin. By establishing the New People's Army on the day that the HUKBALAHAP (People's Army Against the Japanese) had been established in 1942, the CPP affirmed its links to the historic mission of its predecessor party: of armed struggle against foreign invasion and occupation, of armed struggle for the seizure of political power.

The two dates indicated a union of new and old proletarian fighters in the CPP, a dialectical break and continuity in Philippine communist history. They indicated that the new CPP was at a higher level than the old because of lessons learned. And because most party members were in their 20s and 30s, the Party was also reinvigorated.

There was no hesitancy to this new formation. Characterizing Philippine society as semi-colonial and semi-feudal, the CPP immediately raised the banner of armed revolution against US imperialist control over the Philippines and against the country's system of governance by the comprador bourgeoisie, landlords and bureaucrat-capitalists. It identified imperialism, feudalism and bureaucrat capitalism as the principal enemies. It would wage a protracted people's war and encircle the cities from the countryside. Its leading force would be the proletariat; its main force the peasantry. Upon this basic alliance would be built the national united front to draw in the urban petty bourgeoisie and the nationalist bourgeoisie. Because the peasantry comprised the revolution's main force, agrarian revolution would be its main content.

The CPP itself would demand the strictest discipline of its members. Party cadres and members were bound by the organizational principle of democratic centralism. The collective was the essence of Party life. Social investigation was required as basis for the right to speak. Work was subject to assessment and evaluation along ideological, political and organizational lines. Everyone practiced criticism and self-criticism.

The poet Emmanuel Lacaba, murdered at age 27 by Marcos's military in Davao, Mindanao Island, wrote of his brief sojourn as Party member and NPA fighter as being in "the shining secret eye of the storm." This was true in a profound subjective sense. Under Philippine laws, joining the CPP was punishable by death. This meant that all questions regarding life's options had been resolved. Everything one had and one was were now tendered to the service of the people and the revolution. Highly motivated, highly ideological, with awesome focus, a party of less than a hundred led by Amado Guerrero and an army of 65 fighters led by Commander Dante set about the task of mounting a revolution.

Years later, Jose Maria Sison would acknowledge the party's debt to Bernabe Buscayno (Commander Dante), still referring to his old comrade as *Payat* (the thin man). Buscayno was a slim, wiry man, legendary in his ability to confound the Philippine military. From him and other veterans of the HMB, the urban-raised Party cadres learned how to set up camp, go on forced marches, attack, retreat, harass, ford rampaging rivers, etc.. A lack of such skills would have been costly for the Party.

But the CPP was only a fledgling, still growing wings, talons and beak, while its enemy, the Armed Forces of the Philippines was full grown, numbering tens of thousands and was backed by the strongest power in the world and in human history, the United States of America. It had access to war technology and methodology refined and developed in the actual suppression of entire peoples, from American Indians to Filipinos themselves. In the first years of the CPP's life, it came close to annihilation as its enemy tried to develop a purely military situation between 5,000 army regulars and some 200 NPA warriors in the province of Tarlac, birthplace of the CPP. But Sison had anticipated this and, as early as 1969, he had sent cadres to Cagayan Valley to organize. At this time, though, if a cadre survived for a year in the countryside and was neither captured nor killed, he was considered a veteran.

Amado Guerrero had taken the lesson of the PKP's defeat to heart. Even as KM chairman, Jose Maria Sison spoke occasionally of how foolhardy it was to over-concentrate the revolution in Central Luzon. While the area was traditional locale for unrest, dissent and uprisings, it was also studded with military bases and forts. Precisely because of that tradition, the enemy was strongest there.

The Philippine military appeared to be gaining the upper hand in Tarlac province, capturing men and weapons, killing NPA fighters, when, in late 1970, Sison directed a raid on the armory of the Philippine Military Academy, the country's elite school for military officers. Rifles and machineguns were seized. A special NPA commando team, in cooperation with then Lt. Victor Corpus, carried out the raid. Corpus was at the time a member of a secret CPP cell within the government military. This was the beginning of a high profile pattern of military officers and government officials defecting to the underground.

The CPP and the NPA flourished in Isabela Province, whose interior was still forested and undeveloped, where the terrain was difficult and which barely registered in the national awareness. The spine of the Sierra Madre allowed them a clandestine, if perilous, route from north to south of Luzon. Here, within three years, the Party created a strong base among villagers and the peasantry. The province served as training center as well, with cadres sowed and scattered all over the archipelago after their education. In due time, these cadres would create over 60 guerrilla fronts, all waging armed struggle and organizing in practically all the major islands of the archipelago

Making revolution was certainly no dinner party. Rain forests did not evolve for humanity alone. Amado Guerrero survived more than a dozen near misses with the enemy. His commitment was not to be gainsaid. He once forded a river, clinging to a rope, seconds ahead of a mountain torrent which washed away two comrades, who were never found. He crossed a stretch of the open sea in a flimsy boat, to escape a thousand-soldier encirclement. Considering that Jose Maria Sison could not swim a stroke, this was great daring, indeed.

Outside of this deadly cat-and-mouse, the open mass movement carried on its own form of struggle, holding one demonstration after another.

In 1971, as campaigning for senatorial elections reached its peak, two grenades were hurled at the opposition Liberal Party grand meeting in Plaza Miranda, Manila. Scores of people were killed and injured; among them the LP's top leaders and media people. National condemnation was immediate and public. Marcos, whose party was obviously losing the elections, was held culpable. He responded by suspending the writ of habeas corpus. Military intelligence listed those who were to be arrested and detained.

Faced by this threat to civil liberties, the national democratic movement established a broad united front to oppose fascism in the country. The Movement for a Democratic Philippines agreed to form the broader formation, Movement of Concerned Citizens for Civil Liberties. Among those who joined were two senators who led the fight against US bases, Jose W. Diokno and Lorenzo Tanada; and Chino Roces, publisher of the largest circulation newspaper in the country. Bowing to pressure, Marcos lifted the writ suspension, only to declare martial law the following year.

The Long Night of the Dictatorship

1972, the year of Presidential Proclamation 1081 (PP 1081 imposing martial law) was a strange year. The Philippines was struck by 22 typhoons and Central Luzon nearly returned to the sea. Students collected relief goods for the disaster-stricken peasants only to have them stolen by the military. There were reports that dikes on various rivers had been opened to protect Clark Air Base from the torrential floods. A small ship was found aground on the reefs off the shoreline of Isabela Province.

Because Marcos's second term was ending and the Constitution provided for only two terms, he called for a convention to amend it. Delegates had to run for seats at the convention. Unfortunately for him, candidates reputed to have his support all lost, while nearly a dozen winning delegates declared their opposition to any amendment which would allow Marcos to run for president again. Among them were the nationalist businessman Alejandro Lichauco, member of the Movement for the Advancement of Nationalism, and Enrique Voltaire Garcia, who as a student had led the October 24th Movement in 1966.

Among those gearing up for presidential candidacy were Sen. Benigno Aquino, now head of the decimated Liberal Party, and Sen. Salvador Laurel, Jr.

With the exception of the last named, all were promptly arrested when PP 1081 was issued, at midnight of September 21, 1972, part of OPLAN (operation plan) Sagittarius. Almost 5,000 names were reportedly on the list of those to be arrested and detained in one fell swoop: senators and congressmen, convention delegates, mayors and councilors, media men and women, student leaders and activists, and even those who only had names similar to those on the list. The raucous city of Manila fell absolutely quiet. All radio and television stations were silenced, all newspaper offices closed, building entrances blocked by coiled razor wires.

Marcos's term-end was coinciding with the end of the Laurel-Langley Agreement, the enabling law of the parity rights provision in the Constitution—those rights which gave American business the same status as Filipinos in the acquisition and exploitation of Philippine resources. The Philippine Supreme Court, under the unsung but great Chief Justice Roberto Concepcion, had ruled that Americans would not have the right to own property in the Philippines upon the agreement's expiration.

As quickly as he had all legal opposition arrested and suppressed, Marcos solved both questions. The new constitution gave no term limit. Marcos ran unopposed. Actually, he didn't even run. A fake referendum as to whether he should continue in office—vote yes or no—was held. He claimed over 90% approval. Then, he extended Laurel-Langley by presidential fiat. The way was now open for his, his family's and his friends' lifetime dictatorship.

Urban-based activists descended on the CPP in the countryside by the hundreds, straining resources. In one guerrilla front, Party cadres fed student and community activists, sat them down and interviewed them one by one, to determine as accurately as possible whether he/she was indeed in danger of arrest and detention. Those who weren't were sent back to organize—in secret this time, creating a shadow network ranging from just beneath where the Marcoses stood to the homes of the poorest in the cities. Those in real immediate danger were integrated into the countryside struggle.

Martial law triggered an internal debate within Lava-led formations. Some 70 members of the Lava youth formation refused to accept collaboration with the Marcos Dictatorship. They were executed. In 1974, the Lava-led party surrendered and its cadres and officers joined the government.

The CPP's membership, on the other hand, expanded from its initial hundred to thousands, cadres scattered all over the archipelago, all working to create storm centers. Because secret communications between islands were complicated—the CPP's National Liaison Committee in Manila was periodically busted, its staff imprisoned—to be a party member at this time meant being a cadre, with high organizing skills and even higher political consciousness. Going through the CPP's *Basic Mass Course* and *Basic Party Course* was only the beginning of one's education.

No doubt to help the work along (regions, by and large, were operationally autonomous, so that a breach by the military in one area did not spill over to the next; or the capture of one organ didn't lead to the capture of other organs), Amado Guerrero issued *Specific Characteristics of Our People's War* in 1974. This document codified the lessons of the Party's first five years of armed struggle and defined tactics and methods for a protracted people's war in an archipelagic terrain.

That Filipino Muslims in Mindanao began their own war of liberation relieved the CPP to some extent of the intense and intensive military pressure. At certain times, the AFP withdrew battalions from NPA fronts and poured them into Mindanao and Jolo islands, in a futile quasi-blitzkrieg. Jolo City was napalmed, the dead and injured untallied. American expertise in counter-insurgency was manifest in death squads, paramilitary groups, vigilante groups, cults and other aberrations. A transvestite military man, playing rock music and claiming to be Christ, sowed terror among villagers; cults frightened by their own barbarity practiced ritual cannibalism to appease the spirits of those they murdered. An unleashed military wallowed to satiation in pain and death. It slowly grew insane from its own orgy. Men and women were tortured large-scale and the killing count soared in a prolonged holocaust for which few have been held responsible.

At the same time, the Marcos Dictatorship shrouded itself in mythomania. Spray-painting grass green in summer time for Imelda Marcos's extravaganza; staged television reports of her distributing houses to the homeless; building scores of vacation houses for the family and their guests; Marcos allowing a Japanese company to relocate its "dirty" plant to the Philippines—the list of travesty went on and on. And like a contrapunta, there were the periodic loans from the IMF/WB, as the dictatorship mortgaged the seas, the land, the mountains, the rain forests and the people. Most of the money was pocketed privately. Incredible amounts remain stashed to this day in Hong Kong, Swiss and other foreign banks, under various names.

The relentless pillage, the destruction and depletion of the country's resources (90% of the rainforest destroyed to enrich 450 persons) and the people's deepening poverty made revolution urgent and imperative. Strikes had been banned under the dictatorship but barely two years into martial law, workers at a liquor corporation, one of the country's largest, laid a picket in front of the company compound. Nuns and priests joined the picket line even as it was assaulted by police and hired thugs. This open defiance broke the silence imposed by fascist terror. Strikes would follow fast, one after another, in 300 workplaces from October 1974 to January 1975. This surge of worker resistance would presage the formation of the *Kilusang Mayo Uno* (KMU—May First Movement). This militant trade union movement would be a favorite Marcos target, its officers repeatedly arrested and detained, members and lawyers abducted and disappeared.

In 1976, the first major blow to the CPP-NPA came when Commander Dante was captured. The following year, Amado Guerrero was captured. The currents of the revolution swirled momentarily in distress; the talk in Manila was that it took seven men to fulfill all the responsibilities that the chairman carried. Nevertheless, Party cadres were certain that by this time, the revolution was "over the hump;" it was well on its way. CPP membership had grown to 5,000, spread out among ten regional organizations; the NPA had a thousand rifles and nine regional commands. Let the Marcos Dictatorship indulge itself in momentary success, showing off captured CPP officials, including Jose Maria Sison and Bernabe Buscayno; the process of arousing, organizing and mobilizing the masses continued.

As to be expected, Sison was beaten up, subjected to the water cure and death threats. His long poem, *Fragments of a Nightmare*, nearly surreal in its use of demon imagery, detailed the experience. He endured prolonged mental torture, during which he was deprived of his eyeglasses, shackled to a cot, was isolated in a prison cell with boarded up windows. In such circumstances, the only strength was keeping faith with one's self, keeping faith with the others who continued to struggle. More, he fought along with them, sending out advice, smuggling out analyses and essays.

Charges of rebellion and subversion were lodged against Jose Maria Sison. It was a joke, certainly, because they were filed before military tribunals which had no respect for rules of evidence. Sison and his lawyers followed a strategy of jamming procedures with paper, filing petition after petition before the Supreme Court, pitting it against the tribunal. The hearings were useful in breaking his isolation, allowing him to leave his cell, to see people, and speak to them.

In December 1981, the Sison's last child was born in prison. At the end of March 1982, following a mass campaign of almost a year, Julieta de

Lima with her infant child was released. She returned periodically for visits with her husband. She brought news and information and brought out his words.

The following year, Senator Benigno Aquino, Jr., who had been allowed to leave prison and the Philippines for a quadruple by-pass operation in the US, refused to remain in exile any longer. He returned on August 21, 1983 and was gunned down at the Manila International Airport. His wake and funeral were attended by nearly a million people.

Shortly thereafter, 10,000 women, some from the upper-class, most from the lower-income classes, marched together through the streets of Manila, demanding justice for the murdered senator and others killed by the Marcos dictatorship. This event was swiftly followed by intense organizing of open formations all over the country: Justice for Aquino, Justice for All (JAJA); GABRIELA, the women's alliance; the Nationalist Alliance for Justice, Freedom and Democracy; etc... The stench of a decaying regime was pungent throughout the land. Marcos himself was reported to be stricken with lupus, though he kept denying it, and was supposedly on his second transplant, though he kept denying that too. One man who saw him just after the Aquino assassination said he looked "like death warmed over."

Overthrow, Freedom and Exile

The peso rate to the dollar was a disaster; the foreign debt had ballooned to an amount impossible to repay. The Philippines had shifted its export emphasis from bananas, garments and copper concentrates to exporting men and women, sending them to indentured slavery overseas. The social costs of the so-called pillars of development—tourism, export processing zones and labor export—were as staggering as their economic costs. Prostitution, drugs, slavery accompanied all three pillars. With 100% repatriation of profits for transnational corporations, the national economy was depleted. With poverty afflicting nearly 70% of the population, the quick buck became standard operating practice, as survival became the paramount, if not the only, virtue.

The United States, which had backed the Marcos Dictatorship for nearly 14 years and Marcos himself for two decades, was not a disinterested bystander. Coming swiftly down the road was the end of the agreements which enabled the US to maintain Clark Air Base and Subic Naval Base. With government at a virtual standstill, demonstrations happening with such fury and of such dimensions, young and old braving guns, water cannons and razor wire barricades, all under the Left's leadership and inspiration, it was obvious that something had to be done. Removing Marcos was a problem fraught with implications. Because he had pampered the military, he held its loyalty. His overthrow would require splitting the military. This seemed too high a cost but eventually, a strategy to isolate Marcos-loyal troops was adapted. In 1985, the Reform the Armed Forces Movement (RAM) was launched by graduates of the Philippine Military Academy, generally regarded as comprising the military elite.

Marcos then was pressured to agree to hold snap elections, instead of waiting out the 1987 end of his term. He didn't want to hold elections; his subalterns didn't want him to hold elections; he was too weak to mount a national campaign. But in a live telecast via satellite on a US news-analysis show, he was dared to hold elections. Being a vain man and in constant denial of his unpopularity, Marcos agreed.

Corazon C. Aquino, widow of the murdered Benigno, was chosen to be the opposition presidential candidate. She and her supporters were carefully weaned away from the Left, which had borne the brunt of the struggle against Marcos. From his prison cell, Jose Maria Sison issued a long analytical essay, calling for broad united front tactics and critical collaboration with Mrs. Aquino. This was not heeded. The Left issued a boycott policy, unable to accept the idea of yet another landlord in office. Mrs. Aquino owned one of the biggest sugar plantations in Tarlac Province—and a sugar landlord was just about the worst landlord in the country.

Marcos won, of course, and for a day or two, the country was quiet, seething in defeat and unsure of what to do. The Left was the first to issue a call for the overthrow of the Marcos regime. It was followed by a pastoral letter from the Catholic bishops, calling the regime illegitimate and immoral; then the Aquino group called for civil disobedience. At this point, the US-rigged plans went operational. Gen. Fidel V. Ramos and Defense Minister Juan Ponce Enrile, supported by RAM, launched a mutiny. The Catholic Church, through Jaime Cardinal Sin, lent its support and, in a perverse manner of arousing and mobilizing the populace, called on the population of Manila to surround in their hundreds of thousands the military camps to protect the soldiers in mutiny.

But the ranks of organized workers, youth and other people surrounded the presidential palace itself. Hemmed in and unable to have his orders implemented, Marcos fought his battle through the media. In this war of words, Enrile implicated Marcos in the Plaza Miranda bombing and confessed that the supposed attack on his car, the excuse used to declare martial law in 1972, never happened. He had to know; he was one of the "Rolex men" who approved the martial law imposition, so labeled because Marcos gave each a Rolex watch afterwards.

All governance came to a standstill. All work came to a standstill. In the impasse, a plane attacked the palace with a few rockets. That was all it took for Marcos, et al, to pack bag, baggage, jewelry, crates of money, etc., board a US transport plane and fly off to Hawaii. Marcos would remain there until his death and beyond, for an enraged people refused to let his body have a state funeral or be buried, as Imelda wanted, in the Heroes' Cemetery.

Jose Maria Sison, held incommunicado in his cell, overheard a radio report to which his guards were listening. Turning towards an adjacent cell, which held Alex Birondo, another political prisoner, he cupped hands about his mouth and shouted: "Crisis! The end of Marcos is about to come." Analysis and evaluation were instant and accurate.

On February 25, 1986 Aquino was proclaimed president and on March 5, 1986, Jose Maria Sison and Bernabe Buscayno were released. They were brought to the new head of state, who giggled, says Sison, like a schoolgirl. Aquino wanted peace talks with the National Democratic Front, the umbrella formation of the 14 underground revolutionary organizations, including the CPP and the NPA.

The two, as well as other political prisoners, came out to a country still buoyed up by the overthrow of the dictatorship. Dinners in their honor were hosted by some of the 60 ruling families. On May 1,1986, Labor Day, Sison sat on the left side of Mrs. Aquino while Gen. Fidel Ramos sat on her right. At one point, they watched a huge hammer and sickle appear among the workers as the Internationale was sung. Wherever he appeared, Sison was greeted with thunderous applause and by autograph seekers.

In part, to meet the demand for his lectures and speeches, Jose Maria Sison accepted a fellowship at the Asian Center of UP, regained the title of professor, and delivered a series of ten lectures. These lectures helped a befuddled Left find and regain its bearings, in the midst of its anguish, as the old comprador and feudal lords returned, having used the revolutionary movement's work as springboard to regain power. The Left was immersed in self-flagellation, blaming one another for the boycott error. The fractious boycott debate would obscure a far worse problem, *Kampanyang Ahos*, a bloody witchhunt raging in Mindanao. Members of the CPP

Mindanao Commission, in the wake of defeats, ascribed responsibility for disastrous errors to suspected deep-penetration agents of the military. It was a fratricidal undertaking.

The Aquino government was plagued with the twin threat of the RAM and remnant Marcos loyalists. Even as a constitutional convention's hand-picked delegates struggled to draft a basic document for the land, Marcos loyalists tried to duplicate the February 22-25 mutiny. They holed up at the Manila Hotel with their guns and later abjectly surrendered to Gen. Ramos in July. RAM, on the other hand, saw the presence of a few liberals in the Aquino administration as indication that the Left had penetrated the government. Even as a new Constitution was forged and candidates began lining up to run for office, RAM came up with OPLAN God Save the Queen. The idea was to show off RAM strength through assassination of the leaders of the Left. Sison was an immediate prime target.

One reason for RAM's hysteria was the Aquino government's avowed willingness to engage in peace talks with the National Democratic Front. By hindsight, the NDFP strategy in the first peace talks appeared tentative. For one, prior even to laying down a substantive agenda for the talks, it already acquiesced to Aquino's demand for a 60-day ceasefire. It would set demands one day and retract them the next day. Towns and villages under NDFP control were exposed when underground officials visited. Later, the military subjected such territories to intense suppression. It was a most confusing and reckless period.

The abrupt expansion of democratic space, however, enabled Jose Maria Sison to launch yet another organization in 1986, a political party called the *Partido ng Bayan* (PnB—The People's Party). Through the PnB, people's organizations managed to field candidates in 1987 for the new legislature and to gain experience in electoral politics. The senatorial candidates were limited by controllers of the Commission on Election computers to only 10% of the votes. Thus they lost. Two congressional candidates won, despite the assassination of six other candidates, the kidnapping of staff and campaigners, the bombing of PnB offices nationwide, and military control of voting in nearly 700 towns classified as bailiwicks of the revolution. In the subsequent elections for executive officials, PnB advised its candidates to run under other parties. By this means, hundreds of seats at the municipal and provincial level were won.

Immediately following the PnB founding, Professor Sison left for a university lecture tour of New Zealand and Australia. He was gone throughout the month of September. He was in Thailand in October, to receive the Southeast Asia Write Award for poetry. He returned to the Philippines for a week, from October 15 -22, to pick up his visa to Japan. Throughout his first tour, he was hounded by black propaganda from then Defense Secretary Juan Ponce Enrile. And once back in Manila, he came to know he was primed for assassination under OPLAN God Save the Queen.

He was in Japan in November 1986 when RAM struck, torturing and killing Rolando Olalia, head of the KMU, then mutilating his body. In Professor Sison's absence, RAM had chosen another high-profile target. The NDFP promptly announced suspension of the peace talks. But eight days after Olalia's funeral, the NDFP agreed to ceasefire, indicating that there were negotiations after all. Jose Maria Sison learned about the ceasefire only from a news agency reporter. He was so dumbstruck he didn't know what to say. Olalia's murderers were to go scot free. He wanted to return home but both friends and comrades advised him to remain overseas.

From Japan he went to Hong Kong in December, then to India in January, and later in the month, to Europe. Landing in Holland on January 23, 1987, he was met by Luis Jalandoni, later head of the NDFP negotiating panel, with news of the massacre of peasant demonstrators in front of the presidential palace. By February, Aquino had declared total war on the revolutionary forces. It was, for the reactionary forces, an opportune moment. Despite bloody coups launched by RAM and the threat of Marcos loyalists, General Ramos had kept only a minimum military force in Manila and deployed most of his forces in the countryside. He would launch one military campaign after another to contain and paralyze the CPP and NPA whose mass base was already weakened.

The revolutionary movement did not emerge unscathed from the overthrow of the Marcos dictatorship. In the cities, its band of allies from the middle and upper classes narrowed abruptly, many electing to join the Aquino government. The influx of money from funding agencies overseas also affected the usual practice of moving activists from the city to the countryside. More activists stayed in the urban areas, staffing nonprofit organizations and tailoring projects and programs to funding agencies' specifications.

Under the dictator, the movement had guarded information and documents stringently, maintaining its clandestine nature. Now, documents, even Party documents, were making their way to the mainstream media, often even before the intended recipient got them. Papers critical of this or that CPP decision or policy were circulating openly. *Ang Bayan*, the CPP's journal, suddenly lost the phrase "guided by Marxism-Leninism-Mao Zedong Thought" from its masthead. Basic documents of the first congress of the NDFP talked about pluralism. The adversarial language was evolving from Marxist to what the Left itself would call Gorbachovite and bourgeois-liberal.

Worst was the continuing efforts of highly placed CPP officials, including two members then of the Political Bureau and a former member to cover up the criminal consequences of the most grievous errors of line. In Mindanao, nearly a thousand men and women had been decimated from 1985-1986 in an orgy of "house-cleaning"—i.e., winnowing presumed military deep-penetration agents from the revolutionary ranks. A similar campaign occurred in Eastern Visayas, then Southern Tagalog, albeit with lesser casualties. Some activists and cadres were abducted from Manila and taken north, to be investigated and tried. Some were killed. Some, traumatized by torture inflicted by their own purported comrades, broke down. Some fled and abandoned their responsibilities. In one region after another, towns and villages complained about the burden of having to feed and house large concentrations of armed fighters.

Professor Sison would say, years later, that he felt he was being made to wallow in crap, as he came to know of the witch hunts, the shrinking of the mass base, the unjustifiable special operations of some special units, the breakdown of morale and discipline. One by one, the most basic principles of the CPP were violated; one by one, the iron rules of NPA discipline were broken. Even by-standers were appalled. Criticizing the phenomenon of self-constriction and alienation from the masses, he expressed, in 1988, the need for a rectification movement.

From Holland, where he was stranded when the Aquino government canceled his passport, he began tracing the sources and causes the revolution's affliction. By late 1991, the Second Great Rectification Movement was ready for launching—a process in which every component of the national democratic revolution, sector by sector, organization by organization, organ by organ, went into self-examination. This process consisted of an ideological, political and organizational summing up, of identifying strengths and weaknesses, of successes and failures, of criticism and self-criticism. It was a harrowing one, a cleansing away of extraneous ideas picked up and adapted through the decades. At the core of the Rectification Campaign was the document *Re-affirm Our Party's Basic Prin-*

ciples and Rectify Errors.

In the course of the process, Professor Sison was among the, if not the most, vilified person of the national democratic movement. Even as the Philippine government continued its attempt to destroy his character and his legacy, so did some members or former members of the CPP itself, who could not accept the conclusions drawn by the rectification campaign. But the committed remained in the movement; those who understood the history of the Party and the history of Jose Maria Sison remained; they studied and learned and set out with fresh eyes to continue with the tasks of the revolution.

At the end of this process, which was partly a grief-keening for all those wrongly killed or punished, the CPP and the NPA emerged stronger than ever. They are, as Professor Sison himself adjudged, on an even keel. And that was answer enough to all the criticisms and name-calling he endured.

Even the most reluctant observer would admit that as a result of the rectification process, the CPP is now ideologically, politically and organizationally stronger. With the renewed expansion of its mass base, 128 guerrilla fronts have been established while both the urban-based mass and underground organizations have grown. It was fortuitous that the rectification campaign came at the time it did: when the East Asian economic crisis broke out, the CPP had strength enough and clarity of vision enough to become a source of hope for the impoverished and disaffected of the Philippines.

A Personal Note

A recitation of facts, a recounting of events—these are a poor approximation of what the national democratic movement has meant to Filipinos like me. My personal metaphor for the Philippine revolution is that of St. Elmo's Fire, whipping into existence in every one of the 7,100 islands. Impossible to capture, impossible to exterminate, it comes into being because conditions call for it. It is a people's affirmation of the will to freedom, to life, to creativity, as opposed to the ignorance, slavery and death imposed upon the country by colonialism and neo-colonialism.

I have known Jose Maria Sison since the 1960s, nearly the duration of the national democratic movement itself. I was a member of SCAUP, KM and a host of other organizations. This could be construed as bias in his favor. I prefer to think of it as being a witness—to a man and his time, to

Sison Time. It is a much more accurate label to those years of sacrifice than "Marcos time."

I've heard and read both praise of and attacks on Professor Sison, some with a kernel of truth, some pure hogwash. One newspaper report about his supposed villa in Holland I actually read in the efficiency apartment he, Julie and their son Jasm shared with various visiting friends. That kind of black propaganda from Philippine military intelligence was understandable, even acceptable. What is not is the grievous vilification from those who had been with and fallen out of the national democratic movement. They, of all people, would know best the time, effort and sacrifice that have characterized Sison's 40 years of revolution. Nevertheless, the most recent Philippine military plot to assassinate him was reportedly planned with the help of a former NPA leader.

A chronology of Jose Maria Sison's life is only a poor approximation of the man's complex character. In the course of research for this book, I spent two months in Europe, with Sison's community of exiles. Two incidents during this time illustrated how varied circumstances can be, when one sojourns with the men and women of the Philippine revolution.

On a ferry trip back to Holland from Oslo, Professor Sison suggested that we all relax at the restaurant-club on board. He and two companions went ahead, as I needed to do something in my cabin. I followed about a half-hour later. The club had a bar, a small dance floor, a female singer and a live band. Professor Sison liked to dance; still does. We had just come off the dance floor when the singer announced the band would do the birthday song in honor of—yeah, right—this writer, whose birthday was six months away. As I looked around in utter surprise, one of our companions pointed at Professor Sison and said he'd set it up in my absence. As the band blared "*happy birthday to you!*", I had to stand, bow, blow kisses at the applauding crowd, as my three companions, including Ka Joma, convulsed with laughter. It was a prank characteristic of the innocence of maybe twenty, thirty years ago.

But even as I thought of this, another image of the man came to my mind. In Oslo, Norway, when the government panel unilaterally recessed peace talks with the NDFP, there was consternation and dismay. To bring NDFP personnel out of the Philippines involved long and tedious preparations; to bring Professor Sison, Luis Jalandoni and the top NDFP echelon out of Holland involved even longer and more tedious preparations. Some of us couldn't help wondering whether something could have been done, whether they could have done anything, to forestall the government action.

The NDFP secretariat room in the hotel was always a noisy one, with people talking and laughing, going in and out, bringing coffee, food, cigarettes, working on the computers, answering phones—in direct contrast to the government secretariat room which was always quiet, its doors firmly shut. On this particular afternoon, following the talks' cancellation, the telephones were ringing insanely, with overseas calls from Philippine media asking for interviews.

Jose Maria Sison walked in, still wearing rubber flip-flops, sat down and waited for the phone-patch interview call from a radio station in Manila. When it came, he answered, mildly and slowly at first. As he explained the true reasons behind the recess, analyzed the government's actions and voiced the NDFP's indignation, his voice gained strength and passion, rising gradually until it filled the room; himself growing oblivious to the presence of so many men and women. The room fell quiet. Men and women began listening, then listening intensely; then sharing his contempt for the arbitrary silliness of the Manila government; and at last, feeling his outrage that the death of a military torturer outweighed in gravity—as far as the Manila government was concerned—discussions regarding peace, development and justice for the Filipino people. The sidelong glances men and women traded in the room were suddenly fierce and fiery, the hangdog look gone. By the last ten minutes of the phone interview, only Sison's voice was regnant in the room. That he spoke not only for all those present was clear. He spoke for a multitude, that sea of the anonymous, the poor and "the powerless" who nevertheless comprised the source of power for the revolution.

NINOTCHKA ROSCA
Utrecht, Holland;
New York City, USA
2001-2003

Julie and Joma walking on the beach in Cuba (top) and at the Rodin Museum in Paris, March 1987 (Sison family photo collection)

Jose Maria Sison (2nd from right) at the 64th anniversary celebration of the Union de Impresores de Filipinas (UIF) of February 6, 1966 when he delivered the comprehensive history of the Philippine labor movement. He was vice chairman for education of the Workers' Party. Others in the photo are Felixberto Olalia (second from the right), president of the National Federation of Labor Unions (NAFLU), Amado V. Hernandez (fourth from the right), former president of the Congress of Labor Organizations (CLO), and Juan F. Cruz (standing behind Olalia), UIF president. (Courtesy of KMU)

Receiving the Southeast Asia WRITE Award for poetry in Bangkok, Thailand, October 1986. (Courtesy SEA Write Award Committee)

Left: Taking a pause for a snapshot during the Central Luzon Regional Party Conference held in July 1977 in the border mountains of Bataan, Zambales and Pampanga. (NDF International Office photo collection)
Right: Joma reciting his own poems at the 1994 International Poetry Park Festival in Rotterdam, Netherlands.

At a military commission hearing Joma is flanked by lawyers Juan T. David (right) and Joker Arroyo (left). Behind is a close-in guard of the Military Security Unit. (Courtesy, Mike Yabut)

"Wanted: dead or alive" poster offers one-million pesos for the head of Professor Sison and half a million for Julie's. Dutch journalist Henk Ruigrok of Nieuwe Revu claimed that a Filipino colonel offered him US$200,000 (then the equivalent of four-million pesos) for the capture of Sison.

Chapter One

A Dangerous Existence

Q1. You have lived dangerously for most of your life, since becoming known as an anti-imperialist militant, and especially since you were suspected of being a communist. When did you first sense a serious threat to your life? Were you afraid?

When I decided to dedicate my life to the Philippine revolution in 1959 by starting to organize secret Marxist study circles, with the hope of reviving the Communist Party and the revolutionary mass movement, I was aware that the Anti-subversion Law stipulated the death penalty for officers of the Communist Party.

That law was a threat to my life. But instead of being intimidated, I felt challenged to defy the threat. At the same time, I knew I had to be careful since under the law, two corroborating witnesses testifying that one is an officer or member of the CPP or any related organization would suffice to incriminate that person.

I estimated that for some time I would be able to form clandestine study circles before the authorities could somehow detect my work and take punitive action.

Q2. Were you young enough not to have intimations of mortality? What made you daring? What actually happened when the results of your discreet work came into the open? What consequences did you face?

A combination of moral outrage over the oppression and exploitation of the people, intellectual courage and youth made me daring. You would not be afraid of a reactionary law when you are convinced of being scientifically and morally on the correct path and you wish to fight for national liberation, democracy, social justice and development, all in the interest of the people. You become restless and driven to act when you learn what is wrong and what is the correct thing to do.

The authorities started to pay serious attention to the members of the Student Cultural Association of the University of the Philippines (SCAUP) and particularly to me after the March 15, 1961 demonstration of 5000 students, which literally scuttled the congressional hearing of the Committee on Anti-Filipino Activities.

From then on, I noticed close enemy surveillance. In 1961, the anti-communist reactionaries who dominated the faculty of the English Department of the University of the Philippines refused to renew my graduate scholarship and teaching fellowship.

Subsequently, I took a language scholarship to study the bahasa Indonesia in 1961 but could not leave immediately because the National Intelligence Coordinating Agency blocked my application for a passport. I was able to get the passport only after an uncle, Sixto Brillantes, former governor of Ilocos Sur and then chairman of the Commission on Elections, asked President Carlos Garcia to order the Department of Foreign Affairs to issue my passport in late 1961.

I left for Indonesia in early 1962 and stayed there for nearly six months. Upon my return, the government intelligence agencies placed me under closer surveillance. I had difficulties holding on to any paying job because of intelligence dossiers fed to my employers.

When I got a job in 1963, I rose very quickly from the position of public relations officer of the Araneta University to executive secretary of the university president and owner, Dr. Salvador Araneta. As executive secretary, I assisted him in running not only the school but also all his other business enterprises. But he asked me to resign as soon as government intelligence agents fed him with dossiers accusing me of encouraging the strike of students and employees at the FEATI University, another academic enterprise of the Araneta family.

I suppose that being deprived of a paying job constituted a threat to life, not only for me but also Julie and our two children. But I went into trade union work in 1963 and received a small monthly allowance that augmented the salary of my wife who worked as a librarian. I also gained the time to edit the *Progressive Review*, a magazine of social, political, economic and cultural studies.

Enemy surveillance increased upon the suspicion that I was a communist cadre aside from being openly involved in workers' strikes and protest rallies of the youth. I must have been detected attending small and big meetings in Manila and in some provinces of Central Luzon.

My participation was surely noticed in public gatherings of workers in Manila and peasants in Central Luzon, in workers' strikes, student strikes and in various forms of mass protest actions initiated by the organizations to which I belonged. I had to make strenuous efforts to evade enemy surveillance to be able to attend secret Party meetings or conduct study meetings of veteran worker and peasant cadres to whom I gave refresher courses in the early 1960s.

Q3. Please mention some of the mass actions in which you participated in the 1960s so we can gain an idea of both the extent of your involvement and the level of mass activism then.

After the anti-CAFA rally of 1961, I was in the mass action of around 500 workers and students protesting President Macapagal's maneuvers to extend the validity of the Laurel-Langley Agreement in 1962. We marched into the grounds of the presidential palace where presidential guards with fixed bayonets forcibly dispersed us.

We organized mass actions against the US-RP military bases agreement whenever US troops killed Filipinos inside or close to the US military bases. We held a demonstration of 5000 people in Angeles City in the vicinity of the Clark Air Force Base in December 1964. In the spirit of international solidarity, we also held protest actions against aggressive actions of the US in Cuba, Vietnam, Laos, Indonesia and other parts of the world in the entire decade of the 1960s.

We reached a new high in the mass movement when, in January 1965, we succeeded in mobilizing 20,000 workers, peasants and youth to demonstrate against all-round US domination of the Philippines and against continuing feudal domination. We demonstrated in front of Congress and proceeded with a torch parade to demonstrate in front of the US embassy and further on in front of the presidential palace.

I participated in the October 23, 1966 picket in front of the Manila Hotel against US President Lyndon Johnson's visit and the US war of aggression in Vietnam. We were arrested and detained for several hours. The following day, we were back with more than 5000 students. The police and the military viciously attacked us.

To be brief, let me say that I attended every major mass protest action against the US imperialists and the reactionary government until I went underground in late 1968. While underground, I continued to monitor the mass actions from 1969 to 1972. I am proud to have made contributions to the planning and conduct of the First Quarter Storm of 1970 and the subsequent mass actions up to the declaration of martial law in 1972.

Under the assumed name Amado Guerrero, I commented on each of the major mass actions in the First Quarter Storm of 1970. Taking proper safeguards and without revealing themselves, some members of the Executive Committee of the newly reestablished Communist Party of the Philippines discussed and planned the mass movement together with representatives of the youth organizations, trade unions and other mass organizations.

Assassination Attempts

Q4. When was the first serious attempt on your life?

In early 1968, I experienced the first serious attempt on my life. This happened in downtown Manila. One of three men in a passenger jeepney I had boarded tried to stab me with a fan knife aiming for my heart. Another tried to block my way out of the jeepney. I parried the attack, automatically shielding my left chest with my right arm while kicking at my assailant. I suffered a stab wound just below my right elbow.

I jumped out of the jeepney. Had they used a gun or guns, I would have been finished. But they used a knife perhaps to make the physical assault look non-political. Upon the advice of Senator Lorenzo Tañada, who was then chairman of the Movement for the Advancement of Nationalism, I went to the headquarters of the Manila police to report the incident and put it on public record. But the police were not helpful.

Q5. *After this incident, how did you protect yourself? How did this affect your life?*

Of course, after this attempt on my life, I had to be even more careful. All members of my household became alert to new faces and vehicles in the neighborhood. I could no longer take public rides or walk the streets by myself.

Comrades with handguns and cameras accompanied me when I went out for appointments. I made my schedule unpredictable to outsiders. I had to improve my skills at self-defense, such as toppling a bigger opponent and using a handgun. At any rate, for most of 1968, I was in the company of comrades already preparing to go to the field of armed struggle.

Q6. *Have you ever faced death threats from elements other than those associated with the US and the Filipino ruling system?*

Of course, there were such death threats. I came to know of some very serious ones. The Lava revisionist renegades tried to kill me several times from 1967 to 1968.

Once they set up a trap, sending a mutual friend to invite me to a so-called reconciliation meeting where they planned to grab me. But they called it off as soon as they noticed that I had companions with me for security.

Later, the Lavas again plotted to ambush me in the vicinity of my office at the National Association of Trade Unions in 1968. But they failed again because, since the knife attack earlier that year, comrades had always accompanied me. They were ever alert and ready to repel the assassins. I came to know of several Lava plots since the mutual friend who had brought me the reconciliation invitation eventually broke away from the Lavas. He told me of their treachery.

Commander Sumulong (Faustino del Mundo) of the degenerated *Hukbong Mapagpalaya ng Bayan* (HMB—People's Liberation Army), using the pretext of seeking cooperation against the Lava revisionist renegades, invited me twice in 1967 for a meeting. Out of sympathy for me, Sumulong's representative, whose son was a member of *Kabataang Makabayan* (KM), deliberately fouled up the arrangements for each of the meetings. This frustrated Sumulong's scheme to have me killed.

I came to know later from Bernabe Buscayno that Sumulong had planned to kill me because he regarded my work for the CPP as a threat to his "independent kingdom" in Angeles City where he was running a protection syndicate. He saw me as among those chiefly responsible for organizing in Central Luzon the Malayang Samahan ng Magsasaka (MASAKA—Free Association of Peasants), a peasant association outside his control.

Q7. In the 1960s when you were still aboveground, character assassination was more consistently and more often launched against you than attempts at physical assassination. Please recount these.

The most consistent line of attack used by reactionary politicians and by columnists in the reactionary press against me in the 1960s was that I was a communist. At that time, being called a communist was tantamount to being called the devil. Cold war hysteria in our country was running high.

My detractors in the political establishment, press and academe rose to a high pitch of anticommunist propaganda against me every time there was a mass action against the US and the reactionary regime. Some lines of attack were more specific. After I came back from Indonesia in 1962, the most rabid anticommunist columnists in the *Philippines Herald* called me an agent of the Communist Party of Indonesia because I was the secretary general of the Philippine-Indonesian Friendship and Cultural Association.

After Sukarno came to Manila for the Maphilindo conference in 1963, one yellow tabloid started to call me an agent of Sukarno and even accused me of fronting for him as buyer of a Forbes Park mansion for an alleged Filipino girl friend of his, the prominent socialite Amelia de la Rama, whom I did not know from Eve. The only time I was in the company of Sukarno and a pretty woman was when I sat between him and the movie actress Josephine Estrada at a brunch tendered for him in 1963 by then Speaker Jose Laurel at his Shaw Boulevard residence.

Coming back from a short trip to Indonesia in 1963, I was accosted at the Manila airport by intelligence agents who confiscated from me a luggage full of books. I was subsequently attacked in the media for attempting to bring communist books into the country.

After I came back from a visit to China in 1966, the longtime witch hunter Carlos Albert, director of the National Intelligence Coordinating Agency, and some anticommunist columnists in the most reactionary newspapers started to call me an agent of the Chinese Communist Party and Mao Zedong.

These attacks did not at all discourage but simply amused me. I went to China again in 1967 for a study tour and spoke at the conference of the Afro-Asian Writers Association to celebrate the 25th anniversary of Chairman Mao's "Talks at the Yenan Forum on Literature and Art". I had the distinct honor of meeting Comrade Mao and having a photograph taken with him.

Q8. *Is there a reason why the response to your political activities by powerful forces in the US and the Philippines was particularly intense? After all, there were other activists and dissidents.*

There was practically no revolutionary mass movement from the time it was crushed in the early 1950's until 1961. I was a sort of pioneer promoting the resurgence of the anti-imperialist and anti-feudal mass movement. I presume that this is why Filipino reactionaries and US imperialists harbor a deep-seated hatred of me to this day.

They had the illusion that they had completely destroyed the Communist Party of the Philippines and the revolutionary movement in the 1950s. And they passed the Anti-subversion Law in 1957, with the explicit purpose of preventing any revival and of wiping out every sign or trace of any organization that could be deemed a successor, front, extension, affiliate or whatever, of the communist party.

The law merely served to underscore the pro-imperialist and anti-democratic character of the ruling system and challenged us to generate a revolutionary mass movement. Since the early 1960s, the enemy has consistently held the CPP responsible for the revival of the revolutionary mass movement.

Q9. *One accusation was that you could dare to challenge the Philippine ruling system because you were banking on military and financial aid from the People's Republic of China and the Communist Party of China.*

We dare fight US imperialism and the local ruling classes not because we depend on any foreign country or party for military and financial assistance. We rely on the Filipino people fighting for their own national and democratic rights and interests. We trust them as having the motivation and capability to free themselves from oppression and exploitation. We see them as the inexhaustible source of strength for their own revolutionary struggle for national and social liberation.

We are inspired by the revolutionary teachings of Mao Zedong and by the successful revolutionary practice of the Chinese people under the leadership of the Chinese Communist Party. From among the teachings of Mao, we have learned the principle of self-reliance in carrying the Philippine revolution forward. We need moral and material support from abroad but we are not dependent on it.

Q10. Under the Walter-McCarran Act, you were blacklisted as a foreign communist and barred from entry to the US since the 1960s. When the term "terrorist" supplanted the term "communist" in the 1990s in the US law on immigration and naturalization, the US automatically labeled the Communist Party of the Philippines, the New People's Army and you as terrorist. What is your view of terrorism? And what has it meant to you personally to be labeled a terrorist?

US imperialism is the No.1 terrorist force in the entire world and in the entire history of humanity. It is culpable for the killing of tens of millions of people through wars of aggression, the use of the atom bombs and other weapons of mass destruction, the instigation of massacres and the setting up of puppet regimes of open terror. The use of imperialist violence guarantees the daily terrorism that is imperialist plunder and exploitation, victimizing billions of people.

The US has no basis whatsoever to label as "terrorist" the Communist Party of the Philippines (CPP), the New People's Army (NPA) and individuals like me who fight for national liberation and democracy against US imperialism and its puppets in the Philippines. The Filipino people can never forget the killing of 1.5 million Filipinos from the start of the Filipino-American War in 1899 to the waning years of the US pacification campaign in 1913. The US is responsible for the 14 years of Marcos fascist dictatorship, from 1972 to 1986. US terrorism is a daily phenomenon in the Philippines through plunder and exploitation and victimizes the entire Filipino people.

It is not the CPP and NPA but the US imperialists and their puppets that are responsible for terrorism, which we may define as the willful and systematic infliction of violence or threat to inflict violence on civilians and noncombatants in an armed conflict. This violates human rights and the humane treatment of civilians and hors de combat under circumstances of war. It violates the norms and standards set forth by international conventions and the customary law on armed conflict.

The CPP and NPA have steadfastly fulfilled the duty of respecting the bill of fundamental rights set forth by the Guide for Establishing the People's Democratic Government. They are further bound by the Geneva Conventions and its protocols and by the GRP-NDFP Comprehensive Agreement on Respect for Human Rights and International Humanitarian Law.

The NPA is the revolutionary army of the Filipino people and the people's democratic government. It is under the political leadership of the Communist Party of the Philippines and has a well-developed system of command. It is bound by the principle of revolutionary service to the Filipino people and by strict rules of discipline.

With regard to myself, it is utterly unjust and a lie for anyone to call me a terrorist. US authorities have tagged me as a terrorist to discredit me and to bar me from entering their country. This vindictiveness is their reaction to my consistent anti-imperialist stand. They are vindictive against anyone who resolutely fights for national liberation and democracy.

In the Battlefield

Q11. I presume that while you were underground, you had to divide your time between doing office work as Chairman of the Central Committee of the Communist Party of the Philippines and being out in the field with the New People's Army. In either circumstance, were you prepared to shoot it out in case of an enemy attack? Were you always armed? With what?

I did sustained office work either in a forest camp secured by units of the NPA or in an underground house in a barrio or in a suburb. I also had to march with the New People's Army quite often in order to know the situation on the ground or go to important meetings in a rural area secured by units of the NPA.

In all circumstances, I relied on comrades who were assigned to take charge of my security. These were either a small team in a reliable mass base or a full platoon in a forest camp. The first rule was for my guards to take me away to safety in the event of an imminent attack or an attack in progress. But if the first rule could not be carried out, then the second rule was for me to join the fight and fire my gun to defend myself or cover my retreat.

I usually had a handgun essentially for self-defense at close quarters.

When I moved with a unit of the NPA, I was issued a rifle like the fighters in the unit.

Q12. One prevailing stereotype of you is that of an intellectual, with little to do directly with revolutionary armed struggle; that all you did was to write and talk about it. Can you say something more about your being with the NPA? Were you ever directly involved with actions of the New People's Army? Did you ever plan, oversee or direct NPA campaigns and operations. Were you ever with the NPA units, or in a firefight or close to one?

As chairman of the CPP Central Committee and as chairman of the Military Commission, I led the process of deciding policy, strategy and tactics for the revolutionary armed struggle. I marched with a security unit assigned to me and other units of the people's army in the villages and forests, on the plains, across rivers and over mountains.

I joined the Red fighters in conducting social investigation and mass work, conducted politico-military training and participated in planning tactical offensives. We shared weal and woe and, of course, dangers to life. In Tarlac, Isabela, Pampanga, Bataan and elsewhere, I was often within the enemy's encirclement and was with the Red fighters in maneuvering ourselves out of the encirclement. A number of times, I was in the midst of firefights. Oftentimes, I was within or near the area of tactical operations against enemy troops to monitor the progress of the operations.

Whenever necessary, I consulted with commanders of the NPA regarding operations. I paid close attention and devoted much time to certain tactical offensives—examining intelligence reports, carefully guiding the building of a mock up for the target area, choosing the Red commanders and fighters for the operation, planning the offensive with them and training them for that purpose. Sometimes, I would suggest that I participate in the combat operations. More often than not, the comrades in the NPA politely refused.

It was in training exercises that I took my share of fire experience. The training officer would ask me to demonstrate my firing accuracy. Thus, I found occasion to repeat my previous high rating as a rifle marksman, with the Garand and Browning automatic rifle, in the Reserve Officers Training Corps (ROTC) of the University of the Philippines. I never found use for my ROTC training as an artilleryman.

Whether out in the field, in an underground house or in transit from one region to another, I faced dangers like all other comrades. In the midst of or close to firefights, I had to be ready to fight. When marching and camping with units of the NPA, aside from my pistol, I usually carried a rifle like the Red fighters.

Q13. Once you were underground, and a declared enemy of the state, you became a target for punitive measures, including death. In fact, there was a prize for your head. How much was it? How many times were you in danger of arrest or death?

In early 1969, when it became known that I was chairman of the Central Committee of the CPP, the enemy offered the price of 200,000 pesos for my capture, dead or alive. That was a lot of money then.

As far as I know, from 1969 to 1977, I was almost captured or killed in at least twenty instances at various places in the provinces of Tarlac, Isabela, Pampanga, Bataan and Zambales. There were probably more such instances. But an exact count would be difficult, considering the very fluid situation of certain periods in those years.

Take for instance the period of 1969 to 1970, when the NPA increased its armed strength from nine automatic rifles to more than 200 through tactical offensives in the second district of Tarlac, the enemy reacted strongly and mustered a full division of army soldiers and constabulary men against us. During this period, my comrades and I went through so many dangers and difficulties. The enemy often raided as many as 10 villages at the same time, carrying out house-to-house searches.

In the early years of the people's war, the guerrilla zones were small and far apart. I often ran the risk of being arrested and killed whenever I stayed too long in one guerrilla zone or whenever I used highways or roads where the enemy was likely to set up checkpoints.

A few times the vehicle in which I was riding would be flagged down at enemy checkpoints or by enemy patrols. But I was almost always properly documented, unarmed, accompanied by respectable people, and ready with an appropriate alibi. Thus I would escape recognition and be allowed to go together with my companions.

At other times, informers would report to their superiors my presence in a specific location, either a house, village or mountain camp. But I would change location and the enemy would miss me by a few minutes. Still at other times, when in the hurry to make an important appointment I would dare to cross—on foot or on a bull cart—areas heavily monitored or patrolled by scout ranger teams of the enemy. In 1977, some comrades and I had to march rapidly for some days to avoid an enemy cordon at Mount Natib. We slipped away from Bataan by riding a pump boat to Subic.

Q14. *Can you recount an incident or some incidents when you felt you were a goner; when, as the cliché goes, your life flashed before your eyes?*

Some remain vivid in my mind. Late in May 1969, an enemy platoon raided Barrio Sta. Rita, Capas, Tarlac to conduct a search of the house of the barrio captain whom the military suspected of belonging to the revolutionary movement. At first, the enemy did not know that I was holding office in that barrio.

After the search yielded some firearms, the platoon radioed for a battalion-sized reinforcement and made a rapid probe of the entire barrio by encircling one house after another. I was able to slip out of the house we were using as my office and transfer to another house only a few seconds before the enemy troops came and discovered office facilities in the building.

But the house (actually a flimsy bamboo and nipa hut) to which I had transferred would soon be encircled for a short while. Had the enemy troops gone in and searched the house, I could have been captured or killed. Fortunately, the enemy troops did not enter the house and then moved on. I was able to move out of the barrio before the enemy battalion arrived to comb the area and conduct house-to-house searches. This was the enemy raid widely reported in the Philippine media to have uncovered the CPP and NPA headquarters and "tunnel" facilities.

Shortly after the declaration of martial law, one evening in November 1972, I was transferring from Northern to Central Luzon. The car I was in was flagged down by enemy troops for inspection. This was at a narrow pass approaching the bridge linking Bamban, Tarlac and Mabalacat, Pampanga. I thought then that I was a goner and that I would either be killed on the spot or elsewhere.

I was in the backseat, behind the comrade driver. Beside me was Julie and beside the driver was his wife-comrade. I was the only one with a gun—a pistol tucked in a small bag at my feet behind the driver's seat. Following a split second of fear or the flash of thought that I was finished, I debated with myself whether to allow myself to be arrested or to resist and shoot at least one enemy soldier. But that would have invited enemy fire on all my unarmed companions.

I continued debating with myself as the comrade driver and his wife were asked to alight from the car and allow the soldiers to inspect the front seat. Just as they finished checking the front seat and were turning to check the back seat, a commotion erupted around a van ahead of our car. The soldiers had discovered guns on board. They called for help and the soldiers abandoned inspecting our car and told us to move on.

The threat to my life did not come only from enemy troops. A natural phenomenon like a mountain torrent almost finished me off in June 1970 in the forest region of Isabela during a forced march to slip through a huge enemy encirclement. We had been marching for four days and four nights and it was raining hard most of the time.

As we were crossing a creek along a mountain gully, we saw a sudden mountain torrent coming down towards us. Comrades quickly dragged me to the bank some seconds before the torrent rolled down the gully with full fury, sweeping away seven comrades and ultimately drowning two of them. Antero Santos, a young instructor of the Party school, who was right behind me, was swept away and drowned. By the way, Lorena Barros (one of the founders of MAKIBAKA, the revolutionary women's organization) was in that long march because she had come to our camp to report on the women's movement. She was later killed during an encounter between the New People's Army and government troops.

The Capture

Q15. *When you were captured in 1977 or later on when you were already in prison, did you think you could or would be killed?*

Yes, of course. When my companions and I were captured on November 10, 1977, the probability did cross my mind that I could be killed at the place of arrest, while in transport to Manila or while already in detention.

I learned later from reliable sources that the group of generals and colonels who were in charge of the prolonged intelligence dragnet for my capture and who were directly under Marcos debated whether I should be killed or not upon capture. What prevailed was the reasoning that to capture me alive and show me off as trophy would be better propaganda for Marcos.

While in prison, I continued to be vulnerable to foul play. At any rate, Marcos ordered my physical and psychological torture. My tormentors subjected me to fist blows and to the "water cure". The intent was to break me. They manacled and shackled me to a cot for more than 18 months. They kept me under solitary confinement for more than five years and in partial isolation for several more years. The fascist regime "tried" me under two military commissions on the charges of subversion and rebellion. Subversion then carried the death penalty.

Q16. *This seems too brief a summation for what was an extremely difficult time. What did being manacled to a cot for 18 months mean? How did you attend to your personal necessities? And how did you deal with the ennui of solitary confinement after being so mobile in the countryside?*

My long poem, "Fragments of a Nightmare" express in lyrical terms my torture experience. The most thorough presentations of my experience of torture were those I smuggled out during the three times that I was brought to the Supreme Court on a *habeas corpus* petition.

Being manacled and fettered to a cot for 18 months was in itself extreme physical violence. My tormentors used shackles that cut into the flesh after I was observed passing some papers to my lawyer Juan T. David. However, the main form of violence was psychological. I did not know then that I would remain shackled for 18 months.

Thus, the uncertainty, boredom, cruel restraint and helplessness combined to fall on my brain as blocks of lead every second, every minute, every day and every month. The figure of speech is precise. Being kept ignorant about how long I would be in solitary confinement, manacled and fettered to the cot, made the pain of psychological torture very acute.

The manacles and fetters were removed only when I needed to take my meal, go to the toilet or take a bath. But the guards always made it a point to rush me through these motions. At times, I had to remain attached to the cot and be carried to the toilet because, as the guards would claim, one of them had inadvertently taken the keys home and the shackles could not be removed.

I fought ennui in solitary confinement by reviewing experiences and articles that I had written or read in the past, by composing poems and reciting them and by working out in my mind plots of novels.

Post-Marcos Threats

Q17. Before leaving the Philippines in 1986, did you ever think of applying for political asylum abroad in order to stay out of danger? At the time, there were already reports that the Reform the AFP Movement (RAM) was out to assassinate you.

Some time before leaving Manila for Japan on October 22, 1986, I got hold of confidential reports that the RAM was planning to kill me under its Oplan "God Save the Queen". The perverse notion of the RAM leadership then was to kill "communists" in the Aquino cabinet and known communists or progressive leaders, in order to teach Aquino a lesson, save her from the communists and make her yield to the demands of then-secretary of defense Juan Ponce Enrile.

At that time, I tended to underestimate those reports regarding Oplan "God Save the Queen". Before I left the Philippines, I did not intend to apply for political asylum in any foreign country. In fact, I wanted to return home immediately even after the RAM started to carry out Oplan "God Save the Queen," kidnapping and murdering Rolando Olalia (Ka Lando), chairman of Partido ng Bayan and Kilusang Mayo Uno, on November 12, 1986.

I was still in Tokyo then and I wanted to attend the funeral of Ka Lando. I considered it a duty to attend his funeral, especially because, as I still think, my absence made the RAM choose him in my stead as prime target for assassination in showing off its strength.

However, Filipino and Japanese comrades and friends prevailed upon me not to return because they estimated that the enemy was not yet satisfied with the torture, mutilation and murder of Comrade Rolando Olalia and his driver Leonor Alay-ay.

From Tokyo, Julie and I went on to Hong Kong in December 1986. It was she who quietly returned to Manila right on Christmas eve to deliver to comrades and friends my objections to the lopsided terms of the ceasefire agreement of the NDFP with the Aquino regime and to seek advice regarding my lecture tour and homecoming.

She rejoined me in Hong Kong in early January 1987, bringing the advice of comrades and friends that I should prolong my stay abroad until further advice to the contrary because the threats to my life were very serious.

Q18. From Hong Kong, where did you go? Was the advice for you to stay away from the Philippines valid? Were your friends' and comrades' fears for your life accurate?

We proceeded to India and stayed there for two weeks. We visited New Delhi, Bangalore, Madras and Madurai where we attended and spoke at solidarity gatherings, delivered university lectures and held press conferences. We flew from New Delhi to Amsterdam in the morning of January 23, 1986. Upon our arrival at Schiphol airport, our welcomers told us that peasants and their sympathizers participating in a demonstration in front of the presidential palace in Manila had been massacred on January 22, 1987.

Subsequently, Mrs. Aquino "unsheathed the sword of war" and declared her regime's total war policy against the revolutionary movement. And General Ramos pushed his "forward deployment strategy" and his national campaign plans of anticommunist suppression. Regular military and police forces were fielded in the countryside. Death squads were unleashed in urban areas.

The enemy forces carried out a series of ambushes of progressive leaders in the legal struggle in Manila. The secretary-general of *BAYAN*, Lean Alejandro, was ambushed and killed. The former *Partido ng Bayan* senatorial candidate Bernabe Buscayno was ambushed and wounded. Although he escaped death, one of his companions in the car was killed and two were seriously wounded.

Nonetheless, in mid-1987, I received advice from comrades to prepare for my secret return to the Philippines. In late 1987, I was supposed to board one or another vessel somewhere, according to a Plan A or B. Neither plan worked. Certain circumstances prevented the implementation of my homecoming. I cannot provide more details because these would prejudice other people.

Q19. From 1986 onward, what made you feel with certainty that your life was threatened?

The ever-intensifying psywar campaigns conducted by various reactionary groups to demonize me in the eyes of the public constitute a threat to my life. Also, the murder of outstanding mass leaders of the national-democratic movement who were close to me, as well as the murder of six PnB congressional candidates and of human rights lawyers made me feel very keenly the threat to my life.

I was definitely among the targets, if not the prime target. The threats came not only from the RAM and Marcos loyalists but also from authorized operatives of the regular structure of the military and police and from secretly authorized death squads and vigilante groups.

Anticommunist excitement ran high among the reactionaries. They were inciting violence against suspected communists. The RAM painted the wall slogan "Kill Joma" around Manila and in major cities from 1987 onward. Cardinal Sin was attacking the PnB as a "social leper" and praising the Civilian Armed Force Geographical Units (CAFGU) and the anticommunist vigilante groups.

The pro-Aquino and anti-Aquino reactionaries were poised to do violence against each other. But behind the scenes, US operatives were directing Generals Ileto, Ramos and De Villa to whip up anticommunist hysteria as a way of glossing over and mending the split among the reactionaries and rallying the reactionary armed forces to close ranks.

Q20. What threats to you clearly came from the military under the Aquino regime?

Generals Fidel V. Ramos and Renato De Villa became quite vocal against me when I was abroad, from the time I was in Australia in September 1986. They started to publicly pressure Mrs. Aquino to cancel my passport. They kept on claiming that I had re-assumed the chairmanship of the CPP Central Committee and that I was touring the world to raise military and financial resources. And they slandered me in so many specific ways.

General Ramos did everything in 1986 and 1987 to bribe and use Victor Corpus as propagandist against me on the false charge of masterminding the Plaza Miranda bombing. Using the Westview Press as conduit, the US Central Intelligence Agency financed Gregg Jones to write a book along the same line. A Manila newspaper used the Jones book as the basis for attacking me in a series of editorial articles.

I was able to obtain a copy of a top-secret memorandum dated January 5, 1989 and signed by the armed forces chief of staff Gen. Renato de Villa endorsing *Oplan Jericho*. The plan was to carry out "special military operations" against suspected leaders of the CPP, NPA and NDF and carry out psywar operations to murder communists and put the blame on their comrades in order to sow intrigue and chaos within the revolutionary movement. US and Philippine intelligence and psywar experts devised Oplan

Jericho in pursuit of the low intensity conflict scheme.

Bounties of one million pesos for my head and half-a-million for Julie's were announced in July 1989. A Philippine military intelligence officer, one army colonel Manuel Oxales, went so far as to offer the Dutch journalist Henk Ruigrok from the Dutch magazine *Nieuwe Revu* a reward of US$ 200,000 in exchange for bringing me dead or alive to the Philippine embassy in The Hague.

The military psywar waged a full blast campaign of character assassination against me. It blamed me even for the hysterical anti-informer campaigns, which I had condemned and which all occurred within the revolutionary movement while I was either under maximum-security detention (in the case of Kampanyang Ahos) or abroad (in the case of Olympia and Oplan Missing Links). They also blamed me for the Digos massacre and similar events, which all occurred while I was abroad. They put up billboards and published magazines attacking me.

Further, they revived Marcos's false claim that the late Senator Benigno Aquino and I were responsible for the Plaza Miranda bombing. In November 1989 Senate president Jovito Salonga pushed the Senate blue ribbon and justice committees to hold joint hearings in order to play up the false charge that I "masterminded" the Plaza Miranda bombing.

Q21. However, after becoming president in 1992, General Ramos seemed to have caused the threats and attempts on your life to abate. He sent Rep. Jose V. Yap and Bernabe Buscayno to you to ask for peace negotiations. Why the change?

General Ramos came to the presidency on a minority vote of 23.5 per cent. He was advised by the people around him to minimize his military image and have a broad appeal by trying to engage the NDFP in peace negotiations.

He was also ordered by the US to carry out the Armacost formula for healing the rifts within the reactionary armed forces by granting amnesty to the RAM and the Marcos-leaning Soldiers of the Filipino People (SFP). To pretend at being evenhanded, he offered amnesty to suspected revolutionaries, whether captured or still at large.

The CPP and NDFP refused the offer of amnesty. But soon after the signing of The Hague Joint Declaration as framework for the GRP-NDFP peace negotiations on September 1, 1992, Ramos ordered the release of a significant number of political prisoners.

The strategic objective of General Ramos against the revolutionary movement did not change. He was merely trying to use counterrevolutionary dual tactics. While he drummed up peace negotiations, his troops were carrying out the most vicious campaigns of suppression against the revolutionary forces and the people even as armed tactical offensives of the NPA decreased from 1992 to 1996 because the CPP concentrated on rectifying opportunist errors and doing mass work in order to recover strength.

Threats from Ex-colleagues

Q22. In 1994, there were media reports of death threats against you from Filemon "Popoy" Lagman, former secretary of the Manila-Rizal Committee of the CPP and Arturo Tabara, former secretary of the Visayas Commission of the CPP. Are these related to the assassination plot ascribed to Romulo Kintanar, former chief of staff of the NPA?

Lagman, Tabara and Kintanar were together up to 1994, collaborating with one another in anti-CPP, anti-NPA and anti-NDFP activities and presumably scheming on how to do away with me politically and physically. But Kintanar became engrossed with intelligence and moneymaking projects with his uncle, General Galileo Kintanar, former chief of the Intelligence Service of the Armed Forces of the Philippines (ISAFP), and distanced himself from Lagman in 1994.

Tabara, together with Nilo de la Cruz, also parted ways with Lagman after a violent dispute over the sharing of the bribe money from the Amari real estate company in exchange for the eviction of an urban-poor community.

I am not sure whether Lagman ever tried to implement his threat to have me assassinated. More highly probable is Romulo Kintanar and Tabara collaborating in one scheme after another to have me assassinated. Both of them have become well connected with the intelligence services, especially the ISAFP, and have wangled contracts as "security consultants" for powerful politicians. Tabara has become notorious as one of the security chiefs of Eduardo Cojuangco in Manila and Negros.

Q23. You had sharp verbal exchanges with the deposed president Joseph Estrada in the media while he was president. But he raised the ante by reportedly authorizing an assassination plot against you. How

was this supposed to be carried out?

I have two different sources of information regarding the assassination plot approved by Mr. Estrada and supervised by General Panfilo Lacson. One source is close to Romulo Kintanar who proposed the plot to Estrada and Lacson and the other source is Colonel Reynaldo Berroya, a high official of the Philippine National Police.

The assassination team came to the Netherlands in March 2000. Some Filipino residents in the Netherlands associated with Kintanar assisted it. The objective was to hit me when the opportunity presented itself or to wait for me to show up and hit me at a big picnic of the Filipino community in the Netherlands in June 2000.

The plot went awry when one of the operatives who had arrived from Manila was arrested at the Schiphol airport for carrying a knife. The Dutch police authorities reportedly detained but subsequently released the operative. They evidently knew nothing about the plot.

But the arrest was enough to disrupt the plot. The head of the team grew nervous although his team continued to conduct surveillance on me around the NDFP International Office until he was recalled to Manila in the last quarter of 2000.

The assassination scheme was supposed to be resumed in March 2001. But Colonel Berroya went on the air at DZBB in Manila to expose the scheme on January 30, 2001. The expose upset the assassination scheme. It also made unnecessary the plan of Filipino and Dutch friends of mine to conduct counter-surveillance and preempt or possibly catch the prospective assassins.

On the Plaza Miranda Bombing

Q24. It was soon after the 1971 Plaza Miranda bombing of the opposition Liberal Party that Marcos accused you and Sen. Benigno Aquino of being the masterminds of the attack. He accused the two of you as terrorists. This same charge has surfaced again and again. Were you responsible for the Plaza Miranda bombing? If not, who do you think was actually responsible for it?

I had nothing to do with the bombing. The Liberal Party was then objectively an important, even if informal, ally of the CPP against the Marcos regime as this became increasingly repressive. There was no reason at all for the CPP or for me to physically attack such an ally.

I also believe that the late Sen. Aquino had nothing to do with the bombing. He would not harm his own party mates, even though he and Liberal Party president Gerry Roxas were intra-party rivals. His closest party mates like Ramon Mitra were at the rally. Aquino had a credible reason for his absence that evening.

It was Marcos who stood to gain and did actually gain the most from the bombing. This provided him with the pretext to suspend the writ of habeas corpus on August 21, 1971 and then to declare martial law in September 1972. Aquino counter-charged that Marcos was responsible for the crime and presented documentary evidence, a secret memorandum on Oplan Double Strike. This was a scheme to launch physical attacks on the legal opposition and make the communists the scapegoat.

Both the National Bureau of Investigation and the Manila Police Detective Bureau conducted the most serious and most sustained investigations into Plaza Miranda. Their findings showed that the CPP, NPA, Aquino and I had nothing to do with the bombing.

In an interview during the 1986 EDSA uprising, Juan Ponce Enrile, who was Marcos's long-time defense minister, publicly admitted that Marcos had masterminded the Plaza Miranda bombing in 1971 and the fake ambush of Enrile's car in 1972. Earlier than Enrile's admission, Primitivo Mijares, the most rabid Marcos propagandist before he broke away from Marcos and shifted to the opposition, declared in his book *Conjugal Dictatorship* that Marcos was responsible for the bombing.

As documented by Raymond Bonner's *Waltzing With A Dictator*, even the CIA did not believe Marcos' accusation that the communists had anything to do with the crime. The findings of the CIA from its own investigation and from its Philippine sources show Marcos was the probable mastermind of the Plaza Miranda bombing.

Q25. In a recently published book, former Senate president Jovito Salonga revived the Plaza Miranda bombing allegation against you. He has been pretty persistent with this. Would you know why?

It is not for me to spell out the motives of the former senate president. It is simply strange to me that he persists in making his false accusations based on hearsay from Ariel Almendral and the uncorroborated testimony of Samuel Paquiz.

Salonga goes to the extent of being blatantly dishonest by making it appear in his book that he has a new mystery witness against me. He tries to make it appear that he is protecting his witness by not mentioning his name. In fact, Salonga is referring to Paquiz whose testimony was ventilated and debunked at the Senate hearings in 1989 and further examined and evaluated by the city prosecutors of Manila.

The book does not present anything new by way of evidence against me; rather, it offers the most outlandish speculations. It makes a long propaganda attack on the CPP as having supposedly carried out the Plaza Miranda bombing in order to generate recruits who would carry the weapons expected from China in 1971 and 1972.

It is strange that Salonga persists in trying to exculpate Marcos from the Plaza Miranda bombing by making baseless and speculative accusations against me. Is it because of sheer belief in the intriguers who have approached him through his son Steve? Or is it because he is such a rabid anticommunist as to hit the CPP every time the latter is able to make advances in the revolutionary struggle?

Asylum in the Netherlands

Q26. Before your Philippine passport was cancelled on September 16, 1988, did you ever consider applying for asylum? Why did you apply for asylum? Why in the Netherlands? Do you accept the label self-exile?

I never seriously considered applying for political asylum anywhere before my Philippine passport was cancelled. I planned to finish my lecture tour in Western Europe and then proceed to the US. But I could not go to the US on schedule in 1987 because I could not get the visa.

After the cancellation of my passport, I had to apply for political asylum in order to frustrate the scheme of the Aquino regime and the military to handcuff and humiliate me upon my return. The passport cancellation was based on the trumped up charge of subversion, which they had filed on September 14, 1988.

It took me a little over a month to consider whether or not to apply for asylum and to consult with lawyers and friends. The preponderant advice from comrades, friends and relatives was for me to apply because those in power in the Philippines were out to imprison or kill me. Thus, I finally sought asylum on October 26, 1988.

It was true that the Aquino regime had calculated that the cancellation of my passport would force my return to the Philippines and allow the military to arrest me. The regime overlooked the fact that I had a well-grounded fear of persecution and that I had the option of applying for political asylum.

I applied in the Netherlands because I happened to be here when my passport was cancelled. Fortunately, it also happened that the NDFP international office is based here.

Some reactionary politicians and journalists call me a self-exile in order to gloss over the fact that I am a political refugee. Of course, I do not accept the label of self-exile. It is a malicious misrepresentation.

The Dutch Council of State (*Raad van State*) has recognized me as a political refugee since 1992 and even the Dutch government has done so belatedly since 1997.

Q27. *Your application for political asylum has created disagreements among various agencies of the Dutch government. Please summarize their bone or bones of contention.*

The Dutch justice ministry in a decision dated July 13, 1990 rejected my application for political asylum. In turn, the judicial branch of the *Raad van State*, the highest administrative court, in a ruling dated December 17, 1992 nullified this negative decision.

The *Raad van State* ruled that I was a political refugee under Article 1a of the Refugee Convention on the basis of the facts and arguments presented by my lawyer Tom Boekman, Amnesty International and the Dutch office of the UN High Commission for Refugees. It nullified the argument of the Dutch justice ministry that I was not at all a political refugee and that I was not under persecution but merely subject to prosecution as the "intellectual author" of the violence of the NPA.

The court also ruled that it was against the principle of fair administration to use against me secret intelligence dossiers that I was barred from scrutinizing and therefore from answering to defend myself. The dossiers alleged that I was responsible for the violence of the New People's Army of the CPP and for contacts with "terrorist" organizations. Dutch, US and Philippine intelligence agencies supplied the dossiers to the Dutch government. The court went so far as to chide the Dutch justice ministry for failing to grant me asylum after nearly four years.

The Dutch justice ministry ignored the 1992 decision of the *Raad van State*. In another negative decision on March 13, 1993, it insisted that I was probably guilty of "crimes against humanity", that there were "indications" that I had contacts with representatives of "terrorist" organizations and that therefore I could not be granted political asylum. Again the *Raad van State* made a decision dated February 21, 1995 upholding its 1992 decision that I am a political refugee and ruling that I must be granted asylum and permit to reside in accordance with the Refugee Convention and Article 3 of the European Convention for the Protection of Human Rights and Fundamental Freedoms.

Both conventions prevent the Dutch government from sending me back to the Philippines. The Refugee Convention carries the principle of *nonrefoulement*[1]. Under Article 3 of the European Convention, the Dutch state is clearly prohibited from sending me back to where I am likely to be subjected to torture and inhuman or degrading treatment or punishment. The *Raad van State* clearly ruled in 1995 that the Dutch state had no sufficient evidence as to exclude under Article 1 f of the Refugee Convention and that it had the obligation to admit me as a refugee and grant me residence if there was no other country willing to take me without violating Article 3 of the European Convention.

Q28. What else has the Dutch justice ministry done regarding your asylum?

Despite the 1992 and 1995 decisions of the *Raad van State*, both of which are landmark decisions, the Dutch justice ministry refused to admit me as a refugee and allow me residence in the Netherlands. It made a new negative decision dated June 4, 1996 and ordered me to leave the Netherlands.

In accordance with the new Aliens Law, I appealed to the Aliens' Court under the district court of The Hague on August 12, 1996. The court decided to refer the case to its chamber for uniform application of the law (*Rechtseenheidkamer*). In the meantime, the Dutch justice ministry took the position that it recognized me as a political refugee under the protection of the Refugee Convention and the European Convention for the Protection of Human Rights and Fundamental Freedoms and that it no longer sought to expel me; but nonetheless it continued to refuse me admission as a refugee and the permit to reside.

On September 11, 1997, the *Rechtseenheidkamer* (REK) rejected my

[1] This means the obligation of states not to return a refugee, in any manner whatsoever, to a country where his or her life or freedom would be threatened.

appeal. It accepted the argument that since the justice ministry recognized me as a political refugee and no longer demanded my expulsion, there was no need to take up the question of my being granted asylum and residence. It circumvented the decision of the *Raad van State* that the Dutch state cannot refuse to admit me as a political refugee and grant me the residence permit if no other country is willing to take me as a refugee.

The REK decision ran against the jurisprudence of the European Court of Human Rights as established in the Soering and Chahal cases that the protection guaranteed by Article 3 and entirety of the European Convention is absolute and that the interest of the Dutch state should not be weighed against the individual interest of the refugee as to negate or put at risk such protection.

Q29. This sounds like so much gobbledygook. What is the status of the case now? What do you think of the Dutch legal system? I heard that you appealed the case to the European Court of Human Rights in Strasbourg. What do you expect of the case?

It is amusing to see how in a country like the Netherlands, where the rule of law is supposed to operate, the Dutch government actually deals with a juridical case like mine as a political case in order to accommodate demands from the US and Manila governments. Such interventionist pressures are supposed to be prohibited by the Refugee Convention.

And the Dutch justice ministry managed to prolong the litigation before the *Raad van State* by serializing allegations and arguments against me that had all been available in 1990. It was also able to wait for certain amendments to be made on the Dutch Aliens Law, creating the Aliens Court and allowing the justice ministry to use this court to admit secret dossiers as evidence, favor the ministry's allegations against me and deviate from the 1995 decision of *Raad van State* on my case.

I appealed my case to the European Court of Human Rights on February 26, 1998. But the court declared it inadmissible on March 14, 2002, after more than four years, because my counsel Professor G.J.H. van Hoof failed to argue against the "obstacles" cited by the court and completely ignored its reference to the decision on the Hilal case against United Kingdom in which supposedly the case-law is established that the issue of admission can be done away with by the assurance of nonexpulsion. My counsel also failed to inform me about the court decision until September 2002 when I inquired from him how my appeal, the case he was handling, would be affected by the US "terrorist" listing.

Q30. In view of the declared inadmissibility of your previous case before the European Court of Human Rights, are you adversely affected in any serious way? Are you in any danger of being thrown out of the Netherlands? Is your way to the same court now blocked?

Had my case won before the European Court of Human Rights, the way my counsel and I had expected, I would have begun to enjoy the legal right of residence and other rights proceeding from it, including the right of employment, free movement and so on without question.

But still I cannot be thrown out of the Netherlands despite the declaration of the case as inadmissible. I continue to be protected by Article 3 of the European Convention on Human Rights against expulsion as well as by the entire convention. The European Court on Human Rights remains open to me as the venue for my complaints against human rights violations.

Q31. I understand that the US made certain allegations and certain moves against you, shortly after you applied for asylum. What were these? Why was the US so ballistic against you?

Through its Manila and The Hague embassies, the US government or the CIA in particular planted stories in the press in 1988 and 1989 that I was probably liable for "inciting the NPA to commit violence against American civilians and military personnel". In a public document in 1990, the US State Department praised the Manila government for advising the Dutch government to refuse my application for political asylum. In fact the US was behind the Manila puppet government.

I presume that the US had such a deep hatred for me because my lectures in various countries exposed and condemned US economic, political, military and cultural domination over the Philippines. I also made it a special point to demand the dismantling of the US military bases.

It was then very timely to make the demand. The Filipino people and the mass organizations were making the same demand. And there were punitive actions being undertaken by the New People's Army against US military personnel.

Once in 1989, a Philippine radio station made a telephone interview with me and asked me who were responsible for the killing of Colonel James Rowe, head of the Joint US Military Advisory Group (JUSMAG), and other American military officers in the Philippines. I answered that I did not know who were responsible. When asked further what possibly could have been the motivation of the killers, I answered that they must have been patriots strongly opposed to the continuance of the US military bases as well as US economic plunder.

Probably, by expressing my opinion, I angered the US authorities enough to cause them even to violate international conventions by pressuring the Dutch government to keep me in legal limbo as a nonperson in the Netherlands. In such a state of legal limbo, I have been deprived of my rights, like the right to employment commensurate to my professional qualifications and the right to free movement.

A CIA Ruckus

Q32. I remember that in 1991, there was a ruckus about the Central Intelligence Agency trying to recruit a Filipino to spy on you. What was that all about?

On October 10, 1991, operatives of the US Central Intelligence Agency and the Dutch BVD (interior security service) approached a Filipino asylum-seeker, Nathan Quimpo, in order to recruit him and turn him into a spy on the Filipino community, especially on the NDFP and myself.

On October 16, 1991, they were caught on videotape at the coffee shop of the Holiday Inn in Amsterdam. The video footage showed the CIA agent telling Quimpo his tasks and giving him US$1000 as initial payment of his monthly salary. At that time, Quimpo cooperated with the NDFP and a Dutch TV program called *Achter Het Nieuws* (Behind the News) in undertaking the video recording and the exposure of the CIA and BVD on television.

However, the US and Dutch intelligence persisted in trying to recruit him in 1992 upon the advice of a long-time Filipino agent of the Bureau of Foreign Intelligence of the US State Department. Thus, according to reliable sources, Quimpo got a grant of political asylum and a travel grant to the US. These were precisely what were promised to him by the US CIA and Dutch BVD operatives when they first approached him. He was also awarded with a scholarship to write a dissertation on the CPP and the Philippine revolutionary movement. Right now, he is a rabid anticommunist propagandist.

Q33. For further clarity, can you explain how you manage to stay in the Netherlands, despite all the official rejection? And how does the unresolved issue of asylum affect you?

On several accounts I can stay in the Netherlands. As I have already pointed out, the Dutch state told the *Rechtseenheidskamer* that it was not expelling me but neither was it admitting me as a refugee nor granting me a legal permit to reside.

I can stay on in the Netherlands as a recognized political refugee and as someone protected by the Refugee Convention and by Article 3 of the European Convention on Human Rights. Furthermore, Julie has been a legal resident without limitations since 1997. The European Convention on Human Rights guarantees the right to private and family life.

I am not at all despondent over being unjustly denied asylum and the permit to reside. I enjoy doing research, writing, participating in conferences and seminars and engaging in other activities. I feel happy being with many compatriots and Dutch friends.

I have enjoyed abundant political support from so many thousands of signatories gathered over the years by the International Campaign for the Asylum of the Sison Family. Supporters include prominent personalities and ordinary people in various fields of activity. With their kind of support, I feel at home in the world.

Q34. What is the status of the charges that have been formally filed against you in the Philippines?

All those charges have been debunked and invalidated. The subversion charge was rendered moot and academic upon the repeal of the Anti-subversion Law in 1992. No court trial materialized from the false accusations about Plaza Miranda because the Manila prosecutors' office issued a resolution dismissing the Plaza Miranda bombing charge as being based on "sheer speculation" in 1994.

So, upon the demand of my legal counsel, the secretary of justice of the Manila government, who was then Silvestre Bello III, issued in 1998 a certification that there was no pending criminal charge against me. I have a clean legal bill of health, so to speak, even in the eyes of the Manila government.

The certification was issued in connection with plans for me to attend a special ceremony in Manila in April 1988 for the signing of the GRP-NDFP Comprehensive Agreement on Respect for Human Rights and International Humanitarian Law (CARHRIHL), which the GRP and the NDFP negotiating panels had initialed on March 16, 1998.

However, I was not able to visit the Philippines because national security adviser General Alexander Aguirre and foreign affairs secretary Domingo Siazon raised obstacles and uncertainties. Also, President Ramos and Speaker Jose de Venecia, who were very much interested in my homecoming, did not comply with our agreement to release all the political prisoners.

Human Rights Case Against Marcos

Q35. *Why did you join the human rights litigation against the Marcos estate in the US judicial system? Was it necessary for you to do so? I ask this question because of the notion that the expectation of some monetary reward is not in keeping with being a revolutionary.*

I did not see any acute contradiction between being a revolutionary and pursuing a human rights case against Marcos. In fact, I wanted to join the human rights litigation against Marcos as soon as I learned about it from SELDA, the association of ex-political detainees, in particular from Julie who was one of the founders and council members. I thought that the litigation was fine because it would put on record thousands of cases of human rights violations under the fascist regime and would ventilate them internationally.

That was the essential reason for my joining the litigation. I recognized that the Aquino regime would not pursue human rights cases against Marcos and his minions in the military and police. General Fidel V. Ramos had been pressuring the Presidential Commission on Human Rights to desist from pursuing such cases.

On the basis alone of my having been a victim of such human rights violations as torture, illegal detention and cruel treatment, it was necessary for me to file the case against Marcos even in the US. But my participation in the litigation had a special usefulness and specific importance.

I was the only political prisoner subjected to torture after having talked with Marcos face to face. My testimony proved and drove home the point that Marcos had personal and direct responsibility for the human rights violations.

I was not included in the class action because the American lawyer Robert Swift made the prejudgment that my supposed prominence as a communist would burden the case. However, lawyers of the American Civil Liberties Union of Southern California headed by prominent human rights lawyer Paul L. Hoffman and Ellen Lutz, approached my brother Dr. Ramon C. Sison, who resides in Los Angeles, California. They advised him that human rights cases could be filed in a direct action against Marcos for my torture and for the disappearance of my brother Francisco.

They said that neither my ideological nor my political views were at issue. The issue was that Marcos was responsible for the kidnap and murder of my brother Francisco and for my torture. The violation of our human rights was the issue.

Q36. The scale of the human rights litigation against Marcos is epic, even if we do not include subsequent efforts to make the Marcoses pay what they owe the victims. Please recount for us the dramatic threads of your own case against the Marcos as it intertwined with the class action suit of 10,000 litigants.

The class action and the direct action cases were filed on March 15, 1986, soon after the fall of Marcos and his flight to the US. In July 1986, a Reaganite judge dismissed these cases on the basis of the "act of state" doctrine. The Ninth Circuit Court of Appeals reversed the decision and remanded the cases to the district court of Hawaii in June 1989.

In 1990, all human rights cases against Marcos were consolidated before Judge Manuel Real for pretrial hearings. In July 1991, the judge granted the request of the class and the direct action plaintiffs for a bifurcated trial so that the processing of as many as 10,000 class damage claims would begin only after a liability verdict. The request was granted. After the liability phase, the bifurcated trial would proceed with the exemplary damage phase to be followed by the compensatory damage phase.

In January 1992, the court ordered that Julie's and my own testimony be taken by videotape deposition in Utrecht, Netherlands. Our lawyer Paul L. Hoffman examined each of us and the Marcos lawyer James Linn cross-examined us, with a US court-appointed stenographer officially responsible for recording and transcribing the proceedings. Also present were our Philippine lawyer Romeo T. Capulong and our other US lawyers, Ellen Lutz and Ralph Steinhardt.

The sessions were held at the office of the Dutch lawyer Bernard Tomlow and lasted for several days. A hired TV crew of the national broadcast company NOS videotaped the sessions. My deposition, including the examination and cross-examination totaled at least 12 hours and Julie's, some 8 hours.

Subsequently in the US, our lawyers and those of the Marcoses went through an extensive court-supervised process of designating and counter-designating portions of the deposition transcripts to be used at the trial.

The Sison and Piopongco cases went on trial with the class action in *Hilao v. Marcos* and two other direct action cases, *Ortigas v. Marcos* and *Clemente v. Marcos*. At the end of the trial, the jury rendered a liability verdict in favor of the plaintiffs in several verdicts for those in the class action and direct action. The jury found Marcos liable for my torture.

The exemplary damages phase of the trial was held in February 1994 before the same jury. No new evidence was introduced in the trial. The jury decided to award US$1.2 billion in exemplary damages. It also decided that this was an aggregate award to be divided pro rata among the class and individual plaintiffs. I was notified of this award.

The compensatory damages phase of the trial was held in January 1995. It was divided between the class action and direct action plaintiffs. The class action went ahead and resulted in a final judgment entered on February 3, 1995.

The compensatory damages phase in the direct action cases took place on January 19 and 20, 1995. In the Sison and Piopongco cases, the estate of Francisco Sison received a jury verdict of US$400,000 and Jaime Piopongco received a jury verdict of US$175,000.

Strangely, the court on its own motion, would not allow the jury to return a verdict for me on the argument that I did not introduce any new evidence of damages in the damages phase of the trial, notwithstanding the rule that the evidence presented at the liability phase is evidence for the exemplary and compensatory damages phases.

The judge went so far as to argue that one could be tortured without suffering damage. He demanded my personal appearance in court and pretended not to remember that he was the same judge who allowed the videotaping of my deposition in the Netherlands because the US authorities barred my travel to the US.

Q37. What did you and your lawyer do to offset it?

Our lawyers went to the US Ninth Circuit Court of Appeals and we won our appeal. On December 17, 1996, the appellate court reversed Judge Real and remanded our case for further proceedings on my damages claims and also on Jaime Piopongco's claims relating to the destruction of his radio station by the armed minions of Marcos.

In August 1997, the Marcos estate lawyer and our lawyer agreed and signed the stipulation for the entry of judgment in my favor (US$750,000) and Jaime Piopongco (US$250,000) on the claims that the Ninth Circuit sent back for retrial in our appeal. The amount stipulated in my favor is equivalent to the highest given to any individual plaintiff. It was also clear from a previous judgment in 1994 that I would get a *pro rata* share from the US$1.2 billion award for exemplary damages.

Judge Real delayed in signing and entering the stipulated judgment for compensatory damages. And it seemed that he would demand a new trial on the exemplary damages just to avoid entering a judgment. Thus, our lawyers had to appeal again to the Ninth Circuit Court of Appeals on March 3, 1998 to seek affirmation that I was entitled to the 1994 judgment on exemplary damages.

The appellate court affirmed my having a pro-rata share in the compensation for exemplary damages in November 1998. My claim against the Marcos estate therefore came close to US$1 million. It is now well beyond this figure because of the cumulative interest.

Q38. Sometime ago, there were reports in the Manila media that you had collected millions of pesos from the Marcoses. Is this true? If you have not yet collected, when do you expect to do so? What about the claimants in the class suit?

Those press reports were false. I did not receive any amount. The Marcoses, Swift and his Filipino sidekicks were sowing intrigue and engaging in slander when they told the press that I had received the amount stipulated in the final entry of judgment.

The said amount is as much a paper amount as the amounts awarded to the class plaintiffs. The individual and class plaintiffs are basically in the same boat, not having received a single cent of the amount due them. However, Judge Real and the lawyer Swift now ignore the individual plaintiffs.

A series of obstacles stands in the way both of the class and the individual plaintiffs. The Marcoses have been fending off all attempts of the plaintiffs to get what is due them. The Manila government also blocks the human rights claimants with its preemptive claim by law that all assets recovered from the Marcoses and cronies are supposed to go to the so-called comprehensive agrarian reform program (CARP).

It appears determined to get for itself alone all assets it can recover from the Marcoses. And yet, it has not taken any effective action to recover all or most of the assets from the Marcoses. Since the time of Jovito Salonga as PCGG chairman, the PCGG officials, with the exception of a few, have been more interested in taking for themselves a share from the Marcos loot.

Not a Drawn Bow

Q39. Attempts at both physical and character assassinations against you appear to be intensifying. Can you provide a possible explanation for this?

The US and Filipino reactionaries are worried by the advances of the national-democratic movement in all forms of struggle, as a result of the CPP's successful rectification movement.

They wish to discredit or intimidate the entire movement by focusing on my person. They think that destroying me politically or physically is a shortcut to destroying the movement. The campaign of character assassination is aimed at discrediting the entire movement and is probably a preparation for my physical assassination.

Q40. Do these attempts to demonize and assassinate you frighten you? Do you have any tension or stress relieving activities, different from writing political prose, delivering speeches and presiding over meetings?

The possibility of untimely death was far higher when I was in the field of battle. Neither slander nor assassination threats frighten me. I enjoy verbal combat with my detractors and outwitting the physical assassins. My revolutionary conviction grows firmer and I become more alert. I am challenged to fight the enemy ever more resolutely and militantly.

I have written some poetry and participated in poetry readings. I have read my poems in the most prestigious poetry festivals in the Netherlands. I have always considered poetry or the entire range of art and literature as an important medium of revolutionary struggle even as I find relaxation in this.

Of course, the most relaxing to me are singing and dancing during get-togethers with comrades and friends. I attend parties of families, the Filipino community and solidarity organizations. Now and then, I still play basketball with younger people or join a pack of joggers or cyclists.

Q41. You have a reputation for working hard like a water buffalo when it is time to work and fight. But it is also rumored that when you relax, you engage in fun beyond norms acceptable to communists or in fun that could compromise your security.

In the late 1980s, anticommunists painted wall slogans in Manila referring to me as the disco king. Until now, some anticommunist detractors depict me as one who habituates pubs and discos. They will say anything to discredit me.

In fact, I work 12 to 14 hours a day, including Saturdays and Sundays. In a year's time, I go to community and solidarity festivities, with singing and dancing, some five to 10 times. When I invite visiting comrades and friends to go out for cultural entertainment that is within the range of three to six times a year.

Among my closest comrades and friends, I have the reputation of being a parsimonious Ilocano and talking more about fun rather than having it. I take security precautions whenever necessary. But I do not live in fear.

When I relax with comrades and friends and we enjoy ourselves, I am simply recharging myself and absorbing facts and insights informally for more work. When I participate in social drinking, singing, dancing and swapping jokes in social gatherings of the Filipino communities, solidarity groups and foreign organizations, it is with the consciousness of developing rapport and cooperation with people.

Q42. You can't sell me on the idea that your fun activities are simply another form of work. Don't you think that a measure of enjoyment and relaxation is necessary for the stamina required by a protracted revolutionary struggle?

Indeed, there has to be a healthy measure of enjoyment and relaxation, distinct from enjoying the kind of work that one loves to do. Workers are entitled to holidays and opportunities for leisure and cultural development. It is not healthy to work continuously even when one loves and enjoys the work. A point is reached when one feels the strain. A bow that is always drawn taut is liable to break or lose its resilience and thus fail to send the arrow straight to the target.

THE GUERRILLA IS LIKE A POET (1968)

The guerrilla is like a poet
Keen to the rustle of leaves
The break of twigs
The ripples of the river
The smell of fire
And the ashes of departure.

The guerrilla is like a poet.
He has merged with the trees
The bushes and the rocks
Ambiguous but precise
Well-versed on the law of motion
And master of myriad images.

The guerrilla is like a poet.
Enrhymed with nature
The subtle greenery
The inner silence, the outer innocence
The steel tensile in-grace
That ensnares the enemy.

The guerrilla is like a poet.
He moves with the green brown multitude
In bush burning with red flowers
That crown and hearten all
Swarming the terrain as a flood
Marching at last against the stronghold.

An endless movement of strength
Behold the protracted theme:
The people's epic, the people's war.

NPA unit on offensive training exercise. (NDF International Office photo collection)

Opening the Partido ng Bayan Founding Congress on August 30, 1986 at the Folk Arts Theatre in Manila. (Sison family photo collection)

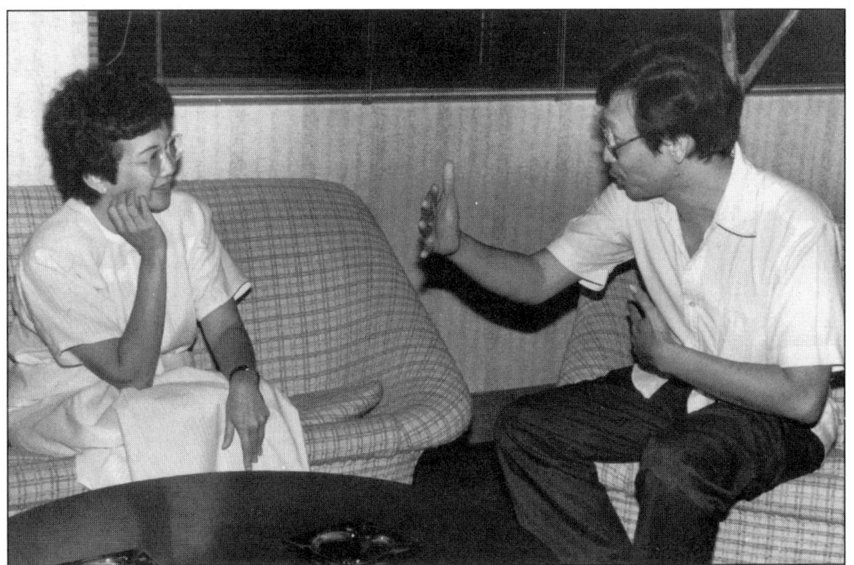

Upon his release from military detention on 5 March 1986, Professor Jose Maria Sison meets President Corazon Aquino. (Courtesy, Bullit Marquez/AP photographer)

Chapter Two

Against One Regime After Another

Q1. As a Marxist, you would be the first to discount the inordinate role attributed to you in the historic process in the development of the revolutionary movement. What do you think of the blame or unintended credit ascribed to you for the growth and achievements of the revolutionary movement?

It is absurd for anyone to simplistically blame or even credit me for the growth and achievements of the revolutionary movement in the Philippines. The people themselves know their own needs and demands. Their revolutionary consciousness and militancy rise because of the intolerable oppression and exploitation that they suffer. The imperialists and the local reactionaries have themselves to blame for the rise of the revolutionary movement for national liberation and democracy.

No amount of theorizing, agitating or organizing by any leader or set of leaders can generate revolutionary forces, unless the objective conditions exist for them. Ideological, political and organizational leadership is, of course, important, but it must above all correspond to the objective conditions.

My detractors reflect their contempt for the people when they credit too much of the rise of the revolutionary movement to my efforts. They refuse to recognize that the people, by their own will and by their own hands, can shape their own destiny. Moreover, they calculate that by subjecting me to character assassination they have a shortcut to discrediting and destroying the movement.

Q2. Why have workers, peasants, women and youth in great numbers joined the revolutionary movement? What are the issues that motivate them to participate in the struggle?

The broad masses of the Filipino people are oppressed and exploited by US imperialism and the local exploiting classes of compradors and landlords. Thus, they join the revolutionary movement in order to struggle for their own national and social liberation.

The toiling masses of workers and peasants are the most oppressed and exploited. They have been the most interested in joining the movement. They comprise at least 90 percent of the population and they know that the movement can succeed only with their resolute and militant mass struggle.

Having the Communist Party of the Philippines (CPP) as its advanced detachment, the working class can grasp the issues involved in the Philippine revolution, from the new-democratic to the socialist stage. The land problem drives the peasantry to become the main force of the democratic revolution.

The revolutionary movement attracts the women because they recognize it as the way to liberate themselves not only from the three evils of foreign monopoly capitalism, domestic feudalism and bureaucrat capitalism but also from patriarchy and male chauvinism.

The movement likewise attracts the youth because the decrepit and decadent social system victimizes the overwhelming majority of them and offers them no bright future. The youth are ever receptive to new and progressive ideas and actions for the benefit of the people as well as for the benefit of the youth themselves.

Q3. The* Biographical Dictionary of Marxism*, edited by American political science professor Robert A. Gorman, cites you as one of the top 210 Marxist thinkers and revolutionaries since the publication of the* Communist Manifesto *in 1848. It is safe to say that you are among the top Marxists in the world today. What would you consider your most important achievements?

I am simply a student of Marxism-Leninism, seeking to apply this theory to the concrete conditions of the Philippines and the concrete practice of the Philippine revolution. I have combined my theoretical and political studies with practical revolutionary work.

I have endeavored to clarify the new democratic character of the current stage of the Philippine revolution. The working class is the leading force and the peasantry is the main force. They fight, as their main adversaries, the comprador big bourgeoisie and the landlord class in the service of imperialism. The main revolutionary task is to defeat imperialism, feudalism and bureaucrat capitalism. Socialism is the perspective of the Philippine revolution in the era of imperialism and proletarian revolution.

With other comrades, I worked hard to revive the anti-imperialist and anti-feudal movement in the early 1960s, after an entire decade of intense reaction in the Philippines. It was some kind of pioneering work for us to break through the anticommunist climate of fear, following the defeat of the armed revolutionary movement in 1950-52 and the intensification of the Cold War by US imperialism.

When I joined the old merger party of the Communist Party and the Socialist Party in late 1962, it had neither a central committee nor a single party branch to speak of. The Party secretary general Dr. Jesus Lava was completely isolated and was in hiding. What remained of the old merger party were small isolated groups and individuals willing to come together. But first, we, young proletarian cadres on our own, had to revive the legal mass movement along the national-democratic line in the early 1960s.

Encouraged by the result of our mass work, we gave refresher courses to senior comrades in the old merger party and recruited Party members from the ranks of the advanced mass activists. Eventually we separated from the old merger party in April 1967 and re-established the Communist Party of the Philippines under the guidance of Marxism-Leninism-Mao Zedong Thought on December 26, 1968. Subsequently, we established the New People's Army (NPA) on March 29, 1969 and the National Democratic Front (NDF) on April 24, 1973.

As an individual, I had some share in the development and victories of the revolutionary movement. But these were basically due to the correct leadership of the CPP and the hard work, struggle and sacrifices of the entire Party and the people.

Q4. *Your best-known personal contributions to the Philippine revolutionary movement are your writings.* Struggle for National Democracy ***has been a bible for activists in the open democratic mass movement since the 1960s. So has been*** Philippine Society and Revolution ***since the 1970s, both for open mass activists and those who join the CPP. What other written contributions of yours do you consider important?***

I consider of crucial importance the drafts of the rectification document, *Rectify Errors and Rebuild the Party*, the *CPP Constitution* and *Program for a People's Democratic Revolution*. These drafts guided the rectification movement from 1967 onward and were the main documents in the reestablishment of the Party in 1968.

Subsequently, I submitted to the Central Committee drafts of Central Committee documents, policy papers and analyses of major political, economic, social and cultural issues, resolutions, policy statements and decisions of the CPP, the NPA and the NDFP. Let me mention some outstanding documents of far reaching significance and consequence: *Guide for Establishing the People's Democratic Government*, *Revolutionary Guide to Land Reform*, *Specific Characteristics of People's War in the Philippines* and *Our Urgent Tasks*.

I also wrote articles on specific ideological issues against the modern revisionists and opportunists in the Philippines and abroad, and on issues arising from the socioeconomic and political character of Philippine society and the strategy and tactics of the Philippine revolution.

I addressed issues pertaining to the working class, peasantry, urban poor, various strata of the Philippine bourgeoisie, women, youth, mass movement, art and literature, science and technology, imperialist globalization, ecology, human rights, peace, and so on.

You can look at a list of my writings in the website run by the International Network for Philippine Studies, www.inps-sison.freewebspace.com. There is now a project to publish in several volumes the listed articles. These can be compiled thematically or chronologically.

Q5. *Aside from writing and doing paper work required by your high positions in various revolutionary organizations, what tasks similar to those of others in the movement did you perform?*

From the decade of the 1960s, I performed concrete tasks to arouse, organize and mobilize the people. I wrote propaganda and delivered agitational speeches. I recruited individuals into mass organizations and the Party. I joined strikes and protest rallies and encouraged other people to do likewise.

I did my share of social investigation among the workers and peasants, integrating with them, encouraging them to join trade unions and peasant associations. I conducted study courses at mass and Party levels and participated in forming mass and Party organizations.

I also had my share of marching and camping with units of the New People's Army in the countryside, doing ordinary chores, doing various aspects of rural mass work, forming people's organizing committees and democratic organs of political power, giving politico-military education to Red commanders and fighters and planning our own defense as well as tactical offensives.

My enthusiasm was always high when I was doing what was new work for me, or following up and checking up on the work of lower organs and organizations, trying to solve problems, making adjustments or rectifying errors.

Q6. *I've heard you say that while lower organs are subordinate to higher organs, they are more interesting. Why so?*

The lower organs and organizations are more interesting in many respects. The basic life, the democratic base and concrete variety of activities are found there.

Leading organs would become isolated without the lower organs and organizations as a broad base. The two levels need each other and must interact with each other.

Those in the leading organs must base their decisions on facts from below. They do so not just by waiting for reports but also by going down to do pilot work, familiarizing themselves with typical and critical situations, and helping solve both ordinary and extraordinary problems.

The development of cadres involves a system of promoting those in lower organs to higher organs in order to bring up to the higher organs knowledge and experience from below.

A Place in History

Q7. As early as the 1960s, you were already considered a historical figure. Your name is in* Brief History of the Filipino People, *the textbook written by the late Professor Teodoro Agoncillo for the University of the Philippines. You are recognized as belonging to the revolutionary lineage of such figures from the working class as Andres Bonifacio and Crisanto Evangelista. How would you evaluate Bonifacio and Evangelista and what is the proper basis for comparison between the two and yourself?

It is an honor to be considered as belonging to the same revolutionary lineage as Andres Bonifacio and Crisanto Evangelista. Indeed, the three of us are recognized as fighters committed to the cause of national liberation and democracy for the Filipino people. What makes us different from each other is the result of the concrete historical circumstances and the corresponding ideological and political requirements for revolutionary struggle.

Andres Bonifacio was a great patriot and revolutionary. He initiated the old democratic revolution by leading the Katipunan and starting the armed revolution for national independence against colonialism. Although a worker, he espoused the bourgeois liberal ideology, as this was the most progressive ideology relevant to Philippine conditions in the 1890s.

The old democratic revolution, which he led, was of great historical significance not only to the Filipino people but also to the people of Asia. It was the first bourgeois-democratic revolution in Asia, foreshadowing the Chinese revolution of 1911, the Indonesian revolution of 1926 and 1945, the Indian national independence movement and so on.

Crisanto Evangelista, also a worker, adopted the revolutionary ideology of the working class. Under the auspices of the Communist (Third) International, he founded the old Communist Party in 1930 and became the chairman of the merger party of the Communist Party and the Socialist Party in 1938.

He had no chance to develop the theory and practice of the new-democratic revolution beyond the rudimentary level. The US colonial authorities repressed him and other communist leaders soon after the Party was established on November 7, 1930. However, he stressed the need for working class leadership in the Philippine revolution under the guidance of Marxism-Leninism.

I had the advantage of learning from Andres Bonifacio and Crisanto

Evangelista. We, the revolutionaries who emerged in the 1960s, learned lessons from the earlier revolutionary struggles in the Philippines and abroad. We benefited from the victories of communist-led revolutions, especially in Russia and the neighboring countries of China, Korea and Indochina. We also learned lessons from the big mistakes in previous struggles in the Philippines and abroad.

Q8. *Like the series of three Lava brothers (Vicente, Jose and Jesus) who became general secretaries of the old merger party in the period of 1942 to 1964, you did not originate from the working class. You came from the landlord class. Do you not find it incongruous and difficult to adopt the working class position?*

Indeed, it is unusual and difficult for someone of my feudal social background and petty bourgeois education to adopt the working class position. Generally, persons with such background and education do not adopt that position; still less the communist position. But you really have to take into account the concrete process of my development.

I had the good fortune of having had certain experiences, like being close to people from whom I heard complaints about how my great grandfather accumulated land, having in 4th Grade a school teacher who opened my eyes to the history of the Philippine revolution, reading in high school an anticommunist book whose logic turned me off but whose quotations from Marx and Engels caught my interest and kindled my curiosity, discovering Marxist-Leninist works in the university, and associating with and organizing other students who took interest in Marxism-Leninism and the revolutionary movement because of the high prestige gained by the socialist countries and national liberation movements.

After getting our bachelors of arts diplomas from the University of the Philippines in 1959, Julie and I lived and supported our young family on our salaries, hers as a librarian and mine as a teacher. Whenever I was out of a job as a teacher, I received a small allowance as a communist cadre, specifically as a trade union activist.

Our proletarian existence was a big factor in my remolding. Certainly, joining a communist party, working in the trade union movement as social investigator and organizer, joining strikes and picket lines with the strikers and striving to build a workers' party like *Lapiang Manggagawa* and the Socialist Party helped me a great deal in remolding myself into a proletarian revolutionary.

In my experience, drawing away from a feudal background was much easier than drawing away from the circumstances, mentality and habits of the petty bourgeois. Until now, I continue striving to remold myself into a proletarian revolutionary.

Q9. Can you explain in the most serious way possible how persons who belong to exploiting classes can become proletarian revolutionaries? What contributions have they been able to make?

The great founders of the revolutionary working class movement, Marx and Engels, did not originate from the working class. But they studied and analyzed working class conditions. From their scientific study of history and capitalist society, they saw the historic mission of the working class in overthrowing the bourgeoisie and building socialism. And, more importantly, they became active partisans of the working class as the vanguard force for revolutionary change and participated in its revolutionary activities.

The revolutionary ideology of the proletariat came from outside the confines of the trade union movement and the economic struggle. It came from Marx and Engels doing scientific investigation and having a comprehensive view of society and adopting the revolutionary vantage point of the proletariat as they studied the contradictions between the proletariat and the bourgeoisie, at the socioeconomic base and superstructure of capitalist society.

Marxism could not have emerged simply from the narrow confines of the trade union movement and the economic struggle. What is likely to emerge from such confines would be a bourgeois laborite or bourgeois-reformist social democratic party in the absence of proletarian revolutionary theoreticians like Marx and Engels.

Of course, thinkers and leaders alone do not make revolution. Revolution is necessarily a mass undertaking. It entails the class leadership of the most progressive class. If under the circumstances, the leading class does not comprise the majority of the people, then it develops an alliance with other classes in order to win the battle for democracy.

To wage the new-democratic or socialist revolution, a revolutionary party must recruit and mobilize the workers through their trade unions, cooperatives, study circles and other forms of workers' organizations, and must link up with non-proletarian masses, including the peasantry and the petty bourgeoisie.

Q10. ***What were the struggles in your mind before you decided to become a proletarian revolutionary? Can you retrace the struggles between your social conscience and your personal ambition before you finally decided to become a proletarian revolutionary?***

Since 4th Grade, I have always been proud of the tradition of patriotism in my family against the colonialists—Spanish, American and Japanese. But I have always been critical of the feudal character of my family.

My father's great ambition, which I accepted then, was for me to become a lawyer and, eventually, president of the Philippines. He thought out loudly the fulfillment of family and personal ambitions, not bothering to mention service to God and country, as other ambitious parents usually would. Echoing populist politicians, I told him that I would become a lawyer and political leader in order to fight for the poor and exploited.

My interest in becoming a lawyer and a politician of the ruling system diminished as I read more Marxist-Leninist works and became more interested in writing revolutionary articles and organizing study circles. I finally gave up the plan to go to law school when I got married to Julie and had to take the teaching fellowship at the English Department of the University of the Philippines.

Q11. ***You are very conscious of the necessary unity of opposites in political work—between the collective and the individual, between your personal contribution and your membership in the revolutionary collective or mass organization. As a poet, do you experience tension between group-oriented activities and the need for solitude? Are you a revolutionary first or poet first?***

I am a revolutionary first rather than a poet. At any rate, I know by experience the tension between collective revolutionary work and the need for solitude at the moment of crafting a poem.

The feelings and thoughts that go into a poem are drawn from one's personal experience and social practice, but when crafting it, you are by yourself as the poet, without the direct assistance of a collective. The more poems you wish to compose, the more time and concentration you need as a poet.

When I concentrate on political prose writing and political work, I tend to forget about writing poetry. During my detention from 1977 to 1986, I gained time for poetry. But after my release, the demands of political prose became overwhelming and once more claimed me.

I also like to sing revolutionary songs. For sheer fun, though, I sing

Spanish love songs and American pop of the 1950s to the 1960s, especially when I'm nostalgic about my youth. I am quite familiar with American pop from the 1950s to the 1970s, but not quite with pop songs from the 1980s and 1990s. My vocal skills are strictly amateurish.

My voice "ranges" from baritone to tenor. I can carry melodies quite well, but my tempo is bad unless I rehearse well enough or get signals from a conductor, follow a co-singer or read lyrics from a karaoke gadget.

Q12. In your poem "The Guerrilla is like a Poet", it seems that the higher metaphor is that of poetry. This is interesting, especially when read side by side with Section III of Emmanuel Lacaba's poem "Letters to the Filipino People," which has always struck me as a mirror image of your poem. Except that here, the ultimate metaphor for the poet is to become a guerrilla. You are familiar with this poem, of course. Would you care to comment?

My poem celebrates the concurrence and harmony of poetry, nature and the people's war. Emmanuel Lacaba's stresses the poet's becoming the guerrilla fighter. We concur in the poetry of serving the people through armed revolution.

Accolade from Unlikely Sources

Q13. In the so-called mainstream Philippine media, you have been a top newsmaker since the 1960s. In political prominence, you were in the same bracket as Ferdinand Marcos and his arch political rival, Benigno Aquino. How do you account for such prominence even in the bourgeois media?

Public attention began to focus on me when I published and edited the Progressive Review in 1963 and became chairman of *Kabataang Makabayan* (KM—Patriotic Youth) in 1964, vice chairman of *Lapiang Manggagawa* (Workers' Party) in 1964, general secretary of the Socialist Party in 1965 and general secretary of the Movement for the Advancement of Nationalism in 1966.

The mass protest actions and press statements against imperialist, feudal and bureaucrat capitalist exploitation and oppression were interesting material for the bourgeois mass media. Such interest lasted and increased as the mass organizations of the national-democratic movement grew in strength and their leaders ably expressed their position. My prominence grew with the strength attained by the national- democratic movement in the Philippines. Had it not been for this basic fact, the bourgeois mass media would not pay any attention to me.

The bourgeois media would give me space under a number of such circumstances as the following: 1) the rulers and mass media lords defend the system and unite in seeking to demonize me or misrepresent my position, 2) editors allow me to talk back to some extent so that they can keep a semblance of liberalism, 3) there is a split in the bourgeois media reflecting a split among the reactionaries and allowing me more frequently to gain access and space in some media outlets, 4) sympathetic and friendly journalists in the mass media skillfully put in my statements, and 5) sometimes an unprecedentedly broad united front against a despotic and corrupt and therefore extremely despised ruler like Marcos is reflected in the media and seeks my stand on outstanding issues.

Q14. In 1985, Kompil (Congress of the Filipino People), which came to be dominated by Jesuits, "social-democrats", in fact by Christian democrats, and businessmen, chose you as one of 15 outstanding Filipinos capable of leading the Filipino people in lieu of Marcos. How do you explain this charming deviation from their anti-communism?

Kompil included my name in the list because it wanted to argue against the line of Marcos and his cohorts that he was irreplaceable despite the fact that his regime was bankrupt in an all-round way and was already a much-hated target of the rapidly surging mass movement for his overthrow.

In line with the united front policy against the Marcos fascist regime, I welcomed my inclusion in the list as it was drawn up in the spirit of the broad united front. I was one of the main speakers at the Kompil convention, with Julie delivering my speech. By the way, Julie was in the background among the organizers of Kompil. In my speech, I strongly condemned Marcos as a fascist puppet of the US and called for a united front to neutralize the reactionary armed forces and encircle the presidential palace by hundreds of thousands of people.

Of course, I had absolutely no illusion that the anti-Marcos reactionaries would actually consider me for the presidency of the Philippines. In the first place, I would never wish to become one under their auspices. In the second place, they merely wanted to use my name as decoration for their real intention of replacing Marcos with someone who represented the exploiting classes but who could masquerade as a democrat while seeking power.

The Best and the Worst

Q15. As chairman of the Central Committee of the Communist Party of the Philippines from 1968 to 1977, what were your most outstanding achievements?

No matter how high the position comrades entrusted to me, I view achievements as something shared among members of the Central Committee and the entire Party.

The achievements include: the First Great Rectification Movement which started in 1967, the reestablishment of the Party in 1968, the founding of the New People's Army in 1969, the founding of the National Democratic Front in 1973 and the continuous formation of mass organizations and organs of political power since the beginning of the armed revolution.

The achievements of the Party and the revolutionary movement would not have been possible without the adoption of the ideological line of Marxism-Leninism-Mao Zedong Thought, the political line of new-democratic revolution through protracted people's war and the organizational line of democratic centralism and all the hard work, struggle and sacrifices of comrades and the people to implement these.

Before my capture on November 10, 1977, developments in the revolutionary movement from 1974 to 1977 clearly pointed to several probabilities: first, a rapid multiplication of guerrilla fronts covering the countryside from 1979 to 1982, with the platoon serving as center of gravity for the guerrilla front and frequently launching tactical offensives; and second, workers in the urban areas would become the most massive and militant force in the urban mass movement.

All those prospects were grounded on the foundational work of the Party from 1968 to 1977. Alas, while I was in prison, certain opportunist elements in 1979 and 1980 were carried away by the purely military viewpoint and spread the notion of building absolutely concentrated companies and battalions, and skipping the full development of the platoon as center of gravity.

Another set of opportunists preoccupied the Party with the question of boycotting or participating in the 1978 elections, caused a split between the central leadership and the Manila-Rizal leadership and the disintegration of the party organization in the national capital region.

Q16. What was your biggest mistake up to 1977?

Let me speak of my personal mistake alone. In the months towards my capture in 1977, I became careless and complacent about security. I moved in and out of three regions too frequently using the national highway. In the few hours before my arrest, I disregarded the advice of comrades not to ride a motorcycle at night.

Jokingly, I used to say that I would not mind being killed after 1975 because by then I had seen the movement making significant advances after overcoming serious difficulties from 1972 to 1974. I anticipated a great leap for the armed struggle in the countryside and the mass movement in the major cities in the last three years of the 1970s.

On November 9, 1977, I decided to drive a motorcycle from Pangasinan province to La Union province from 11 p.m. to midnight. Because motorcycle traffic had dwindled, enemy spotters could easily spot me on the highway. I violated the rule I had long set for myself of not driving or riding a motorcycle at night.

Getting captured was my biggest mistake because it separated me for a very long time from my work and the main flow of events in the revolutionary movement. In my first two years of detention, I was completely in solitary confinement. I made other big mistakes in revolutionary work but none bigger than that which would put me away for so many years, from 1977 to 1986.

Q17. Is separation from the work worse than the tortures and ennui you experienced in prison? Why?

You are referring to aspects of the same thing. There is no need to compare them and say what was worse. As a result of my arrest and detention, I suffered the pain of being separated from optimal revolutionary work and that of being subjected to various forms of torture, including punching, water cure, being manacled and fettered, and solitary confinement.

My detention, torture and defiance of the enemy were part of the revolutionary struggle, notwithstanding my preference to be outside of prison to be able to do more work. I tried to do my best like showing defiance in order to inspire others to fight, issuing political statements whenever possible and writing poetry.

My long poem, "Fragments of a Nightmare" is a crystallization and lyrical rendition of my suffering, struggle and yearnings in prison. Several short poems also reflect my will to resist and revolutionary hope based on the people's struggle.

On the Marcos Regime

Q18. ***Please tell me more about your struggles against the Marcos dictatorship while you were in prison until 1986. What were your most significant actions in this regard?***

I fought the Marcos dictatorship despite the rigors of maximum-security detention. My reasoning was that if someone like me who was in an extremely difficult and dangerous situation could defy and fight the fascist regime, people outside of prison would be inspired to fight the regime even more courageously, militantly and effectively.

I refused to recognize the military commissions (tribunals) trying me for subversion and rebellion. I refused to enter any plea. I turned the military commission hearings into occasions for exposing the tortures inflicted on my person, for denouncing the regime on a wide range of issues and for discreetly sending out articles that I had written in my solitary confinement cell.

In several ways, I was able to send out messages and articles to comrades and friends, especially after I was taken out of solitary confinement. Comrades and friends were also able to communicate with me.

After Julie was released from prison in 1982, I was able to participate even more effectively in the struggle against the Marcos dictatorship. Through her, I communicated with various forces in the broad united front and participated indirectly in its various initiatives to topple Marcos. But, of course on her own account, she also participated in all these initiatives, including leading a broad worldwide campaign for my immediate release, the Free Jose Maria Sison Committee.

Q19. ***A long time has passed since Marcos was overthrown. Please recap his rise and the long-term and immediate process of his fall.***

Marcos rose to the presidency "normally" within the system through the 1964 elections. He bore the usual qualifications of being a lawyer-politician of the big compradors and landlords and of having gained wealth through corruption as congressman and senator.

As president, he implemented the IMF-World Bank scheme of tightening the imperialist chains on the Philippines by preventing national industrialization and genuine land reform, over-burdening the country with foreign loans for "infrastructure development" (building overpriced roads and bridges), and favoring raw-material production-for-export.

He spent a great deal of public funds to ensure his reelection to the presidency in 1969. By then, the country was in severe financial crisis. Social unrest was intense. Marcos opted to beef up the reactionary armed forces and continue the neocolonial and Keynesian policy of building roads and bridges, and mills basically for refining sugar, processing coconut and smelting copper ore. He also declared martial law in 1972.

He started the labor export policy in the late 1970s because the absence of industrial development and decrease of foreign funds for public works brought about rampant unemployment. The global crisis of overproduction in raw materials and the drying up of foreign credit from the late 1970s onward had undermined the Marcos fascist regime.

Benigno Aquino, Marcos's political rival, thought 1983 was payback time and decided to return to the Philippines from exile in the US. Marcos panicked and had him assassinated. This exacerbated the political crisis of the ruling system and further widened and deepened the split among the reactionaries, extending to a split within the military and police forces.

The socioeconomic and political crisis of the ruling system mainly caused the fall of Marcos. But simultaneous to the crisis was the advance of the armed revolutionary movement. This definitely was a decisive factor in the toppling of Marcos.

Fearing the further advance of the revolutionary armed struggle and the militant urban mass protests, the US authorities, the Catholic Church and the majority of the big compradors and landlords decided that it was time to drop Marcos. At the same time, the revolutionary forces and the legal democratic forces intensified the people's resistance.

The culmination of the mass resistance included the people's uprising at Edsa highway, the encirclement of the presidential palace mainly by the organized progressive masses of workers and students and the BAYAN-led[2] uprisings in so many provincial cities, capitals and major towns.

---

[2]. BAYAN was organized in May 1985 as a broad united front organization of progressive forces and some anti-Marcos conservatives as the legal campaign machinery of the antifascist and anti-Marcos struggle. It has since then evolved into what is now the largest alliance of legal progressive and patriotic forces consistently taking up the people's issues in the struggle for national liberation and democracy.

Q20. After their pillage of the country, the Marcoses and their cronies fled. Now they are back in the country while you and so many others, including myself, remain in exile. There must be a lesson to this. Can you think of one?

The Marcoses had no problem returning to the Philippines to run for office, including the presidency in 1992. That is because the Marcoses and the Aquinos belong to the same big comprador-landlord exploiting class. Within that class, factions fluctuate between bitter conflicts and compromises, usually orchestrated by the US.

The Right opportunists erred in characterizing the Aquino regime as liberal-democratic rather than as a big comprador-landlord regime momentarily wearing a liberal-democratic façade. The "Left" opportunists likewise erred in presuming that conditions were available or impending for "fast-tracking" the armed revolution to total victory through urban armed insurrections or for rapidly enlarging NPA units.

In my case, returning to the Philippines means taking the risk of being killed or imprisoned because I cannot be enticed to go against the revolutionary movement. While willingly accepting the risk, I also submit myself to the decisions of responsible entities. At the moment, my duties as chief political consultant of the NDFP in its peace negotiations with the Manila government require me to stay abroad and stand firm with the NDFP in insisting on a neutral foreign venue for the negotiations.

On the Aquino Regime

Q21. The Aquino regime was touted as a big change from the Marcos dictatorship. How different from and how similar was it to the Marcos regime?

The Aquino regime basically was a big comprador-landlord regime, similar to the Marcos regime. Only for a short while did this regime maintain a liberal democratic façade to distinguish itself from the blatantly fascist Marcos regime.

The façade crumbled when presidential security forces massacred peasants and their supporters in front of the presidential palace on January 22, 1987. Subsequently, peace negotiations between the Government of the Republic of the Philippines and the National Democratic Front broke down.

Right from the beginning, the Aquino regime was interested only in a ceasefire agreement to allow Aquino to consolidate her power and embark on an economic policy of accelerated liberalization, privatization and deregulation dictated by the IMF in consonance with the US shift to the neo-liberal policy stress.

The US-Aquino regime could no longer avail of huge foreign loans because the Marcos regime had put the Philippines on bad credit standing and, more importantly, because the neo-liberal policy shift was putting the credit squeeze on third world countries and shifting the money back to the imperialist countries, especially the US. Thus, the regime accelerated domestic public borrowing to cover increasingly large budgetary deficits due to shortfalls in tax collection.

It was not at all interested in national industrialization and land reform. It escalated the exploitation and oppression of the working people. It launched a series of vicious national military campaigns of suppression called *Oplan Mamamayan, Lambat Bitag I, II* and *III* against the revolutionary forces and the people.

The fascists in the military and police who were carried over from the Marcos to the Aquino regime continued the practice of torturing and murdering many mass leaders and activists of the working people as well as human rights lawyers who had survived the Marcos fascist dictatorship.

Choices after Prison

Q22. After your release from military detention in 1986, you rejoined the University of the Philippines as a senior research fellow with the rank of associate professor at the Asian Center of Graduate Studies. You chaired the Preparatory Committee of the Partido ng Bayan. Why didn't you rejoin the revolutionary movement immediately and go underground?

At that time, interest was high in my public meetings, university lectures, seminars, press interviews and other legal activities. Comrades and friends advised me to stay aboveground for a year or so, in order to take advantage of opportunities for open activities in propagating the ideas and policies of the national-democratic movement.

The plan was for me to conduct nationwide campaigns of political education for six months and then go abroad for a university lecture tour for another six months. Thus, I did not go underground right away.

Q23. Were all the contemplated lectures as weighty a task as returning to armed struggle? Then you went overseas. Was it necessary to leave

the Philippines and did you intend to stay out of the country indefinitely? What did you accomplish?

The lectures in the Philippines and abroad had their own importance apart from the armed struggle, which was being conducted continuously by so many other comrades. It was important to speak about the Philippine revolution and seek international support for it in various countries. People took special interest in me then because of my record as a revolutionary leader and because of the significance of the Philippine revolutionary movement.

I went abroad in response to numerous invitations from universities, mass organizations and solidarity organizations. Comrades and friends advised me—and I agreed—that there was such a great opportunity for carrying out an information campaign about the revolutionary movement and for visiting socialist and anti-imperialist countries.

I visited dozens of countries and scores of cities in several continents. I went to New Zealand, Australia, Thailand, Japan, Hong Kong, India, Netherlands, Norway, Sweden, Denmark, Belgium, West Germany, France, England, Albania, Switzerland, Italy, Algeria, Greece, East Germany, China, the Democratic People's Republic of Korea, Yugoslavia, Nicaragua, Cuba, Mexico, Spain and Portugal.

I lectured in nearly a hundred universities and attended important meetings and conferences. My activities included visits and exchanges with parliamentarians, trade union leaders, women activists, progressive writers, representatives and leaders of other national liberation movements, and so many other kinds of people as well as meetings with solidarity groups and Filipino communities. Occasionally, I also attended big and small cultural gatherings where I read my poems or sang.

My lecture tour accomplished a number of things: the strengthening of existing solidarity relations against the growing notion among most of the Philippine solidarity organizations that they had no more reason to exist after the fall of Marcos; and the establishment of new contacts and solidarity relations with organizations in labor, the academic and other fields.

Q24. Why were you unable to stay within the limit of a six-month lecture tour abroad?

After I received word from the Philippines that I should prolong my stay abroad because of the murder of Rolando Olalia, chairman of the Kilusang Mayo Uno and Partido ng Bayan, my plan was to return to the

Philippines after a year abroad. For a while, I waited in the Netherlands for the US State Department decision on my visa application to fulfill a lecture tour in the US.

I did not get the US visa and then comrades and friends further advised me to remain abroad because of growing threats to my life in the Philippines, as indicated by the ambushes on the Polytechnic University of the Philippines president Dr. Nemesio Prudente and former NPA commander Bernabe Buscayno, BAYAN general secretary Lean Alejandro, and so many other human rights activists.

While arrangements were being made for my safe return to the Philippines in 1987, I accepted from a US publishing firm a book contract that I could do in the Netherlands. In the midst of this book project came the decision of Mrs. Aquino to cancel my Philippine passport on September 16, 1988, after she ordered the filing of a complaint for subversion against me. The actions of the Aquino regime forced me to apply for political asylum in the Netherlands on October 26, 1988.

Q25. How did you struggle against the Aquino regime? What were the issues?

In the Philippines in 1986, I analyzed and criticized the Aquino regime in so many public meetings and press interviews. In a comprehensive and deep-going way, I criticized the Aquino regime and the Philippine ruling system in a series of 10 lectures delivered at the University of the Philippines from April to May 1986. These lectures are compiled under the title *Philippine Crisis and Revolution*.

Abroad in the latter part of 1986 and onward, I exposed the pro-imperialist and reactionary character of the Aquino regime. As early as September 1986 while I was in Australia, Generals Ramos and De Villa were already pressuring Mrs. Aquino to cancel my passport.

The issues that I raised against the Aquino regime included puppetry to the US, adoption of the "neoliberal" or "free market" dictates of the IMF, the sham character of the "comprehensive agrarian reform program", corruption of the new ruling clique, escalation of human rights violations and the plan of the regime to retain the US military bases.

Q26. You personally knew both the late Senator Benigno Aquino and former President Corazon C. Aquino before you went underground in 1968. Please describe your relationship with each or both. Is it true

that the Aquinos cooperated with the CPP and NPA?

In 1967, Senator Aquino invited me to his home through his assistant Raul Roco. Thus, I met Aquino for the first time. He proposed that I join him in a hunger strike to call attention to the people's demands. I declined because among other reasons, I was then preoccupied with so many strikes of workers and students, mass protest actions and more urgently, the struggle against the Lava dynasty within the old merger party of the Communist and Socialist parties.

I knew the Aquinos enough as allies against the Marcos regime and as allies who happened to have economic and political interests in Tarlac province where the CPP and NPA had a strong revolutionary base.

Q27. Despite your criticism of her government, Mrs. Aquino nevertheless sent a peace emissary to you in 1990. Why?

By then, Mrs. Aquino was in deep trouble. She was afraid of being engulfed by the coup threats and social calamities for which her regime was responsible as well as by natural calamities (like the Mt. Pinatubo eruption in Central Luzon and the earthquake in Northern Luzon).

So, she sent Rep. Jose V. Yap twice to meet me in the latter half of 1990 and explore the possibility of opening peace negotiations between the Manila government and the National Democratic Front of the Philippines. The exploratory talks were progressing until the mutiny of Col. Alexander Noble in Mindanao in December 1990 seemed to discourage Aquino.

On the US Bases

Q28. When the US wanted the Philippine Senate to extend the life of the US-RP Military Bases Agreement, you were already in exile. How were you able to participate in the struggle to frustrate this US move?

I participated in the struggle not only by issuing press statements to encourage the broad popular movement but also by cooperating directly with BAYAN, former Senator Lorenzo M. Tañada and his son, then Senator Wigberto Tañada, in the campaign to raise sufficient votes in the Philippine Senate to defeat the extension of the US-RP Military Bases Agreement.

Senator Tañada came with peace advocate Ms Maris Diokno, daughter of the late Senator Diokno, to meet with Luis Jalandoni and myself at the Tricontinental Centre in Louvain, Belgium in March 1991. The head of the Centre, Professor Francois Houtart, provided us with the meeting place but did not participate in the meeting.

Senator Tañada told us that Senate President Jovito Salonga would be encouraged to exercise leadership and get a majority of the senators to vote for the non-extension of the agreement, if the NDFP would announce its willingness to engage the Manila government in peace negotiations and to declare a unilateral ceasefire.

Luis Jalandoni and I agreed to the proposed announcement. Just before the Senate voted on the resolution on the US bases in September 1991, the formal announcement of the NDFP was dramatically read on the Senate floor. It was met with a resounding ovation. This encouraged most of the senators to vote against the bases.

On the Ramos Regime

Q29. General Fidel V. Ramos was a key player in the Aquino regime. What was his role and function?

General Fidel V. Ramos was the point man of the US in the Aquino regime. As chief of staff of the reactionary armed forces and then as secretary of national defense, he was in charge of lining up support for Aquino among the military and police. With every coup attempt, Mrs. Aquino became increasingly dependent on him.

He was the transition or continuity man from Marcos to Aquino and eventually from Aquino to himself as president. The US designated him to play that role. Under the 1984 Armacost formula[3] of the US State Department, the US authorities expected him to "mend" the rift within the reactionary armed forces. Previously, they had encouraged a split within the Philippine reactionary armed forces, between the Marcos-Ver faction and the Enrile-Ramos faction, in order to break the prolonged personal hold of Marcos over the military.

When Ramos became president in 1992, he amnestied the officers and men of the Reform the Armed Forces Movement (RAM—renamed *Rebolusyonaryong Alyansang Makabansa*) and reinstated them in the military and police services.

---

3. Armacost was former US ambassador to the Philippines 1982-84 and undersecretary of political affairs, US State Department, from 1984–89. The Armacost formula was a concept for mending the rift within the Armed Forces of the Philippines (AFP). The US State Department designed it to assure the Pentagon that the overthrow of Marcos would not indefinitely fracture the AFP.

Q30. *How would you characterize the Ramos regime? Please point out the policies that he pursued either to the detriment or benefit of the people.*

The US-Ramos regime went full blast with pushing "free market" globalization and implementing the policies of liberalization, privatization and deregulation. It promoted low value-added and export-oriented semi-manufactures (garments, semiconductors, shoes, toys and the like) and a temporary boom in private construction and real estate speculation.

It bargained away state assets and encouraged foreign monopoly and big comprador firms to go on a borrowing spree from the foreign commercial banks, with "sovereign guarantees" from the puppet state. To generate dollar cash flow in the face of the growing foreign trade deficits, it further pushed Filipinos to become migrant workers abroad. Nevertheless, the Ramos regime increased foreign and local public debt at a rate faster than did Marcos and Aquino.

Ultimately, the economic collapse came in 1997. A global overproduction in garments had emerged in 1994 and in electronic components in 1996. The private construction boom went bust in 1997 in the whole of Southeast Asia. The trade deficits and defaults on debt service payment came crashing on the Philippines. The foreign monopolies themselves shifted their speculative capital to their home grounds.

The Ramos regime had talked much about a medium-term development plan since 1992. This plan was bound to fail. It did not carry a single national industrial project. Neither did it offer genuine land reform. It was a lot of neo-liberal crap about "leveling the playing field". This in fact meant bulldozing national entrepreneurs to give way to foreign monopolies.

The regime opposed the people's aspirations for national industrialization and land reform. It accelerated the reduction of tariffs on industrial and agricultural monopolies. It aggravated the problem of unemployment and intensified the exploitation of the working people.

The Ramos regime had a propensity for campaigns of military suppression against the revolutionary forces and the people. Since 1992, it intensified these campaigns from year to year, despite the reduction of NPA tactical offensives from 1992 to 1996 due to the CPP-initiated rectification movement and the preliminary talks for the peace negotiations of the GRP and the NDFP.

Q31. *In what struggles against the Ramos regime did you participate?*

I issued statements, speeches and messages to the Philippine mass organizations, opposing all major policies and actions of the Ramos regime that were detrimental to the people. I always stood in militant solidarity with the broad masses of the people struggling against the regime.

By the time Ramos began maneuvering in 1996 and 1997 to prolong his stay in office through certain amendments to the 1987 Constitution, the forces of the national-democratic movement had gained so much mass strength that it could enter into a broad united front with other forces in order to mobilize greater numbers of protestors nationwide.

I called on the forces of the national-democratic movement to go into a broad united front with all other forces to frustrate Ramos's scheme to prolong himself in power. The progressive forces maintained their independence and initiative and at the same time linked up with all other forces against Ramos to arouse and mobilize the people in their millions.

Q32. *How did you reconcile such struggles with the peace negotiations, which both Ramos and you encouraged? Weren't you offered positions in government? How did you respond?*

The NDFP is consistent in declaring that the struggle for a just and lasting peace is no different from the struggle for national liberation and democracy against US imperialism and the local exploiting classes. There can be no just and lasting peace for as long as the roots of the armed conflict are not addressed. That is clear in the framework agreement called The Hague Joint Declaration of 1992.

It is also clear to the NDFP and all the revolutionary forces that peace negotiations are a form of struggle subordinate to the revolutionary armed struggle and the legal mass movement. As it conducts peace negotiations correctly, the NDFP gains equal footing with the Manila government under international law.

When Ramos was not yet president, he was quite active in sabotaging Aquino's attempts to negotiate with the NDFP. When he became president, with only 23.5 percent of the vote in 1992, he found it necessary to resume exploratory talks about peace negotiations.

Once more, I welcomed Representative Yap when he came back to the Netherlands to conduct exploratory talks and agree with the NDFP on the framework of the peace negotiations. Thus was The Hague Joint Declaration agreed upon and signed by Yap and NDFP representative Luis Jalandoni on September 1, 1992. The principals of the GRP and the NDFP approved the agreement.

Luis Jalandoni and I were offered cabinet positions in 1993 and 1996. But we consistently rebuffed the offers. Different high officials made the offers discreetly as well as openly. We told them that the leaders of the NDFP did not join the revolutionary movement to get high positions in the reactionary government.

Q33. *Obviously, both the NDFP and the Manila government run risks in negotiating for peace. At the very least, the Manila government wants the demoralization of the revolutionary movement; at the maximum, it wants complete capitulation from the NDFP. At the same time, it worries that the NDFP might gain international recognition of the status of belligerency. How important to the NDFP is the status of belligerency and international recognition of such status?*

The status of belligerency is something that the people's democratic government has already gained through the people's revolutionary struggle. The international or diplomatic recognition of such status is important for at least two reasons: first, the Geneva Conventions and its protocols would apply to the civil war between the Manila government and the people's democratic government; and second, the revolutionary government would be able to establish relations of mutual support and assistance with foreign governments, without the latter becoming subject to charges of interference.

Q34. *It was much publicized in 1998 that you would return to the Philippines for a possible public signing of the GRP-NDFP Comprehensive Agreement on Respect for Human Rights and International Humanitarian Law (CARHRIHL). Was there really such a plan? What was the public reaction to that?*

I would have returned to the Philippines to participate in the public ceremony for the signing of the CARHRIHL had the Ramos regime complied with all the requirements.

Among these were the release of all the political prisoners, the issuance of a certification that there was no pending criminal charge against me, the issuance to me of a Philippine passport on the basis of the GRP-NDFP Joint Agreement on Safety and Immunity Guarantees and an agreement on the coordination of security personnel of the NDFP and the GRP with regard to my security.

I did not go to Manila because the GRP was unwilling to release all the political prisoners even as the GRP certified that there was no pending criminal charge against me and assured me of their respect for the guarantees under the GRP-NDFP Joint Agreement on Safety and Immunity Guarantees.

Some of the political prisoners advised me not to go and said they would rather stay in prison than let me take unnecessary risks. But I would have gone had all the political prisoners been released.

On the Estrada Regime

Q35. *As soon as Estrada was elected president, you opposed him. Why? What were the issues against the regime?*

Even before he took his oath of office as president, Estrada announced he would honor Marcos as a hero and have him interred in the *Libingan ng mga Bayani* (Heroes Cemetery). He merely echoed the Ramos policies of liberalization, privatization and deregulation, which had sunk the country further into bankruptcy. His anti-people policies had to be opposed immediately.

He signed on August 7, 1998 the GRP-NDFP CARHRIHL that Ramos had failed to sign. But on October 26, 1998, he dispatched Senator Franklin Drilon to the Netherlands to demand that the NDFP agree to a supplementary agreement by which it would capitulate to the GRP and criminalize itself.

The demand had the effect of torpedoing the CARHRIHL and the entire peace negotiations, long before the Estrada regime betrayed the Filipino people by pushing the Senate ratification of the Visiting Forces Agreement (VFA) on May 27, 1999.

This VFA is even worse than the defunct US-RP Military Bases Agreement. It allows the US military forces to occupy any part of the country for any length of time, to use Philippine territory for aggression against the Filipino people and other peoples, and to commit any kind of atrocity with impunity and without the puppet state having any claim of criminal jurisdiction.

Q36. *In your message to the BAYAN national conference in December 1998, you predicted that the Estrada regime would fall. You even compared him to Abdalla Bucharam, the deposed president of Ecuador.*

How did you reach this conclusion?

From the very beginning, Estrada was scandalously unfit for his presidential position even by the standards of the exploiting classes. He is intellectually and morally a big disgrace. He climbed to power merely because of populist demagoguery and movie-star popularity.

And yet he was so arrogant as to challenge and to fight the legal progressive forces and the revolutionary movement, which could easily puncture his claims to being a champion of the poor. At the same time, he made theatrical provocations against the Catholic Church and the Ayala business group.

It was well known that Estrada had collected campaign money for the presidential elections from criminal syndicates and from such big Marcos cronies as Eduardo Cojuangco and Lucio Tan.

Considering the gravity of the socioeconomic and political crisis of the ruling system since 1997, I estimated that a broad united front could easily isolate and overthrow Estrada.

Q37. Will you explain the line that you advocated in effecting the overthrow of the Estrada regime?

The line is for the people and the revolutionary forces to take advantage of the contradictions among the reactionaries and to isolate and overthrow every ruling clique that works against and undermines the people's interests. In this manner, they accumulate enough strength to overthrow the entire reactionary ruling system.

Short of overthrowing the entire ruling system, it is possible for a broad united front to neutralize the reactionary military and police and to overthrow, through a relatively peaceful mass uprising, a fascist or despotic regime like that of Marcos or an extremely corrupt regime like that of Estrada. To overthrow the entire ruling system, the protracted people's war is necessary.

For the armed and legal forms of struggle, an echelon of alliances can be developed: the basic alliance of workers and peasants; the alliance of progressive forces, including the toiling masses and the urban petty bourgeoisie, the alliance of patriotic forces, including the progressive forces and the middle bourgeoisie, and the temporary and unstable alliance with reactionaries opposed to the ruling reactionary clique as the common enemy.

On the Macapagal-Arroyo Regime

Q38. What do you think of the regime of Gloria Macapagal-Arroyo? How is it similar to or different from the Estrada regime?

The Macapagal-Arroyo regime is as rotten as the Estrada regime. It is another passing regime of a clique of big compradors and landlords. It is a faithful follower of the current neoliberal policy stress of US imperialism.

It treads the same path as the fallen Estrada regime in exploiting and oppressing the people. The puppetry, corruption and brutality of the regime repel the people.

This regime is in a situation more difficult than that of its predecessor. The crisis of the world capitalist system and the domestic ruling system is now acutely worse than before. Under these circumstances, the anti-people, anti-national and anti-democratic character of the regime will appear more conspicuous in due course.

Q39. What tactics is the Macapagal-Arroyo regime using against the revolutionary movement? What is the revolutionary movement's response?

The Macapagal-Arroyo regime is obsessed with having its president retained in 2004. Thus it displays shameless puppetry to the US as it tries to assure its imperialist masters and the local reactionary classes that they can rely upon it and can get what they want.

At the same time, it is trying to echo the anti-poverty demagoguery of Estrada and feigns and avows interest in the peace negotiations. But it is further impoverishing the people, committing human rights violations on a wide scale and launching brutal military campaigns of suppression against the revolutionary movement and the people in the countryside.

The response of the revolutionary movement is to intensify the revolutionary armed struggle and other forms of struggle. At the same time, for as long as possible, the NDFP can engage in peace negotiations with the GRP along the strategic line of struggle for national liberation and democracy.

Q40. How do you compare the Marcos regime and all the post-Marcos regimes, with regard to the issues of national sovereignty and socioeconomic problems? How much have they affected Philippine society for better or for worse?

The Marcos and post-Marcos regimes are all similarly committed to preserving the ruling system of big compradors and landlords and following the dictates of US imperialism directly and indirectly.

They are all instruments of the imperialists and local reactionaries for the oppression and exploitation of the broad masses of the people. They are all corrupt and repressive.

The Marcos regime was a puppet regime under the auspices of the US Keynesian economic policy stress and the cold war strategy. It became a fascist regime propped up by foreign loans for public works and for enhancing raw-material production for export.

The succeeding regimes are much weaker than the Marcos regime economically and politically. This is a consequence of the pillaging done by the imperialists and the Marcos regime. The depredations of each succeeding regime render the next one weaker. Coming on top of the previous Marcos' plunder is the new wave of plunder under the neo-liberal policy stress of the US.

Q41. Nevertheless, these regimes survive, propped up by a military structure that appears to be basically unchanged. Please explain why there have been no military takeovers as a result of the weakening of civilian rule.

The US and the local exploiting classes would go for military rule if they see this as the alternative to civilian rule against an armed revolutionary movement that is strong enough and is about to seize power.

So far, in the history of the existing ruling system, Marcos took the initiative of magnifying his claims about the armed strength of the revolutionary movement and proceeding to impose martial law on the people. However, since the 1980s, in dominating client states, the US imperialists have shown a preference for civilian rulers whom they control and manipulate.

For this purpose, it has applied economic, financial, military and diplomatic pressure, blackmail and punishment on client states. But if the armed strength of the revolutionary movement rises high enough, the US can opt to replace civilian rulers with military rulers and even to commit naked aggression against the Filipino people, using American and other foreign military forces.

THE BLADED POEM

Behold the bladed poem
Tensile and razor-sharp
Cold and glinting silver
In the light or dark.

See how the blackbird
Of a hilt flies
Bedecked with pearls
On the firm mobile hand.

Look at each face
On the leaf of steel,
The virile subtle flames,
Images of incised gold.

On one face are toilers
Varied with pike and ore,
Crucible, hammer and anvil,
Water and whetstone.

Plow and carabao on soil,
The oyster in the sea,
Carving and etching tools,
Bowl of acid on a table.

On the other face
Are the same workmen massed
Upright and poised to fight
Behind the radiant flag.

The uprising completes
The figures of labor
And urges another surge
With the well-versed weapon.

Grasp well the bladed poem
And let it sing in your hands.
This kampilan is a talisman
Of the people in red headbands.

March 1982

The multi-sectoral alliance BAYAN (New Patriotic Alliance) spearheads nationwide demonstrations in the Philippines against US military intervention and the projected return of US military bases. (NDF International Office photo collection)

NOT TERRORIST Militant groups march through Paseo de Roxas en route to the European Consulate in Makati City to protest the European Union's inclusion of Jose Ma. Sison and the Communist Party of the Philippines in its list of terrorist individuals and organizations. PHOTO BY ROLEX DELA PEÑA

Marchers in Manila demand removal of Professor Sison from "terrorist" list. (DEFEND photo collection)

Addressing the Kabataang Makabayan (KM) reunion in 1986.
(Courtesy Pat Roque/Midweek)

Chapter Three

Rectification and Rebuilding

Q1. You have been with the revolutionary movement since the early 1960s when it again began to stir to life. You virtually rebuilt it from zero. What was the situation when you began organizing?

The old merger party of the Communist and Socialist parties had been practically liquidated since 1957 because of the single-file policy of Dr. Jesus Lava, the general secretary, who isolated and hid himself in Manila. Not a single party branch existed. There was no leading organ until Jesus Lava authorized in 1962 the formation of the executive committee.

He had issued in 1955 the order for the liquidation and conversion of the armed units of the old people's army, the *Hukbong Mapagpalaya ng Bayan* (HMB—People's Liberation Army), into 'organizational brigades'. Thus, he cut himself off from any armed unit. The remnants of the people's army did not heed the order and they found no reason and no way to keep in touch with him.

There was no progressive mass movement to speak of, until the mass action against the congressional Committee against Anti-Filipino Activities (CAFA) took place on March 15, 1961. The enemy had destroyed the progressive trade union movement, the peasant associations and other legal progressive forces as it destroyed the backbone of the armed revolutionary movement in the period 1950-52.

Q2. You were central to the revival of the revolutionary mass movement and ultimately in rebuilding the Communist Party of the Philippines. How did you proceed?

I started doing revolutionary work where I could, by forming study circles among young faculty members and students at the University of the Philippines in 1959. We openly studied Philippine history and current conditions with the purpose of starting a movement to complete the struggle for national liberation and democracy. Secretly, we studied Marxism-Leninism to be able to apply it.

When CAFA launched a witch-hunt against progressive writers, the Student Cultural Association of the University of the Philippines invited other campus organizations to a meeting. The meeting decided to fight the witch-hunt by carrying out the anti-CAFA protest action in 1961. This encouraged dormant progressive forces to speak up and act against US imperialism and the local reactionaries. Thus was the progressive mass movement ignited in the 1960s.

By the way, among those so-called subversive articles targeted by the CAFA was one of mine written under a pseudonym and published in the *Philippine Collegian*. The article was a tribute to Patrice Lumumba, the outstanding Congolese patriotic leader, and a condemnation of the US and Belgian imperialists who were responsible for his murder. Among the articles deemed subversive, the most significant was one on the history of the peasant war in the Philippines, published in the social science journal of the UP College of Arts and Sciences faculty.

Following the anti-CAFA mass action, we created more study circles in other universities. We trained ourselves to debate with the reactionary faculty members. We engaged in cultural activities with revolutionary message. Our members became leaders of campus organizations, officers of the student government and editors of the student publications.

From 1962 onward, we started to have links with the trade union movement, particularly the National Association of Trade Unions led by Ignacio Lacsina, the Philippine Association of Federated Labor Unions led by

Cipriano Cid and the National Association of Free Labor Unions led by Felixberto Olalia. In 1963, some of us integrated ourselves into the trade union movement. We also went into the research and education departments of the Workers' Party and the labor federations.

Also, in 1963, we gave refresher courses to veteran peasant cadres and to newly released political prisoners. In 1964, we organized *Kabataang Makabayan* (KM) as the comprehensive youth organization for young workers, peasants, students and young professionals. This became the seeding machine of the struggle for national democracy nationwide. KM trained young communists and helped in rebuilding the mass movement and the CPP in Metro Manila, Central Luzon and Southern Tagalog from which these expanded nationwide.

***Q3. Where did you get the Marxist-Leninist literature that you used for your studies from 1959 to the 1960s? In terms of immediate need of a resurgent mass movement, how would you weigh the Marxist classics against your own book* Struggle for National Democracy?**

We were able to get a few Marxist-Leninist books and pamphlets hidden by senior communists and also those provided by an Indonesian comrade. Eventually, we were able to arrange the flow of Marxist-Leninist literature from Indonesia, Hongkong, the US and England.

It was of crucial importance that we reproduced and studied the Marxist-Leninist classics on philosophy, capitalist political economy, state and revolution, imperialism, socialism, strategy and tactics and so on. The revolutionary theory of the proletariat is the prerequisite to the revolutionary movement in the era of imperialism and proletarian revolution.

Through theoretical studies, I was able to grasp the scientific stand, viewpoint and methodology of Marxism. Subsequently I applied these in my writings on the history and conditions of the Filipino people. The book, *Struggle for National Democracy*, was read widely by mass activists and helped to generate the mass movement. It was more available than the few Marxist books and pamphlets.

But I would not assert that my book had a more important role than the Marxist-Leninist classics. The Marxist-Leninist classics were necessary and effective in theoretical study. My book was necessary and effective in political education based on the history and conditions of the Filipino people.

Q4. Why did you break from the old communist party? You were its most effective organizer and propagandist in the 1960s. You were then in key positions in the mass movement, simultaneously as general secretary of the Socialist Party of the Philippines and general secretary of the Movement for the Advancement of Nationalism.

We, the young proletarian revolutionaries and a number of the veteran cadres, broke from the old merger party in April 1967 because the Lava revisionist renegades opposed a summing up of experience for the period of 1942 to 1962 and a necessary rectification movement. They wanted to gloss over the history of the Party and cover up the errors of the past. They also took the side of Soviet revisionist renegades in the international ideological debate. They wanted us to follow their revisionist line or else be expelled.

The Lava revisionist renegades opposed the ideological, political and organizational building of the Marxist-Leninist party. They were so afraid of the enemy and bitterly opposed the efforts and determination of the proletarian revolutionaries to resume armed revolution.

Immediately after our break from the Lavas, we started the First Great Rectification Movement in 1967 to prepare for the reestablishment of the Party. We upheld the theory of Marxism-Leninism-Mao Zedong Thought, the political line of a new-democratic revolution through protracted people's war and the organizational principle of democratic centralism.

Q5. What attracted young men and women to become members of the CPP? Why were they so unafraid of the penalties (i.e., death for officers and long imprisonment for members) under the Anti-Subversion Law?

The CPP attracted young men and women because it showed the revolutionary way out of the oppressive and exploitative system. When people recognize a just revolutionary cause and the way to carry it forward, they become dauntless and consider it a duty to work hard and struggle, make sacrifices and overcome the odds.

They become unafraid of the high risks and adverse personal consequences. They become more resolute and militant as they become part of a growing movement, in which more and more people are being aroused, organized and mobilized. Their lives become meaningful and fruitful through the struggle for national liberation, democracy, social justice and other lofty goals.

Q6. During your chairmanship of the Central Committee of the Communist Party of the Philippines, from 1968 to 1977, how far did the Philippine revolutionary movement develop?

We may consider the period 1968-77 as the foundation years of the reestablished CPP and the resurgent revolutionary movement. We established the firm ideological, political and organizational foundation of the Party.

To lay the ideological foundation of the Party, we studied the works of Marx, Engels, Lenin, Stalin and Mao. We continued to carry out the First Great Rectification Movement. We laid out the general political program and the strategy and tactics of the new-democratic revolution.

We produced *Philippine Society and Revolution* and so many other major documents, like *Guide for Establishing the People's Democratic Government*, *Revolutionary Guide to Land Reform*, *The Specific Characteristics of People's War in the Philippines* and *Our Urgent Tasks*.

We started the people's war where we could in early 1969. That was in the second district of Tarlac. Early on, we trained cadres for assignment to other regions, such as Northern Luzon, Southern Luzon and the Visayas. As soon as we could, we formed the regional party committees and the regional operational commands of the New People's Army.

In building the initial units of the NPA, usually in the form of the armed propaganda teams, we gave priority to organizing the people at strategically important points and in terrain favorable to guerrilla warfare. Wherever we could deploy armed propaganda teams, which were subdivisions of NPA squads, we built organs of political power and mass organizations.

The Party and the mass organizations expanded nationwide. The urban-based mass movement facilitated the approach to the peasant masses in various regions. The Party rooted itself deeply among the masses of workers and peasants. It accumulated victories by wielding such weapons as armed struggle and the united front.

Before 1977, the NPA gained the capability to undertake platoon-size tactical offensives in many parts of the country. We used the tactics of the united front effectively to strengthen the people's army, the urban and rural mass movement and the coordination of the forces in both urban and rural areas.

Under Martial Law

Q7. How did the Party operate under martial law? How did the Marcos dictatorship affect the revolutionary movement? What were the methods used to offset or break through the fear generated by martial law?

Since its founding, the CPP had been prepared against the worst. It foresaw the coming of the enemy's open rule of terror and thus continuously maintained its clandestine character. It adopted the strategic line of protracted people's war and built secret Party groups within mass organizations and institutions.

When the writ of habeas corpus was suspended in 1971 and martial law was declared in 1972, we had underground Party organs and units that could preserve and regenerate themselves. However, the most vulnerable to destruction by the fascist dictatorship were the urban-based legal mass organizations. Its strength in the countryside, though limited, enabled the revolutionary movement to preserve itself.

The most difficult years were 1971 to 1974. The fascist Marcos regime launched an all-out suppression campaign in both rural and urban areas. Organized urban communities came under zoning operations, with masked informers identifying Party members and sympathizers. The enemy forces conducted searches and mass arrests without judicial warrants and other formalities of bourgeois law. The few guerrilla zones could not absorb instantly many of the mass leaders and activists being hunted down by the enemy.

We encouraged the people in the urban areas to carry out all possible forms of struggle to resist the fascist dictatorship. Workers used such tactics as work slowdowns and "trooping the offices" (i.e., everyone queuing up to file complaints). The youth conducted lightning rallies and lightning painting of wall slogans and distribution of leaflets.

Statements of the revolutionary forces and reports about NPA tactical offensives in the underground press, such as *Ang Bayan* (The People), *Taliba ng Bayan* (People's Guardian), *Liberasyon* (Liberation) and various regional Party publications inspired and encouraged the people.

In 1974, the Party succeeded in making a dramatic breach in the climate of fear imposed by the fascist dictatorship on the country. As a result of urgings by church people in the Christians for National Liberation (CNL), Cardinal Sin exposed and denounced human rights violations. The same church people participated actively in carrying out the historic

La Tondeña workers' strike that led to a nationwide strike of workers in more than 300 workplaces, from October 1974 to January 1975.

Q8. *That the Marcoses ravaged the country's economy is pretty well known. That they wreaked havoc on people's lives isn't. Has there ever been a final tally on how many were actually imprisoned, injured and/or killed during the Marcos regime?*

By surpassing his predecessors in collaborating with multinational firms and banks in ravaging the economy, the Marcos fascist dictatorship intensified the daily violence of exploitation inflicted on the broad masses of the people in their tens of millions.

Incalculable violence was inflicted upon the people when the Marcos dictatorship deprived them of economic, social and cultural rights—whether they were workers and peasants forced to produce wealth while suffering ever lower levels of subsistence, or women or national minorities forced to suffer multiple forms of exploitation and discrimination.

With regard to the most blatant forms of violence such as violation of political and civil rights, human rights organizations have made tabulations of victims of arbitrary arrest, torture, summary execution, involuntary disappearances, displaced communities and so on. But these tabulations fall short of the real score as martial law imposed restrictions and difficulties on human rights organizations undertaking fact-finding, data collection and documentation.

One estimate puts those illegally arrested and imprisoned for at least one week at 500,000 and those imprisoned for one month to several years at 70,000. Those summarily executed and disappeared number more than 100,000.

Displacement of entire communities, if reported, was often underestimated. Still, in the early 1980s, the Philippine National Red Cross reported to the International Committee of the Red Cross that fascist military campaigns displaced some five million people. Hundreds of thousands of Moros fled to Sabah.

The military, police and private security guards forced people from their homes and land not only to suppress the armed revolutionary movement but also to deliver the land and other natural resources to the imperialists and the local exploiting classes.

Violence continues to this day against economic, social, cultural, political and civil rights of the people. The Marcos fascist dictatorship is gone but the oppressive and exploitative ruling system remains.

Q9. *Is it true that after you wrote* Specific Characteristics of People's War *in 1974 you were taking too many risks? Had you been captured in 1974, how costly would it have been for the revolutionary movement? Looking back at your capture in 1977, do you think it could have been avoided? What led to your capture?*

I was running bigger risks from 1974 onward because quite a number of comrades in the Central Committee had been either killed or captured and because so many personnel of the general secretariat were being reassigned to the regions to strengthen the regional forces.

Before 1974, certain members of the Central Committee and scores of personnel of the general secretariat assisted the office of the chairman and provided it with layers of support and protection. From 1974 to 1977, the personnel of the general secretariat thinned out mainly due to redeployment. It became necessary for me to move frequently from one region to another and within a region from one guerrilla front to another.

Both prudence and pressure of work necessitated my frequent movement. The safest place for me would have been an underground house in Manila but this would have prevented me from meeting cadres from various regions and looking at actual work on the ground.

Had I been captured in or before 1974, the consequences would have been disastrous to the Party. The Party and other revolutionary forces were still in the process of overcoming the most adverse conditions under martial rule. But by 1975 they had overcome those adverse conditions and had I been captured then, the Party and the revolutionary movement would have been able to continue advancing.

My capture in 1977 could have been avoided had I stayed put in a forested camp or in an urban underground house or at best only moved within the range of guerrilla bases close to one another in the same region. But meetings with central cadres in various regions in the countryside and consultations with urban-based national staff organs necessitated my frequent movement.

Q10. How were you captured?

A renegade informed the Philippine Constabulary (PC) headquarters in Camp Olivas that I was attending the Central Luzon Regional Party Conference in July 1977 at the mountainous border area of

Pampanga, Zambales and Bataan. But, the enemy couldn't raise enough troops on time to seal off the mountainous and forested venue of the conference. Before the enemy military could mobilize more than a thousand troops, all of us in the conference area were able to move out of the loose encirclement.

However, the same informer told the enemy that I had arrived at the conference with comrades from northwestern Luzon (Ilocos-Cordillera-Pangasinan region). Based on this info, the enemy launched an intelligence dragnet against me from July to November 1977 in Pangasinan, La Union, Baguio City and Ilocos Sur.

Enemy intelligence established my presence in the general area and concentrated its personnel there. Then I made the mistake of driving a motorcycle from 11:00 p.m. to midnight of November 9, 1977 from Pangasinan to La Union, necessarily with my eyeglasses on. Enemy spotters caught sight of me at 11:55 p.m. in Bauang, La Union. At around 02:15 a.m. of November 10, 1977, the enemy raided the house where I was.

On the Salas Leadership

Q11. Is it true that the revolutionary movement reached its peak from the late 1970s to the mid-1980s under the chairmanship of Rodolfo Salas? In the mid-1980s, the NPA was alleged to have 25,000 fighters and so many company formations in Mindanao.

The big quantitative increases of Party members, Red fighters, guerrilla fronts and so on from 1977 to 1986 were due to several factors. These were the worsening crisis conditions of the ruling system, the good ideological, political and organizational foundation of the party and the revolutionary movement and the continuing revolutionary struggle of the Party and the people.

But the increases would have been bigger, more solid and stable if the correct ideological, political and organizational lines were followed and had grave errors not occurred hand-in-hand with quantitative growth. Those errors brought about increasingly bigger disasters from 1983 and onward. They overlapped with the achievements, which were what caught more attention. An all-time peak nationwide was reached in 1983-86 but was followed by a drastic decline due to underlying errors.

In 1985, the NPA had 5600 high-powered rifles; in 1986, it had hardly

6000 in the hands of full-time Red fighters. In Mindanao, successive military setbacks starting in 1984 and Kampanyang Ahos starting in 1985 resulted in the loss of large numbers of firearms. The figure of 25,000 Red fighters in the mid-1980s is a pure invention of the reactionary armed forces to magnify the subsequent so-called victory of Lambat Bitag I, II and III—the national military campaigns of suppression launched by the US-Aquino regime from 1987 to 1992.

What the NPA easily had in abundance then were the people's militia in the barrios and self-defense units of the mass organizations. However, these were not organized and trained as thoroughly as they should have been. The NPA could have had tens of thousands in the people's militia and hundreds of thousands in the self-defense units. But these numbers were not realized.

On the 1986 Boycott of National Elections

Q12. In Manila in 1986, there was so much distress in some urban "Left" circles over a so-called "marginalization" due to the boycott policy in the 1986 presidential elections. There were even those who said that had the Party played its cards right, the revolutionary movement could have gotten a big share of power, or could have seized power itself. When I expressed doubts as to its capacity to seize and much less hold political power, I was assured repeatedly that the revolutionary forces had the capacity. Could the Left at that time have wrested and held political power in the Philippines?

In the period of 1983-86, from the assassination of Aquino to the fall of Marcos, the forces of the Left could not have wrested power to complete the new-democratic revolution. It was just right for them to participate in the broad antifascist united front in order to strengthen themselves in the process of overthrowing the despotic regime.

The broad antifascist front succeeded in overthrowing Marcos through mass protest actions. But it would take far more strength than these to overthrow the ruling system of big compradors and landlords and replace it with a people's democratic government. Certainly, the NPA then was not strong enough to smash the military and bureaucratic machinery of the reactionary government.

Under conditions where the ruling system and its armed forces were intact, it was not possible for communists openly to take a share of power in the coalition government under Aquino. Earlier, in November 1985, US authorities had told her to keep communists out of her electoral campaign machinery and her prospective cabinet.

The boycott policy was a major tactical error that took effect only for the duration of the electoral campaign period in the 1986 snap presidential elections. It was not a strategic error that caused a permanent or long-term "marginalization" of the legal and illegal forces of the national-democratic movement. Immediately after the elections, BAYAN was able to take the initiative in calling for a people's uprising to oust Marcos and played the major and decisive role in the process of overthrowing Marcos.

Q13. What was wrong with the boycott policy? And what was wrong with the views of the "Left" and others regarding the boycott error of 1986?

The adoption of the boycott policy was a "Left" opportunist error. The policy separated from Bayan itself the BAYAN-led masses that responded to the electoral calls of the pro-Aquino alliance. Sen. Lorenzo M. Tañada had to take a leave of absence from his position as BAYAN chairman to join the pro-Aquino alliance and go around the sectarianism of the boycott policy.

BAYAN could have maintained its independence and initiative, mobilized its own masses and allowed them to join up occasionally with the pro-Aquino masses. And like Tañada, other BAYAN leaders could have mounted the same platform with Aquino and the rest of her slate to denounce Marcos and US imperialism. BAYAN is different from the underground forces. It can wage legal struggle, use the tactics of the broad united front and cooperate with certain reactionaries in order to isolate and defeat the worst of the reactionaries categorized as the enemy.

However, Right opportunists were wrong in presuming that were it not for the boycott error, Aquino would have rewarded BAYAN and the like with lots of cabinet and other posts in the reactionary government. Aquino was an ally against Marcos, albeit a temporary and unstable ally, soon to come under the tight control of the US and the influence of her fellow anti-Marcos reactionaries. Certainly, they would have blocked the appointment of any BAYAN leader to her cabinet.

The "Left" opportunists were also utterly wrong in presuming that had it not been for the boycott policy, an armed insurrection would have occurred in Manila and elsewhere and allowed the people to seize power after Marcos cheated in the snap elections.

The NPA from the countryside and/or armed city partisans simply did not have enough strength to overpower the Reform the Armed Forces Movement (RAM) and the entire structure of the reactionary armed forces. The "Left" opportunists did not include in their calculations how their putschist line and Kampanyang Ahos had already destroyed a large part of the NPA in Mindanao from 1985 onward.

Q14. Is it true that because of the boycott policy, the forces of the Left were so marginalized that they were practically absent from the "People's Power" uprising from February 22 to 25?

That is completely untrue. The leaders and members of BAYAN were among the first, if not the first, to respond to the call for people to assemble at Isetann in Cubao on the night that the anti-Marcos military coup of the RAM failed.

BAYAN chairman Tañada and other leaders of BAYAN were very much in the planning room, together with the representatives of other forces, in Camp Crame. Some 500 BAYAN Quezon City chapter members accompanied former Colonel Santiago of the Land Transportation Commission and they seized TV Channel 4. The seizure was very crucial in rallying the people to rise up against Marcos.

BAYAN members and sympathizers constituted at least 20 percent of the crowd at EDSA and some 85 percent of the people pressing on Malacañang Palace. They were the most organized and persevering in camping at EDSA and around the presidential palace.

The people organized by BAYAN stopped the tanks of General Palafox in Angeles City. In so many cities in the entire country, BAYAN mobilized the people to denounce Marcos, split his forces and paralyze the regime. It is utterly ridiculous how the reactionaries try to airbrush BAYAN or the progressive forces from the so-called EDSA I.

On the Movement's Decline

Q15. During the Aquino regime, there were large-scale mass actions and there was intensification of the armed struggle. In 1991, mass actions were launched against the US military bases and effected their removal. How do you reconcile such facts with the contrary view that

the revolutionary movement suffered a decline?

Let us review the facts. Mark well the time, place and limits of the phenomena. I will also point out the essence behind the façade of events. From the time Benigno Aquino was assassinated in 1983, the legal mass movement of progressive forces gained strength and surged forward. By the time Marcos fell in 1986, the strength of BAYAN, KMU, KMP, ACT, GABRIELA, LFS and other progressive organizations was at a relatively high level.

The single biggest mass action that BAYAN organized was the funeral march of Rolando Olalia, chairman of KMU and Partido ng Bayan in November 1986. Close to a million people joined the funeral march. Partido ng Bayan held sizeable election rallies nationwide in 1987. KMU spearheaded nationwide strikes against oil price increases and by the teachers for salary increases.

But by 1988 the basic urban-based mass organizations had weakened and mass protests had dwindled. Long-running errors in line and policies combined with vicious assaults by the enemy to weaken the mass organizations. The military and police wiped out the youth organization KADENA in Manila and killed mass leaders and human rights lawyers.

In 1987 and 1988, the urban insurrectionists, who were in the leadership of the armed city partisans, went overboard in increasing the armed city partisans units. They recruited elements who had little or no understanding of the revolutionary movement, no experience in revolutionary mass work and who were, in many cases, lumpen proletarians (street people). They used these city partisans to kill policemen at so rapid a rate that at one time, 200-300 policemen were killed in only two months' time.

Starting from 1988, the urban-based mass movement declined from year to year. In 1991, the biggest mass action against the US military bases in Manila numbered no more than 25,000. The factors that led to the removal of the US military bases included the long-running opposition of the people, the anti-bases majority in the Senate, and the volcanic eruption of Mt. Pinatubo. Also, the US imperialists were self-satisfied with their huge bases in Guam, South Korea and Japan and with the satellites that made the San Miguel electronic facility dispensable.

Q16. You use the terms "Left" and Right opportunism to characterize certain errors. Can you define these, please?

"Left" and Right opportunism are errors in political line. In the concrete circumstances of the Philippine revolutionary movement, these are errors committed by cadres, organs or the entire Party as a result of deviations from the correct line of new democratic revolution through protracted people's war.

The "Left" opportunists exaggerated the prospect of quick military victory through urban-centered insurrection by the spontaneous masses and by a few armed city partisans and/or through premature enlargement and regularization of concentrated combat units divorced from the peasant masses in the countryside.

"Left opportunism is Left in appearance but Right in essence. The desire to get quick results or win a quick victory amounts to impetuosity and overreaching. Left opportunists overestimate the strength and capability of the revolutionary forces and underestimate those of the enemy. In other words, the results sought are way beyond the objective or material situation of the forces being marshaled to accomplish them. Such an overestimation of the capability of the revolutionary forces results in defeat or failure and weakens rather than strengthens the revolutionary forces.

Unlike "Left" opportunists, Right opportunists overestimate the strength of the enemy and underestimate the strength and capability of the revolutionary forces and the people. Their subjective view leads them to seek the transformation of the exploitative and oppressive system through an indefinite series of peaceful reforms and compromises with the exploiting classes. They may ride on a revolutionary armed struggle but use this as a secondary form of struggle, subordinate to the legal forms of struggle. Subsequently, they seek to reduce, avoid or stop revolutionary armed struggle altogether.

Q17. What type of opportunist error proved to be most damaging from the 1980s to 1992? What kind of damage was inflicted upon the CPP, the NPA and the entire revolutionary movement?

The most damaging type of opportunist errors from the early 1980s to 1992 was of a "Left" character. The errors included the line of "strategic counteroffensive" pushed by the central leadership until 1986 and various types of putschism, especially urban insurrectionism, which directly opposed the line of protracted people's war and pushed the old theory of spontaneous masses.

The "Left" opportunists were led astray by their purely military viewpoint. They claimed that the Party had done enough mass work and that it was time to build larger units of the people's army and step up tactical offensives without considering the breadth and depth of the mass base. In particular, the urban insurrectionists wanted to intensify armed city partisan warfare and to call on people in the urban areas to carry out armed urban uprisings. They ignored the necessity of painstaking mass work and solid mass organizing in both city and countryside.

The "Left" opportunists played into the hands of the enemy. They were responsible for the erosion and contraction of the revolutionary mass base, the isolation and passivity of prematurely built NPA companies and battalions and ultimately, the over-suspiciousness and panic resulting from military setbacks, which triggered the anti-informer hysteria campaigns.

An assessment made by the Executive Committee of the CPP Central Committee states that the mass base was down by at least 15 per cent in 1988. By 1991, 60 per cent of the mass base had been lost.

Q18. *Could not the decline of the mass base and other revolutionary forces have been simply the result of better social conditions and the effectiveness of the strategy and tactics of the Aquino regime?*

No, certainly not. For a short while in 1986, the people were happy or even euphoric over the overthrow of the Marcos regime. But the economic and social conditions grew worse from month to month and from year to year under Aquino. Like its predecessor, the new regime was subservient to multinational firms and banks. It was corrupt and repressive. The new regime was under the weight of the accumulated foreign debt of the previous regime as well as adjusting to the neoliberal policy of the US, which meant less available foreign loans from official sources.

The enemy forces continued to adopt the offensive strategy appropriate to their size and strength. General Ramos carried out what he called "forward deployment strategy" and fielded as many troops as he could. His new recruit, the renegade Victor Corpus, called for a "war of quick decision," complemented by "gradual constriction". After the enemy forces took perimeter control over a certain area and undertook "search and destroy" operations, they fielded "special operations teams" (SOTs) to "consolidate and develop" the area. The SOTs tried to imitate the mass work and tactics of small NPA units. But for one thing, they could never imitate nor did they even try to imitate the NPA campaign for land reform in areas where NPA units were still following the correct anti-feudal line of the democratic revolution.

The response to the enemy's strategic offensive was fundamentally wrong. The "Left" opportunists who were dominant in the NPA national command and in some regional executive committees of the CPP played into the hands of the enemy by forming absolutely concentrated NPA companies, which were divorced from mass work and led astray by a purely military viewpoint. They abandoned the strategic line of protracted people's war. They abandoned the NPA practice of doing painstaking mass work, building the mass base and carrying out genuine land reform.

They chose to ignore the strategy and tactics of encircling the cities from the countryside and accumulating strength over a long period of time by launching and winning tactical offensives in order to advance from one stage to another until power can be seized in the cities.

The strategy and tactics suitable to the enemy forces became effective whenever and wherever the revolutionary forces committed the error of trying to fight in the same way as enemy forces, i.e., prematurely building larger military formations, disregarding mass-base building and land reform, and going for putschism of one kind or another.

On "Left" Opportunism

Q19. I presume that this impetuosity, as you call it, this overreaching in pursuit of a quick military victory without a solid base, has ideological roots. From what, then, did "Left" opportunism spring, ideologically speaking?

"Left" opportunism arose from petty-bourgeois subjectivism. The "Left" opportunists exaggerated the infrastructure-building projects and the sham land reform program of Marcos as having caused the dissolution of the semi-feudal character of the Philippine economy and the invalidation of the line of protracted people's war in the countryside. From this false premise, they spun their notions of a quick military victory, exaggerating their capability to seize power through an urban armed uprising, even without people's war in the countryside.

They spread the notion in the late 1970s and early 1980s that Philippine society was no longer semi-feudal; that it was more urbanized than pre-revolutionary China and therefore, the strategic line of protracted people's war was no longer valid and necessary for carrying out the new democratic revolution.

One implication of this subjectivist view was that the comprador-landlord economic policy of Marcos had so industrialized and developed the Philippines that it was no longer semi-feudal. The "Left" opportunists wanted a quicker way of seizing political power and lost patience with the line of developing people's war in stages over a protracted period of time in the countryside.

They went so far as to credit Marcos for what they themselves imagined to be "industrial capitalist development" and land reform. In fact, Marcos' big comprador-landlord economic policy for two decades devastated the Philippine economy and deepened its pre-industrial, agrarian and semi-feudal character. The Marcos regime was dependent on the production of raw materials for export, incurred high trade deficits due to the unequal exchange of raw material exports and manufactured imports and resorted to foreign borrowing to cover trade and budgetary deficits.

Q20. *Is it known who specifically were responsible for "Left" opportunism?*

At the Party center, the proponents of "strategic counteroffensive" were headed by Party chairman Rodolfo Salas. The NPA was still trying to develop fully the early phase of the strategic defensive. But the exponents of the "strategic counteroffensive" claimed in 1979 informally and at the 1980 plenum formally that the NPA was already aiming for the advanced phase of the strategic defensive. They subsequently claimed at the Politiburo meeting in 1981 that they had reached the advanced phase of the strategic defensive and were aiming for the "strategic counteroffensive" as the third and final phase of the strategic defensive.

In the 1985 plenum, a three-year program was adopted to fulfill the requirements of the "strategic counteroffensive". In effect, the "Left" opportunists sought to run down the NPA by forcing it to run faster than it could.

In the Mindanao Commission of the CPP were exponents of the "Red area-White area" schema. They regarded the people's army as a purely military force and sought to conjure an urban insurrectionary movement, supposedly a politico-military force, combining the spontaneous masses and the armed city partisans. They echoed Joaquin Villalobos of the Farabundo Marti Movement for National Liberation (FMLN) who pontificated the nonsense that the people's army is a purely military force while armed urban insurrection had the dignity of being a politico-military force, having the participation of the spontaneous masses as its political component.

The Party center under Salas paid lip service to people's war but shared with the "Left" opportunists in the Mindanao Commission the purely military view that the time for building the mass base and guerrilla fronts was over. The supposed objective of the "strategic counteroffensive" was to exhaust the possibilities of guerrilla warfare and rapidly move on to regular mobile warfare as the main form of armed struggle.

The "Left" opportunists in the Mindanao Party Commission had the same bias for quick military victory as the Party center. They outrightly considered the NPA a purely military force and wanted to subordinate it to an armed urban insurrection consisting of armed city partisans and spontaneous masses. They worshipped the successful anti-authoritarian insurrection in Nicaragua as a model of armed revolution, without sufficient consideration of the requirements of social revolution.

The "Left" opportunists sought and placed undue emphasis on foreign military and financial assistance for speeding up the armed revolution. In the early 1980s, they abandoned the principled anti-revisionist stand of the CPP and considered the Soviet Union as socialist and the Soviet party as Marxist-Leninist—all in the vain hope that by doing so, they would secure Soviet military and financial aid.

On Right Opportunism

Q21. What about Right opportunism—i.e., being downright obsequious to the ruling system? How did that develop within the CPP? Can you elaborate on the ideas and actions that went into Right opportunism?

Like "Left" opportunists, Right opportunists long for an easy way to power. Supposedly, their easy way is bloodless and painless, while that of the "Left" opportunists is bloody but quick. The rightists wish to win victory by seeking to change society peacefully through an indefinite series of reforms. Right opportunism can develop in a communist party because persistent petty-bourgeois elements can take advantage of the natural desire for easy victory and can churn out the notions, plans and scenarios for changing society peacefully.

In the Philippines, like the "Left" opportunists, the Right opportunists based themselves on the line that the Philippine economy was already industrialized and highly urbanized and no longer semi-feudal. In line with their subjective view, they exaggerated the importance of urban-based *legal* struggles and considered these the main form of struggle, at the expense of rural-based armed strugggle.

Eventually, they started asserting that the legal form of struggle was either the sole or the principal means of empowering the people. They sought to liquidate the working class leadership in the united front, supposedly to make the revolution more attractive to the bourgeoisie and the entire people. They wanted to convert the NDFP to their concept of New Katipunan, drop the working class leadership and recycle the old democratic revolution. They wanted both legal progressive forces and the underground revolutionary forces to beg for accommodation in the post-Marcos regimes.

Ultimately, they systematically tried to put the name of the NDFP at odds with the CPP. They considered the united front rather than the CPP as the vanguard of the people in the legal mass movement as well as in the urban uprisings in some vague future.

The Right opportunist trend grew from year to year gradually from 1981 to 1987 under the shadow of "Left" opportunism and then grew rapidly from 1988 onward, especially under the influence of Gorbachov. The Right opportunists emerged as unabashed revisionist renegades as they opposed the principle of proletarian revolutionary leadership and called for the liquidation of the CPP. They became more emboldened, especially in the years 1989 to 1991, when the revisionist-ruled countries were in turmoil and the revisionist regimes were imploding.

Take note that the worst of the "Left" opportunists responsible for the barbarities swung to Right opportunism, further on to Gorbachovite or Trotskyite anticommunism and still further on to joining the reactionary government. Using the slogan of anti-Stalinism, they sought to wreck the CPP and imitate the anticommunists in Eastern Europe from 1989 to 1991.

Damage from "Left" and Right Opportunism

Q22. You have said that "Left" opportunism did more damage than Right opportunism. How? Given ample chance, could not Right opportunism have been more devastating to the CPP?

From the first half of the 1980s to the start of the Second Great Rectification Movement in 1992, "Left" opportunism did far more damage than Right opportunism. It abetted the purely military viewpoint and recklessness. It brought about the unsustainable and self-defeating premature formation of absolutely concentrated companies in the NPA.

This caused the loss of mass base and rapid depletion of supplies. With dwindling political and material support, the companies became easy prey for the enemy forces to detect and attack.

When the NPA companies met serious setbacks, the "Left" opportunists in Mindanao failed to look into their erroneous line and instead blamed "deep penetration agents" as the cause of setbacks. They launched a massive witchhunt, called Kampanyang Ahos (Garlic Campaign). This was destructive to the revolutionary movement in a large island, reputed in the first half of the 1980s as having one-third to one-half of the armed strength of the movement.

As for the Right opportunists, you are correct in saying that given ample chance they would have posed a bigger threat to the CPP and the revolutionary movement. If there had not been preparations for the rectification movement before 1992, the Right opportunists could have totally liquidated the CPP and the revolutionary movement. They would have followed the path of liquidationism taken by the Gorbachovite revisionists on a global scale. The Right opportunists wished for an easy life and an easy victory through parliamentarism and appointments in the post-Marcos reactionary regimes.

Q23. How did Right opportunism pose a threat to the revolution?

After the fall of Marcos in 1986, the long running Right opportunists, especially the so-called popular democrats, attempted to rationalize their line of parliamentarism by counterpoising it to the 1986 boycott error and the strategic line of protracted people's war. They complemented the urban "insurrectionists" who spoke of the need for parliamentarism as preparation for urban-based insurrections.

In 1988, former "Left" opportunists whose own putschist line had caused them frustration and who had openly become Rightists reinforced the long-running Right opportunists. They united in opposing the principles, policies and line of the Party and came under the influence of Gorbachovite revisionism, Trotskyism, anti-Stalinism and liquidationism.

Were it not for the alertness and resistance of proletarian revolutionaries, the Right opportunists and revisionist renegades would have liquidated the Party any time from 1992 to 1994. The worst of the revisionist renegades had already usurped editorship of *Ang Bayan*, the official organ of the Party's Central Committee. There they published anti-Party articles in 1991. They also wrote lengthy letters attacking the Party in the same year.

By launching the rectification movement in 1992, the Party stopped the Right opportunists from destroying the Party and causing far worse damage than the "Left" opportunists had previously done.

Atrocities Within

Q24. How could such barbarities as Kampanyang Ahos, Olympia, Operation Missing Link and the like transpire under the auspices of a disciplined Party?

Materialist dialectics teaches us that every Party, even the most correct, united, and disciplined, will always have contradictory aspects. The CPP is not exempt from the law of contradiction and the law of uneven development. Even if the overwhelming majority of the CPP cadres and members are good, there will always be a minority of fictitious communists and degenerates who will try to mislead the Party through opportunism, "Left" or Right, and may even manage to mislead sections of the Party.

The barbarities you mentioned arose in the wake of frustrations due to "Left" opportunist errors. The impetuosity and recklessness of the "Left" opportunists made it easy for the enemy to attack the organs and units of the revolutionary forces. But instead of reexamining their erroneous line and recognizing its disastrous consequences, the "Left" opportunists covered up their responsibility and conveniently spread suspiciousness, blaming deep penetration agents for setbacks, and eventually igniting hysteria.

Kampanyang Ahos from 1985 to 1987 followed the eventual frustration of the 1981 insurrectionist and militarist line in Mindanao from 1983 to 1985. The so-called June breakthrough and Olympia in 1988 followed the arrests of major cadres in February 1988 and on March 29, 1988 in the national capital region and the ensuing panic among cadres.

Operation Missing Link followed certain setbacks in the 1980s in the Southern Tagalog region and Manila-Rizal. Such setbacks became compounded by an intense desire of some cadres to hunt down those suspected of collaborating with the enemy in its successful intelligence operations against the revolutionary forces since the 1970s.

Q25. Had the CPP not confronted such barbarities, what could have happened? How are collective and individual responsibilities in such cases weighed?

The CPP would have violated revolutionary principles had it not confronted the barbarities. It would have nullified its reason for being. It would have condoned and thereby become complicit with wrongdoers. It would have totally discredited and destroyed itself.

The appropriate party organs looked into the causes of the barbarities and weighed the collective and individual responsibilities of those involved. Educational and disciplinary measures were immediately undertaken even before the Second Great Rectification Movement. In late 1988, the Central Committee drew up the necessary guidelines for the investigation, trial and sentencing of those accused of counter-revolutionary crimes. The implementation of these guidelines put a stop to Operation Missing Link and other witch hunts and ultimately led to the reinvestigation of Kampanyang Ahos.

From published CPP documents, you can read that the judicial organs of the people's government uphold the right to due process, evaluate the evidence and weigh the varying degrees of culpability of those found guilty. The mitigating and aggravating circumstances and the varying degrees of remorse or lack of it are also taken into account.

The party and judicial organs concerned make it a point to preempt any hysteria against those accused of committing the barbarities and apply the guidelines for the correct conduct of investigation, prosecution, trial and evaluation of evidence and appropriate penalties.

Q26. Why do workers and peasants in Mindanao and other parts of the Philippines, who experienced bitter setbacks and tragic losses associated with "Left" and Right opportunist errors, remain loyal and rally again to the CPP banner? Where does this resilience come from?

The resilience comes from the acute need and determination of the workers and peasants to liberate themselves from the exploitation and oppression imposed by the imperialists and the local exploiting classes. The toiling masses recognize the revolutionary movement as their own. They have raised the level of their revolutionary consciousness and militancy under the leadership of the CPP.

Their experience has taught them that the overwhelming majority of CPP cadres and members are worthy revolutionaries and, in comparison, only a few elements stray off the revolutionary road, violate principles and commit serious errors and crimes.

In opposition to the incorrigible opportunists, revisionists and incorrigible wrongdoers, the CPP takes responsibility for reaffirming basic principles, rectifying errors and rendering justice to the victims. Thus, the CPP maintains and builds the trust of the workers and peasants. The rectification movement has reassured them that the CPP is determined to stay on the road of new-democratic revolution through people's war to uphold, defend and carry forward the rights and interests of the workers and peasants.

Forging the Rectification Campaign

Q27. *How does the First Rectification Movement differ from the Second? And what is great about them?*

The First Great Rectification Movement (FGRM), which was carried out from 1967 onward, guided and prepared the reestablishment of the Communist Party of the Philippines. It was thus an event of great significance to Filipino communists and the Filipino people.

The FGRM upheld Marxist-Leninist principles, analyzed the history and circumstances of the communist party and the Filipino people, criticized and repudiated the Lava revisionist renegades and the Taruc-Sumulong gangster clique and thus paved the way for the rebuilding of the Party and all other revolutionary forces.

Following the road of the FGRM, the Second Great Rectification Movement (SGRM) reaffirmed basic Marxist-Leninist principles. Unlike the FGRM, which repudiated the opportunists of the old merger party and led to the reestablishment of the Party, the latter saved the Party from destruction by incorrigible opportunists and revisionists.

The CPP would have been destroyed had it not undertaken the rectification movement because the anti-Party ideological, political and organizational work done by the incorrigible opportunists and revisionists while they were still in the Party would have led to the liquidation of the Party.

The greatness of the SGRM lies not only in saving the Party and the revolutionary movement but also in inspiring, guiding and revitalizing them for a full decade. As a result, great victories in ideological, political and organizational work have been won.

Q28. *The seminal document of the First Great Rectification Movement was* Rectify Errors and Rebuild the Party *and of the Second Great Rectification Movement,* Reaffirm Our Basic Principles and Rectify Errors. *If you were to isolate the essence of these documents, what would*

be their central admonition to the revolutionary movement?

It is to "uphold the ideological line of Marxism-Leninism, oppose revisionism, empiricism and dogmatism; uphold the political line of the new-democratic revolution through protracted people's war, oppose 'Left' and Right opportunism, putschism and parliamentarism; and uphold the organizational line of democratic centralism, oppose bureaucratism and ultra-democracy."

The foregoing ideological, political and organizational lines are central to both rectification movements and run through them. At any rate, let me enumerate the 10 points of principle guiding the SGRM:

1. Uphold the theory and practice of Marxism-Leninism-Mao Zedong Thought
2. Pursue the anti-revisionist line consistently
3. Confront the semi-colonial and semi-feudal character of Philippine society
4. Carry out the general line of new democratic revolution
5. Build the Party as the vanguard force of the proletariat and the people
6. Wage the protracted people's war in stages and carry out extensive and intensive guerrilla warfare based on an ever widening and deepening mass base
7. Pursue the revolutionary class line in united front work
8. Follow the principle of democratic centralism
9. Look forward to the socialist future of the Philippines
10. Carry out the Philippine revolution in the spirit of proletarian revolution.

Ideological Problems

Q29. What ideological problems were discernible in 1992?

The subjectivist view that Philippine society was no longer semi-feudal was extended to a denial of the validity of the anti-imperialist struggle and the struggle for national liberation in the Philippines. The renegades started to claim in 1992 that the issue of national sovereignty had become passé in this period of neo-liberal globalization.

As revisionist regimes fell and the Soviet Union disintegrated, the Gorbachovites preached that the class struggle had been outdated and marginalized by such supra-class concerns as nuclear disarmament, ecology, gender, ethnicity and the like. They waxed enthusiastic over the capitulationist trend in Central America.

The Trotskyites played along with the Gorbachovites. They shared a common platform with the Gorbachovites and bourgeois-liberals in using the line of anti-Stalinism to oppose Marxism-Leninism-Maoism and the CPP.

The hodgepodge of renegades from the CPP banded together as a petty-bourgeois claque for the big bourgeoisie against the CPP. They had all the makings of a future fragmentation among themselves. They preyed on the urban petty bourgeoisie and tried to lead them astray from the national-democratic movement. They rode on the imperialist ideological and political offensive in the wake of the political turmoil in China, the fall of the revisionist regimes and the disintegration of the Soviet Union.

They celebrated Gorbachovism as the way to socialism even as the revisionist regimes were pushing an anticommunist ideological and political offensive against the working class and the socialist cause. Articles to this effect appeared in *Ang Bayan*, the publication of the CPP Central Committee.

Q30. *How were these ideological problems confronted and solved? Please specify issues and methods used.*

When the Second Great Rectification Movement was launched in 1992, the CPP had to confront not only the major errors and shortcomings of 1980 to the end of 1991 but also such major international issues as the turmoil in China, the fall of the revisionist regimes and the disintegration of the Soviet Union in the 1989-1991 period.

The CPP put forward the ideological line of Marxism-Leninism-Maoism and urged the Party rank and file to study the line and reaffirm the basic principles of the Party. The CPP Central Committee clearly defined the character of the SGRM basically as an education campaign in Marxism-Leninism-Maoism within the Party. It was conducted as a campaign of study, summing up of experience, and criticism and self-criticism. The Party Central Committee issued the rectification documents to guide the Party rank and file.

The revolutionary ethic of serving the people and of self-sacrifice was merged with the historic mission of the working class to build socialism. The works of Marx, Engels, Lenin, Stalin and Mao were reproduced and circulated. Formal study courses were conducted at the primary, intermediate and advanced levels. Study aids were made for the benefit of workers and peasants. Selected works of the great communists were translated into Pilipino and other Philippine languages.

Political Problems

Q31. What political problems were conspicuous in 1992?

The incorrigible opportunists and revisionist renegades opposed the general line of new-democratic revolution through protracted people's war. All of them denied the semi-feudal character of the Philippine economy. Also, some of them began to deny the semi-colonial character of Philippine society.

The attacks and wrecking operations launched by the incorrigible opportunists, revisionists and Trotskyites were compounded by the erosion of the revolutionary movement's organized mass base due to prolonged errors of "Left" and Right opportunism. The 1985-86 mass base of about seven million people dwindled by 60 percent.

Mass work was neglected in the regions where absolutely concentrated NPA companies were prematurely formed and where anti-imperialist and anti-feudal education and mass mobilization were scarce.

The systematic or programmed deployment of worker and educated youth cadres from the cities to the countryside had stopped or had been discouraged since 1981. The "Left" opportunists drummed up the line that such cadres were more needed to prepare for the urban armed insurrection.

The Right opportunists based in foreign-funded "non-governmental organizations" (NGOs) enticed party cadres and young activists to salaried positions. They also gained undue influence in the urban-based mass movement by pushing sweeping protest campaigns to the exclusion of painstaking mass work and solid mass organizing.

Q32. How did the Party handle these problems?

As you can read from CPP publications, the CPP called on all Party cadres and members to persevere in the general line of new-democratic revolution through protracted people's war. It conducted a vigorous study campaign to criticize and repudiate the various currents of "Left" and Right opportunism.

The NPA was reoriented, reorganized and redeployed. The Red commanders and fighters reaffirmed the line of serving the people, putting revolutionary politics in command and abiding by the mass line from the masses to the masses. Service to the people for the revolutionary cause inspired the CPP and the NPA.

In every guerrilla front, the platoon was designated the center of gravity, divisible into squads, within a relatively short radius for the purpose of mass work. Two other platoons, also divisible into squads and further, into armed propaganda teams, within a relatively larger radius were designated for extensive mass work.

The NPA took the line of waging intensive and extensive guerrilla warfare based on ever-widening and deepening mass base, launching tactical offensives within the current stage of strategic defensive, while carrying out land reform and building the mass base. Efforts were renewed to undertake painstaking mass work and solid mass organizing in both urban and rural areas.

The CPP pushed for the further development of the united front in order to advance the revolutionary armed strength. It clarified the series of alliances to be built under the leadership of the proletariat: the basic worker-peasant alliance, the progressive alliance of the toiling masses and the urban petty bourgeoisie, the patriotic alliance of the progressive forces and the middle bourgeoisie, and the temporary and unstable alliance with certain reactionaries in order to isolate and defeat the enemy or the worst of the reactionaries.

Organizational Problems

Q33. *And how were the political and ideological problems manifested organizationally?*

"Left" and Right opportunism had long undermined and weakened certain parts of the Party and the revolutionary movement. The Party was in danger of being liquidated completely. Well-placed elements were promoting Gorbachovism and Trotskyism, and some of them were coordinating with psywar and intelligence agencies of the enemy.

Bureaucratism and ultra democracy were rampant simultaneously and were taking their toll on Party cadres and members. The initiatives of lower Party organs and units were stifled by so-called political officers who formed a layer of individualized authority between the higher and lower organs. In reaction to bureaucratism, certain elements generated liberalism and ultra democracy in the name of democracy.

For a long time, the opportunists did not care about increasing Party membership. They were satisfied with organizing and reorganizing layers upon layers of staff and task forces. The tendency towards carving out independent kingdoms and generating disputes over turf grew. Party cadres and members were being attracted to salaried jobs in the foreign-funded NGOs. The number of personnel deployed for long-term work in the countryside and in the people's army dwindled.

When the rectification movement was launched, the incorrigible opportunists and revisionists imitated the revisionist rascals of the Soviet Union and Eastern Europe by separating personnel from the Party and privatizing or appropriating for themselves the funds and other assets of the Party. Even as they had different political tendencies and belonged to different factions, all of them tried to band together using the slogan of anti-Stalinism for a wrecking campaign against the Party. But they failed and then they began to bicker and quarrel among themselves. The splinters splintered further.

Q34. *What solutions to the organizational problems came out of the rectification movement?*

The rectification movement reaffirmed the principle of democratic centralism. All Party organs, units and individual members educated themselves further in the practice of combining conscious discipline and democracy in pursuing Marxism-Leninism and the revolutionary cause.

Only a few diehards opposed the rectification movement and sought to disorganize and wreck the Party. Against them stood loyal Party cadres and members who firmly upheld democratic centralism and enthusiastically carried out the rectification movement. The Party moved quickly to frustrate the renegades' schemes and attempts to wreck it.

By launching the rectification movement, the Central Committee took full initiative in rebuilding the Party ideologically, politically and organizationally. Organizationally, the Party remained a nationwide organization and became ever closer to the toiling masses of workers and peasants.

Painstaking mass work and solid mass organizing were emphasized. From the expanded and consolidated mass base, the most advanced activists were recruited into the Party.

The Party made it a point to recruit more Party members from the ranks of the workers and peasants. More cadres from the working class and the educated youth in the cities were deployed in increasing numbers to serve in the countryside and to join the people's army.

Resistance to Rectification

Q35. ***Resistance to the Second Great Rectification Movement seemed very strong, at least to those outside the Party. Some say that the resistance was even more damaging than the impact of long-running "Left" and Right errors. Why was the resistance so adamant?***

The resistance and wrecking operations undertaken by the Lagman faction in Manila-Rizal and by the Tabara faction in Central Visayas were relatively the strongest and most damaging. But the damage wrought by long-running errors, especially the erosion of the mass base, was much bigger than any further damage dealt by the renegades from 1992 to 1994, after the rectification movement was launched.

Had the CPP not waged the rectification movement, had it tried instead to retain or accommodate the incorrigible opportunists and revisionist renegades, it would have incurred a much bigger cost: its own demise or complete liquidation.

The opposition put up by the worst opportunists was so adamant because they wished to conceal and evade their criminal responsibilities. They feared being held accountable for their crimes, apart from their ideological and political errors.

Key elements among the "Left" opportunists were remorseless perpetrators of atrocities like Kampanyang Ahos, Olympia and Operation Missing Link (OPML). Some of them, especially Romulo Kintanar, Arturo Tabara and Filemon Lagman, profited personally from gangsterism. Also key elements among the Right opportunists engaged in thievery, stealing funds and resources from the Party and from NGOs.

Q36. ***How true is the claim that the rectification movement was undemocratically decided and undemocratically launched, and that it was unjust in targeting certain personalities of the revolutionary movement? Why did you have to come out swinging against those opposing***

the rectification movement?

The Party Central Committee made the call for rectification as early as 1988, on the CPP's 20th anniversary. Before that and afterwards, Party organs at various levels, units and individual Party cadres and members pressed for a rectification movement. A fundamental criticism was explicitly made against the phenomenon of the Party's self-constriction as early as 1987.

The decision to launch the rectification movement was long overdue by early 1992. Had not the draft rectification document been prepared in late 1991, the renegades would have run far ahead in attacking the CPP and would have succeeded in wrecking its Marxist-Leninist and revolutionary character.

In formulating the central rectification documents, the Party Central Committee based itself on reports and recommendations from lower organs and organizations as well as those from the interaction between higher and lower organs and units through formal meetings and consultations in writing. The reports and recommendations were collected over a long period and updated.

From the last quarter of 1991 onward, the draft of the rectification documents first circulated among the Central Committee members who in turn made their proposals. Finally, the CC held a plenum in the middle part of 1992, in order to discuss and decide on the draft. But the renegades preoccupied themselves with attacking the rectification movement and demanding that the Central Committee stop it. They concentrated their attack on the Central Committee chairman Armando Liwanag in their effort to discredit and destroy the rectification movement and the entire revolutionary movement.

It was only on December 6, 1992, after the appearance of an article attacking me in the November 22, 1992 issue of a Manila newspaper, that I came out with public statements against the worst and most active detractors who had circulated smear propaganda against me. I came out swinging against the renegades because they were spreading lies. Had I allowed them to attack from the dark, they would have succeeded with their foul tactics.

Q37. The CPP leadership was accused of conducting a purge; actually, there was talk of how the CPP was undertaking a "Stalinist" purge, suggestive of a lack of due process and bloodshed. Was there any truth to this?

In European history, both bourgeois and proletarian parties have used the term "purge" or "purge from the list" of members. It simply means that according to its own principles and rules of discipline and due process, the Party removes from its roster those members who violate the Party's principles or have ceased to perform their duties and responsibilities.

The renegades practically removed themselves from the CPP by violating the principles of the Party, trying to cover up their grave errors and crimes, and then by demagogically drumming up their opposition to the CPP in the name of democracy. After failing, in most of 1992, to hoodwink the public with their self-depiction as victims of persecution, they proceeded before the end of the year to declare their autonomy and, by 1993, their separation and independence.

As I pointed out earlier, the Gorbachovites and Trotskyites combined in attacking and accusing the Party of being "Stalinist." They thought that they could gain an advantage by riding on anticommunist prejudices. Let me say forthrightly that Stalin is definitely a great communist, the complete opposite of such anticommunist traitors as Gorbachov and Trotsky.

Results of Rectification

Q38. What has been the ideological impact of the rectification movement?

The Second Great Rectification Movement has been a resounding success as an education campaign in Marxism-Leninism-Maoism and the new-democratic revolution among Party cadres and members. The level of theoretical knowledge in Marxism-Leninism has risen among Party cadres and members. They have a better grasp of the Marxist-Leninist stand, viewpoint and method.

They are ideologically well armed against modern revisionism, empiricism and dogmatism, as well as against imperialism and the latest trends of pro-imperialist petty bourgeois ideas. They have benefited greatly from the rectification documents issued by the Central Committee, the summings-up and analyses of experience undertaken by the lower organs and units, the assessment of current work and concomitant criticism and self-criticism and the formal study courses at various levels.

They have acquired a comprehensive and profound understanding of the history of humankind, and of the modern proletariat in particular, the current world and domestic situation, the evils of imperialism, modern revisionism and all reaction, the tasks and prospects of the working class in fighting for and building socialism for the ultimate aim of bringing about communism.

In ideological rebuilding, the CPP has developed thousands of Party cadres and members who guarantee its continuity and further advance. It has also been outstanding in combating the imperialist ideological and political offensive. It has thwarted the objective of such an offensive to demoralize proletarian fighters in the aftermath of the turmoil in China, collapse of the revisionist regimes and disintegration of the Soviet Union in the 1989-1991 period.

Q39. *What political successes has the CPP garnered because of the rectification movement?*

The Party membership has a deeper understanding of the semi-colonial and semi-feudal character of current Philippine society and the urgent need for the new democratic revolution through protracted people's war. The Party now is leading the people in their millions in both urban and rural areas.

Under the absolute leadership of the CPP, the NPA has expanded and consolidated its mass base. Now 128 guerrilla fronts nationwide cover portions of more than 90 per cent of the provinces of the Philippines. The NPA is waging extensive and intensive guerrilla warfare based on an ever widening and deepening mass base. It is carrying out tactical offensives within the strategic defensive stage.

Since 1992, the NPA has significantly increased its armed fighting units. It has seized weapons and other war materiel from the enemy. It has also captured enemy officers, up to the rank of general, and has treated them leniently in accordance with the revolutionary principles and tradition of the NPA, as well as in keeping with the Geneva Conventions and its protocols, which the National Democratic Front of the Philippines has undertaken to observe in its Unilateral Declaration of 1996.

The NPA has successfully conducted mass base building and land reform, and has integrated these with the armed struggle. Mass organizations of workers, peasants, women, youth, cultural activists and children have been formed. These support the organs of political power. Through mass base building, the revolutionary forces are able to raise the level of the appointive barrio organizing committee as provisional organs of political power to the level of the elective barrio revolutionary committee as regular organs of political power.

The legal mass movement has developed rapidly. Great mass struggles have been waged against the policies of General Ramos and his presidential successors. The democratic mass organizations have accumulated such strength that they have been able to oust the Estrada regime from power and elect progressives to congressional and local executive offices.

The united front is advancing in both the armed and legal forms of struggle. Under the leadership of the Party, the basic alliance of workers and peasants, the alliance of progressive forces (toiling masses plus petty bourgeoisie), the alliance of patriotic or positive forces (progressive forces plus middle bourgeoisie) and the unstable and temporary alliance with the reactionary opponents of the current enemy have been successful in isolating the enemy and maximizing the strength of the Party and the people.

Q40. And in terms of organizational victories, what did the rectification movement bring?

The CPP is more than ever bound by the principle of democratic centralism. It exercises centralized leadership based on democracy and democracy under the guidance of centralized leadership. Within the Party, the constructive balance and interaction of conscious discipline and freedom are maintained.

The CPP is more than ever national in scale and deeply rooted among the toiling masses of workers and peasants. Its membership has increased in number and has a higher quality than ever before because the mass movement from which the Party recruits its members is growing, intensifying and advancing.

A good number of Party cadres and members put into effect the leadership of the Party in the New People's Army in the countryside. So do a good number of them put into effect the leadership of the Party in the trade union movement and other mass movements based on class, sectoral and multi-sectoral issues.

More and more workers and educated young people are joining the Party. They are eager to serve the people in the countryside and serve in the people's army.

On the Youth

Q41. One very visible impact of the rectification movement is the rise of a new wave of young mass leaders and activists in every sector of the national-democratic movement in the legal arena. Is this true as well in the underground?

Yes, according to our most reliable sources. The great number of young people in the legal mass movement indicates an increasing number of young people also in the urban and rural underground. I am happy to learn about the renewed interest and enthusiasm of the youth in joining the people's army.

The progressive mass leaders and activists in the open mass movement recognize the importance of the underground. They recognize the need to have a refuge to which they can go in case of any development like the suspension of the writ of habeas corpus, declaration of martial law or all-out state terrorism coming from the reactionary state. Such a refuge is also the base for active resistance.

On Women

Q42. Among the organized sectors, which took its time in summing up its experiences, was the women's sector. What is the role of women in the revolutionary movement? What was in error with the women's movement before rectification? What kind of correction was done?

The role of women is as important as the role of men in the revolutionary movement. Women are capable of performing the same revolutionary functions as the men. It is a matter of history and social circumstances that men have preempted many social functions. It is a matter for women to struggle and assert their rights.

I have always considered as a manifestation of progress in the revolutionary movement when women assert their rights and assume responsibilities under the principle of equality with men. The revolutionary movement can become stronger only if a full half of the people is actively integrated and working in the revolutionary movement.

Women suffer the oppression inflicted by imperialism, feudalism and male chauvinism. When they assume their due role in the national-democratic movement, they have the opportunity to struggle against these three types of oppression. Their achievements are truly significant because they confront and prevail over more types of oppression than men.

In the rectification movement, Party cadres and Party organs have been criticized for assigning women only to such limited and stereotyped traditional functions for women as child care, nursing the sick and aged, handling funds, sewing, cooking, doing the laundry and so on. For instance, Kintanar and other militarists were denounced for disqualifying women from fighting units of the NPA on the ground that menstrual periods make women inefficient and a burden to army units.

Even in leading organs and units, where women have earned a significant proportion of the positions and functions, the rectification movement has made both women and men alike conscious of the need to further increase and enhance the role of women. Given the same circumstances and opportunities, women are equal to men in achieving competence in the fields of ideology, politics and organization.

The national democratic movement and in particular the women's movement must give full play to the women of the working class and peasantry. Progressive women from the urban petty bourgeoisie should support the women of the toiling masses in generating a strong mass movement of women at the grassroots level and producing women cadres capable of assuming responsibility at various levels.

Q43. Menstruation as an expression of women's inferiority went passé 40 years ago. Nevertheless, even I will grant that while there is work that women may find difficult, there are also lines of work in which they excel. Unfortunately, engaging in the furtherance of Marxist theory does not appear to be one of them. Can you think of a reason why there seems to be a paucity of theoretical or analytical writings by women in the Philippine revolutionary movement?

The apparent paucity of women's theoretical or analytical writings in the Philippine revolutionary movement may be a part, reflection or consequence of men's preemption of women within the movement. There is also such preemption related to household chores and other traditional preoccupations expected of women within the existing society, which in fact is related to men's traditional preemption in the entire society.

As a matter of principle and policy, the CPP keeps open to women the door to all kinds of revolutionary activity, including theoretical work. Actually, many women write for revolutionary publications. Their writings are subsumed within the collective or they write in anonymity. At any rate, your question should be a reminder to the CPP and a challenge to women in the revolutionary movement.

In the bourgeois world, a lot of women do masteral and doctoral dissertations and off-campus writings of high theoretical and analytical value to the bourgeoisie. Why shouldn't Marxist women come forward with more of their written work in the service of the revolution?

Armed Struggle and Peace Talks

Q44. How does the CPP or NDFP reconcile the intensification of the armed struggle with the peace negotiations? On the other hand, will not ceasefire paralyze and debilitate the NPA?

The intensification of the armed struggle does not go against the policy of peace negotiations. It is precisely because of the growing strength of the revolutionary armed movement that the reactionary government finds it necessary to hold peace negotiations with the revolutionaries.

The framework of the GRP-NDFP peace negotiations allows for fighting while talking and does not allow the enemy to obtain the paralysis, capitulation or pacification of the revolutionary forces under the guise of an indefinite ceasefire before addressing the roots of the armed conflict.

However, there may be short-term ceasefires, which are not in any way debilitating to the NPA. These are for limited purposes on grounds of humanitarianism and goodwill, such as the celebration of Christmas and New Year, the safe and orderly release of prisoners of war, appreciation for the Senate vote to deny the renewal of the US-RP Military Bases Treaty in 1991, the safe evacuation of casualties across the battlefield and pre-arranged medical missions.

Q45. From year to year since 1996, the CPP has called for the intensification of the revolutionary armed struggle. How can this be done?

In my view, the intensification of the revolutionary armed struggle can be carried out only with the successful ideological, political and organizational building of the CPP. Thus, the CPP can effectively wield the weapons of armed struggle and the united front and integrate armed struggle with land reform and mass base building.

The CPP Central Committee is the organ that decides the strategy and tactics of the revolutionary armed struggle. It sets the general guidelines and allows the regional Party committees to apply these in their respective regions. Under the overall operational command of the national military staff, the regional commands and guerrilla front commands are authorized to undertake such tactical offensives as they are capable of winning.

To be sure of winning, the NPA always uses the element of surprise and superior force in ambushes, raids and arrest operations. It gives high priority to seizing arms from its enemy. Units of the NPA are mandated to carry out intensive and extensive guerrilla warfare, make the enemy bleed in so many parts through surprise offensives, accumulate armed strength and prepare the basis for a higher phase in the strategic defensive.

THE FOREST IS STILL ENCHANTED

The fickle-minded spirits and fairies
Have fled the old trees and groves,
Dark caves and mounds in the shadows,
Mossy rocks and whispering streams.
The gnarled balete and the blackbird
Have lost their intriguing power.

The uncertainties of the past ages
No longer lurk to exact awe and fear.
In the forest throbs discreetly
A certainty above the certainties
Of chopping wood, hunting boar and deer,
Gathering fruits, honey and even orchids.

But the forest is still enchanted.
There is a new hymn in the wind;
There is a new magic in the dark green,
So the peasant folks say to friends.
A single fighting spirit has taken over
To lure in and astonish the intruders.

June 1981

As chairman of the International Initiative Committee, Professor Jose Maria Sison presides over the founding of the International League of Peoples' Struggle (ILPS) in Zutphen, Netherlands on 25-27 May 2001. (ILPS Secretariat photo collection)

This is a part of the delegates to the First International Assembly of the ILPS. More than 240 organizations worldwide are represented in the assembly. (ILPS Secretariat photo collection)

Demonstrators in Paris, France protest "terrorist" listing of Professor Sison and demand his de-listing. (ILPS photo collection)

Chapter Four

The Global Situation and Revolutionary Internationalism

Q1. Are you a nationalist or an internationalist first? How does the Filipino people's struggle for national liberation relate to revolutionary internationalism?

As a communist, I am a proletarian internationalist first, one interested in the worldwide victory of socialism over imperialism, in order to make way for communism. I uphold the principle that the workers of the world must unite as the leading class to fulfill the historic mission of building socialism and that the oppressed peoples of the world must also unite as the main force with the workers against imperialism.

I am at the same time a Filipino patriot fighting for national liberation and democracy against US imperialism and its puppets. In fighting for national liberation from US imperialism, the Filipino people cannot and must not fight in isolation from the rest of the people of the world. They are held captive in a world capitalist system dominated by US imperialism. US imperialism is the No. 1 enemy of the people of the world. The Filipino people must unite with the people of the world to fight that common enemy.

In waging revolutionary struggle, they contribute to the common struggle of the people of the world and draw support from this. To fight for national liberation is to perform a duty for one's own people and for other peoples in the spirit of revolutionary internationalism.

In my view, revolutionary internationalism has two components. One is proletarian internationalism, which means the unity of workers who comprise the leading class in the world proletarian socialist revolution. The other is the broad anti-imperialist unity of the peoples of the world. In the era of imperialism and proletarian revolution, I follow Lenin's call for the workers and oppressed peoples of the world to unite.

Q2. What is the guiding principle when internationalism collides with the national interests of a people on the path to socialism?

To stop or avoid the collision of internationalism against national interests, the guiding principle is for the revolutionary forces and the people to fight in common against imperialism; to cooperate with each other in bringing about the progress of every revolution in various countries and to carry forward the broad anti-imperialist movement and the proletarian socialist revolution on a global scale.

It is not narrow national self-interest for the oppressed peoples and nations to fight for national self-determination and independence against imperialism. National-democratic revolutions are a decisive component of the general advance of humankind for socialism against monopoly capitalism. Necessarily, a number of countries march ahead in undertaking socialist revolution and construction.

But the proletarian revolutionary parties, and the proletariat and people in each of these countries should be guided by the principle of proletarian internationalism and anti-imperialism, provide the revolutionary example and extend moral and material support to the proletariat and people of other countries. They should make their advances without sacrificing the revolutionary struggles of other peoples and without being carried away by the notion that socialism can advance into communism without the prior defeat of imperialism on a global scale.

Broad anti-imperialist solidarity and proletarian internationalism are complementary. National-democratic revolutions can succeed and proceed to a higher stage of revolution only with the leadership of the revolutionary proletariat. The ultimate goal of communism is possible only upon the global defeat of imperialism.

Q3. How do the proletariat and people of the Philippines contribute to the development of the world proletarian revolution and the worldwide anti-imperialist struggle?

The new democratic revolution in the Philippines is part of the world proletarian revolution and the broad anti-imperialist struggle of the peoples of the world. The revolutionary victories of the Filipino people are the victories of the peoples of the world, as much as the victories of the latter are those of the former.

As they wage the new democratic revolution through protracted people's war, the proletariat and people of the Philippines can make important contributions to the world proletarian revolution and the broad anti-imperialist movement. They serve as a revolutionary example and a source of revolutionary experience and lessons for study. The real advances of the Philippine revolution are inspiring to others and can contribute to further revolutionary developments worldwide.

The revolutionary forces and people in the Philippines demonstrate to those in semi-colonial and semi-feudal countries that it is possible to wage a new-democratic revolution through protracted people's war even under conditions where the imperialists and puppets appear to be so strong and so capable of preventing any direct military and financial assistance from revolutionary forces abroad.

Q4. How much did you take from Marx, Engels and other acknowledged greats of the international communist movement? How much came from the study of successful revolutions overseas and from involvement in international issues? How are these lessons changed by the lessons of Philippine history and conditions?

To become a communist, I had to study hard and learn the fundamentals of Marxism-Leninism from the great communists like Marx, Engels, Lenin, Stalin and Mao, from successful and unsuccessful revolutions abroad and from taking up international issues.

I would not have been able by my writings to shed light on the road of the Philippine revolution if I had not learned philosophy (dialectical and historical materialism), political economy (from capitalism through socialism to communism) and social science (from class struggle leading to proletarian class dictatorship) from the great communist teachers. By learning from the history and current struggles of the working class and oppressed peoples of the world, we gain a better understanding of the current revolutionary struggle within our respective countries.

The science of Marxism-Leninism has a universal character. It is the indispensable guide of the world proletariat for realizing its historic mission of building socialism, bringing about the world victory of socialism over imperialism and enabling humankind to enter the threshold of communism. But such a science has to be integrated with the concrete conditions of particular countries and the concrete practice of a revolutionary movement.

Marxism-Leninism needs to be applied on the concrete conditions of the Philippines and on the concrete revolutionary practice of the Filipino proletariat and people. That is the only way that we can effectively carry out the new democratic revolution. Principles and lessons learned from revolutionary practice abroad must serve the needs of the Philippine revolution and the Filipino people. In turn, the Philippine revolution and the Filipino people make direct and indirect contributions to the revolutionary struggles abroad.

Support and Solidarity

Q5. Both you as a revolutionary leader and the CPP in its entirety have always been supportive of revolutionary movements overseas. You personally actively supported the Chinese and Korean peoples, the Cuban and Congolese revolutions and more tellingly, the Vietnamese struggle against the US war of aggression in the 1960s. Did you and/or the CPP ever receive any expression of gratitude for those acts of support?

The revolutionary forces and people abroad are always grateful for the support extended to them by the Filipino revolutionary forces and people. Whenever the occasion arises, they express their gratitude.

Whenever we receive expressions of gratitude, we also express the gratitude of the Filipino revolutionary forces and people. Revolutionary internationalism involves mutual support and cooperation. It is not a one-way process.

During my foreign trips in the 1960s,—specifically to Indonesia, China and Japan—comrades from Indonesia, Malaya, China, Vietnamese, Japanese, Thai, Burmese, Indian, American, Latin American, African, Australian, New Zealand, British and other comrades warmly received me.

As chairman of the CPP Central Committee from 1968 to 1977, I communicated with many communist and workers' parties and other revolutionary organizations abroad to express admiration for their achievements, inform them of the Philippine situation and seek the furtherance of mutual support and cooperation.

In my travels abroad after my release from prison, I have sought to promote revolutionary internationalism and have exchanged expressions of gratitude.

From Country to Country

Q6. You left the Philippines in June 1986 and returned to the Philippines only to leave again in August of the same year. What was the purpose of these trips?

In June 1986, I left the Philippines for Singapore to participate in a seminar on Philippine political and economic trends, sponsored by the International Research Center and Institute of Southeast Asian Studies. I was one of the speakers among whom were officials of the Aquino government and university professors.

On August 31, 1986, immediately after presiding over the two-day founding congress of Partido ng Bayan (PnB—People's Party), I left for New Zealand and Australia to deliver lectures in almost all major universities in various cities of the two countries. I also gave talks to the Filipino community, solidarity and workers' organizations in these two countries. This work lasted from September 1 to October 8, 1986.

In the second week of October, I proceeded to Thailand to receive the Southeast Asian WRITE Award for poetry, specifically for my book of poems, *Prison and Beyond*. The award came from the Thai royal family and respectable Thai institutions. I also spoke at a university in Bangkok.

On October 15, I returned to the Philippines to pick up my visa for Japan. On October 22, I left for Japan and from there proceeded to so many other countries in Asia and Europe.

Q7. So in Thailand, how did you like wearing a tuxedo and bowing to a

king? It must have been a sticky situation.

The award ceremony was a very formal event, with the crown prince, in representation of the king or the entire royal family, presenting the awards. Fittingly, the awardees wore their own formal national dress. So I wore a barong tagalog. As a matter of social grace and courtesy, I nodded my head in a slight bow to the crown prince when he presented me with the award. This is how we formally show courtesy or respect in our particular part of Asia.

While receiving the award, I was amused at the irony of the situation. I thought to myself, here I am, very recently released from more than 8 years of imprisonment and heavy torture under the regime of the autocrat Marcos and now being praised and awarded by the Thai monarchy for poems most of which I had written in prison.

At any rate, the hospitality to all the literary honorees was overwhelming. Julie and I were accommodated in the favorite room of Somerset Maugham at the Oriental Hotel. Relatives and friends who would later stay at the Hotel told me they were astonished to find my name on a plaque honoring world writers at the hotel lobby.

Q8. What did you do in Japan and the countries you visited afterwards?

Julie, who was then international secretary of Partido ng Bayan, and I visited Japan for about two months from the last week of October to the second week of December. My lecture tour began with a lecture series at Todai (Tokyo University), followed by a quick succession of lectures in more than a dozen major universities in Tokyo and other Japanese cities. I also spoke before labor and other mass organizations, political parties and grassroots organizations, and gave media interviews in so many cities.

Subsequently, we went to Hong Kong where I gave one lecture at the Hongkong University. We had a relaxed schedule among Filipino migrant workers most of December 1986 until the first week of January 1987.

Julie left Hongkong for a short visit to the Philippines in order to consult with friends and relatives whether I should return to Manila. She returned to Hongkong with their advice for me to proceed with my tour. We departed for New Delhi, India on January 8 for a 2-week quick tour of a few major Indian cities.

Julie and I helped establish relations between Philippine and Indian parties and mass organizations. We had a hectic round of university lectures, press conferences and speeches at events organized by different Indian organizations in various cities, including New Delhi, Bangalore, Madras and Madurai.

From India, we proceeded to the Netherlands on January 22, 1987. We made this country the base for my West European tour. We went to more than 20 European countries to give university lectures and speeches before varied audiences and also gave media interviews. Until 1988, our travels brought us to scores of European cities and some 30 universities. We must have gone to a total of 60 universities in Oceania, Asia and Europe.

From Western Europe, we visited countries in various continents in order to exchange views and experiences with different political forces. We went to Algeria, as guest of the leadership of the Palestinian Liberation Organization. We went to North Korea and China, East Germany, Yugoslavia, Albania, Nicaragua, Cuba and Mexico as guest of the ruling parties or the appropriate governmental or nongovernmental institution.

Q9. *What overriding reason compelled these trips?*

The people's uprising that overthrew the Marcos fascist regime generated among peoples abroad great interest in the Philippines, particularly in the legal democratic movement and the revolutionary forces. In the press and among progressive organizations, there was also some keen interest in me as the so-called number one political prisoner of Marcos and as the founding chairman of the CPP Central Committee. Many people could recognize me from appearances on international television and newspaper front pages soon after the fall of Marcos.

So, I got so many invitations, especially from various entities in the United States. But I could not go there right away because I could not get a visa. I went to other countries while I waited for the US visa, which never came. As international secretary of Partido ng Bayan, Julie had her own program of activities even while she traveled with me from country to country.

In the course of my travels, I explained Philippine history, current situation and prospects. I called for mutual support and cooperation between Philippine organizations and host organizations. I took the opportunity to thank all the individuals and organizations, which had campaigned to save my life or defend my rights and to demand my release while I was in the clutches of the fascists.

The single most important reason for my travel was to seek international solidarity for the Philippine revolution and promote the cause of revolutionary internationalism. My objective was to share the revolutionary experiences of the Filipino people with other peoples and to promote proletarian internationalism among communist and worker parties and broad anti-imperialist solidarity of the people.

Q10. Did your travels and sojourn outside of the Philippines have any impact on your way of thinking? I ask this because I notice a marked difference in the scope of what you wrote while in the Philippines and what you've written since settling down in the Netherlands.

My travels or sojourn abroad have not changed my basic principles and way of thinking. But certainly they have had some impact on me in terms of knowledge further gained from the big changes in the international situation and from interaction with progressive forces.

Your observation is correct regarding the marked difference in the scope of my writings now that I am abroad and previously when I was in the Philippines. The wider scope of the issues and subjects covered by my writings since 1986 is because these were written for various international conferences and seminars on a wide range of issues and subjects.

In terms of content, my political writings from 1986 to 1988, especially on the relationship between the revolutionary forces in the Philippines and those abroad, reflected an optimism that there could be broad anti-imperialist solidarity between the National Democratic Front of the Philippines and the forces in China and the Soviet-bloc countries similar to that between the Palestinian Liberation Organization (PLO) and these forces.

But from 1989 onward, the desire of the CPP to broaden its anti-imperialist relations with forces in the revisionist-ruled countries came face-to-face with the turmoil or fall of the revisionist regimes in those countries. Subsequently, the CPP was globally at the forefront explaining the phenomenon of modern revisionism and capitalist restoration in socialist countries in connection with the rectification movement in the Philippines.

Since then, various parties have asked me to write articles or deliver speeches concerning the conditions of the proletariat and people and the course of revolutionary struggles for national liberation, democracy and socialism in the aftermath of the disintegration of the Soviet Union, the restoration of capitalism in former socialist countries and the global dominance of a single superpower waving the piratical flag of "free market" globalization and becoming more and more aggressive amidst a new world disorder.

Solidarity Versus Meddling

Q11. From time to time, the Philippine revolutionary movement has experienced attempts from overseas parties and organizations to change its political line, strategy and tactics, and even its analysis of the situation, whether in part or in toto. As a matter of fact, one casualty of the rectification movement was the vast array of solidarity organizations specifically established for the Philippine new democratic movement. Where is the demarcation between others' expression of internationalism and solidarity, and simply disrespect and meddling? How is this demarcation determined?

The CPP is a self-reliant party that is keenly mindful of its integrity, independence and equality with other parties abroad. It upholds its revolutionary principles and does not cower before any threat or yield to any improper inducement from any foreign party or government.

When in the early 1980s, some members of the CPP Central Committee wanted to seek Soviet support and assistance supposedly for accelerating the military advance of the NPA, it was not because of any offer of support from the Soviet revisionist party. In fact, the Soviet party was quite content with its relations with the Lavaite group of revisionist renegades in the Philippines. The line of depending on foreign military and financial assistance to advance the armed revolution has been criticized and repudiated.

The solidarity groups that have continued to support the revolutionary movement led by the CPP from the 1980s to the present are those based among workers and revolutionaries. Those solidarity groups that started to distance themselves from the CPP and people's war in the Philippines soon after the fall of Marcos and long before the start of the rectification movement in 1992 were based among the petty bourgeois elements, including academics and religious elements.

Those who were merely anti-Marcos or anti-fascist and who were deeply anti-communist did not only distance themselves from the CPP but also attacked it during the Second Great Rectification Movement. They were motivated by certain funding agencies that became blatantly pro-imperialist and anticommunist after the fall of Marcos in 1986 and even more so in the 1989-91 period.

Genuine solidarity groups are internationalist and are based on the anti-imperialist unity of progressive forces and individuals from the working people and the petty bourgeoisie. They are helpful and they make friendly suggestions and criticisms to their Filipino partners and are not arrogant and meddlesome towards them. They do not try to dictate the political line of Philippine organizations with which they relate.

The Philippine revolutionary movement is better off without the sham solidarity of anticommunist hustlers. These hustlers used measly amounts of financial assistance for Philippine projects as levers for pushing their anticommunist, reformist, pro-imperialist or other counterrevolutionary ideas and influences in Philippine organizations.

Q12. Don't you think that some Filipinos working with these organizations are partly responsible for tolerating such a "second-guessing" of the Philippine movement? I'm reminded of the PKP's history of being under the CPUSA.

The reestablished CPP is different from the old CPP in the sense that the former is Marxist-Leninist and that the latter specifically under the leadership of Vicente Lava came under the influence of Browderite revisionism. Also, the CPP is not in any situation similar to that of being put by the Third International under the auspices of the CPUSA.

Some Filipinos working with solidarity organizations abroad were in the first place responsible for "second guessing" the Philippine revolutionary movement. They speculated that the movement would be in dire straits after the fall of Marcos and started pushing the notion of "broad solidarity", by which they meant taking out the Left component, obfuscating the character of the Aquino regime and liquidating the previous anti-imperialist solidarity organizations.

The confusion among some Filipinos abroad was a reflection of the confusion among some CPP leaders in the home front who overestimated the Aquino regime as an obstacle to the revolutionary movement, fretted about the imagined long-term adverse effects of the boycott error or pushed the Right opportunist line.

Q13. Were there solidarity groups in the erstwhile socialist bloc?

Some of those countries had friendship associations that hewed closely to diplomatic relations. There were no militant solidarity groups like those in Western Europe. I learned that ruling parties calling themselves socialist had various types and degrees of responses to appeals for mutual support and cooperation from Philippine organizations.

Some were willing to help the Philippine revolution but had varying degrees of willingness and ability to provide material assistance. I salute all of them.

However, there were also those that were already so concerned with improving diplomatic and trade relations with the US that they would not have anything to do with any kind or degree of support for the Philippine revolution. By 1988, articles outrightly denigrating revolutionary causes and cynical about revolution were already appearing in the Soviet academy of social sciences and the official Soviet press.

Q14. *Did you or the CPP ever approach the Soviet CP for bilateral relations? Or was it the other way 'round?*

I was approached a number of times in the Philippines, in Australia, Japan and Western Europe by representatives of the Soviet CP and parties close to it. They floated the idea of a merger between the CPP and the pro-Soviet revisionist group in the Philippines.

I gave them the opinion that a merger was impossible because of fundamental ideological differences and, of course, because of the total public discredit or political suicide the revisionist group had brought upon itself by collaborating with the Marcos fascist regime for a long time, from 1972 to 1986.

The CPP was willing to have bilateral relations with the Soviet party on the basis of broad anti-imperialist solidarity. It was also willing to allow the NDFP, instead of the CPP, to establish those relations on an anti-imperialist basis.

I was aware that representatives of the CPP occasionally met with representatives of the Soviet CP. But the Soviet demand for a merger of the CPP and the revisionist group in the Philippines became an obstacle to the establishment of relations between the CPP and the CPSU.

Q15. *How could the Soviet CP justify their continuing support of a party that surrendered to Marcos? Or even their support for the Marcos regime? Did they ever give you a justification, ideological or otherwise?*

In the first place, the CPSU had actively supported the Marcos fascist regime up to its end in 1986. It never bothered to give any ideological or other justification. It was public knowledge that the CPSU had approved the surrender of the Lavaite revisionist group to the Marcos fascist regime. Both the CPSU and the Lavaites agreed to support and collaborate with the regime on the inane supposition that Marcos was the representative of the national bourgeoisie and not of the pro-US comprador big bourgeoisie.

They pushed their notion of "non capitalist development," depicting Marcos as the representative of the national bourgeoisie who wished to carry out industrialization with the cooperation of the Soviet Union. And yet self-contradictorily they said that Marcos was going down the road of "neocolonial industrialization" whenever they were confronted by the harsh reality that he was the chief puppet of US imperialism and chief representative of the comprador big bourgeoisie and landlord class.

The ringleaders and pen pushers of the old revisionist group could not distinguish their wish for "non capitalist development" from the reality of big comprador operations, involving "infrastructure building" financed by foreign loans, semi-manufacturing in export-processing zones and import of luxury goods. Pretending to be anti-imperialist, they peddled the muddled line that Marcos was industrializing the Philippines, albeit under the ownership and control of the multinational corporations.

Soviet offers of cooperation with the Marcos regime did not amount to much as the Soviet Union stagnated economically due to bureaucratic corruption, the growth of the new bourgeoisie and the arms race. The Soviet revisionist regime also got sucked further into costly military commitments in Africa and Afghanistan.

On the eve of the fall of Marcos, the Soviet regime awarded him with the medal of antifascist hero. It completely disregarded Marcos' record as a traitor selling scrap metal to the Japanese fascists during World War II and the gigantic mass protests already raging against his ongoing fascist rule.

Getting a Visa to the US

Q16. Can you tell me more about your plan to visit the US after your trip to Western Europe? How many times did you try to get a visa?

As I said before, my plan was to go to the US after my Western European lecture tour. As early as February 1987, I applied for a visa at the US consulate in Amsterdam. I had invitations from respected academic, professional, human rights, trade union and other progressive organizations in major cities of the US.

But after several months, the US consul in Amsterdam informed me that the US State Department had taken no decision on my visa application despite the strength of such inviting organizations as the Human Rights Program of Harvard University and the San Francisco Bar Association.

In 1989, the US publisher of my book, *The Philippine Revolution: The Leader's View,* invited me to the US to promote the book there. Around that time, I also engaged the *pro bono* services of the Boudin Law Office, particularly Leonard Weinglass, to get the US visa for me. Once more the US State Department stonewalled my application.

In 1991, the Most Rev. Edmund Browning, presiding bishop of the Episcopalian Church, personally interceded with US deputy secretary of state Lawrence Eagleburger and then US secretary of state James Baker for the grant of a visa to enable me to visit my mother who was seriously ill in Los Angeles, California. But the US State Department again refused to act on my application for a visa.

In 1992, Paul Hoffman of the American Civil Liberties Union, the lead lawyer in my human rights case against Marcos, invited me for consultations and to attend the trial in Honolulu. At that time, my mother and my eldest sister were terminally ill with cancer in the US and this would have been my chance for a reunion with them while they were still alive. Again, the US refused to give me a visa.

Q17. ***It is not surprising that the US would refuse to give you a visa. But what legal reasons did they give for such an action?***

US authorities used the anticommunist line under the Walter-McCarran Act and then the "antiterrorist" line under the new US immigration law to bar known foreign communists from entering the US. They are ruthless against those who militantly oppose US imperialism and they wish to preempt foreign communists from developing stronger links with progressive forces and the people in the US.

The US position towards me is completely rotten. US authorities did not respect the invitation of US entities to me. They did not give any value to the invocation of humanitarian grounds by religious and other respected people, who endorsed my request to visit my terminally ill mother and sister. Neither did they give any value to my American lawyer's plea that I be allowed to go to the US for legal consultations and to attend the trial of the human rights case against the Marcos estate.

Q18. ***I'm frankly surprised you even tried to apply for a visa to the US. Was there a special reason for you to go to the US? How do you see it, in terms of the world?***

I considered it highly important to accept the invitation of comrades, friends and other people interested in my views and to be in close touch with them. It is necessary to be in close touch with the large number of Filipino compatriots in the US, including my relatives, friends and town mates, who have their own communities.

US imperialism is the number one enemy of the Filipino people and the rest of the people of the world. It is therefore important to seek the solidarity and support of the progressive forces and people in the US.

Q19. At that time, what were the most striking circumstances in the US? How did the US and the Soviet Union confront each other in the Cold War?

The Reagan administration had shifted US economic policy bias from Keynesianism to neo-liberalism. Its objective was to attract funds from its imperialist allies and call back loans from client states in the third world and to deliver more resources and profit to the monopoly bourgeoisie by pushing down wages and cutting down on government social spending.

At the same time, it was giving the highest priority to the production of high-tech weaponry and trying to frighten the Soviet Union with the "strategic defense initiative" using outer space as the base for missiles. It was aggressively counteracting the residual influence of the late Brezhnev manifested in Soviet claims of strategic military parity and Soviet support for governments in Africa, Afghanistan and Nicaragua.

On the side of the Soviet Union, the Gorbachov regime was using every possible means to disorganize the Soviet economy and state and accelerate the full restoration of capitalism under such slogans as perestroika and glasnost. It also paved the way for Soviet withdrawal from Afghanistan, Nicaragua and elsewhere and for the break up of the Soviet-bloc governments in Eastern Europe.

Q20. Capitalism constantly aims to put more resources and profit in the hands of the monopoly bourgeoisie, just as it pushes to cut wages and government social spending. What's new with this shift from Keynes to neoliberalism, a term very much in use in political discourse nowadays?

The shift from the Keynesian to the neoliberal policy stress, starting with Reaganism and Thatcherism in the 1980s, meant putting the blame for the phenomenon of stagflation, which turned virulent in the 1970s, on the so-called wage inflation and government social spending.

In the wake of the crisis of overproduction, resulting from the postwar "economic miracles" of reconstruction in Japan and West Germany and likewise from the cost-push inflation generated by US military production and spending, the imperialist policymakers could not prescribe remedies for the phenomenon of inflation without causing stagnation and likewise stagnation without causing inflation.

Thus the imperialist policymakers decided to make more resources available to the monopoly bourgeoisie through tax cuts, wage freeze, social welfare cutbacks, union busting, privatization of public assets, subsidies, increased state purchase contracts, liberalization, deregulation against labor and the environment and so on.

With more capital in its hands, the monopoly bourgeoisie is presumed to be able to invest more in production and generate employment. The state is supposed to be able to make the "free market" flourish by abstaining from direct investments, labor protection, social welfare measures and environmental considerations and by allowing the central bank a lot of autonomy in manipulating the interest rates to redress imbalances in the economy.

Under the neo-liberal dispensation, the monopoly bourgeoisie has intensified exploitation of the toiling masses of workers and peasants all over the world and accelerated the extraction of surplus value from them and the accumulation and concentration of capital in the imperialist countries.

The imperialists have veered away from the pretense of aiding development in the underdeveloped countries. The neo-liberal dogma is to achieve the public good globally through individual and corporate greed, i.e., giving full play to the invisible hand of self-interest and likewise to the multinational firms and banks in the "free market".

Q21. How did the US stand, in relation to the other capitalist countries you visited in 1986-1988?

The US was very much like what it is today. It was the strongest imperialist power economically, politically and militarily. It stood as the chieftain of all imperialist countries. It was the force that headed the G-7 and the OECD and directed the IMF, World Bank, GATT, NATO, the US-Japan Security Treaty, and so many other agreements and arrangements.

It set the neo-liberal policy direction for the entire world capitalist system. It headed the imperialist alliance against the Soviet Union in the

Cold War, as well as against national liberation movements and Third World states assertive of national independence.

The US was at the forefront of its imperialist allies in inducing the Soviet bloc and China to integrate into the world capitalist system and in unleashing counterrevolutionary violence and terror against revolutionary forces in the Third World.

Japan appeared at times to be so powerful, having risen second only to the US overall, in industrial production, trade and finance, especially because it became the No. 1 creditor of the US and the world and it invested heavily in the US. In contrast, the US became the world's No.1 debtor, as it borrowed foreign funds to help sustain its high-speed military spending and consumerism.

But the US was also rebuilding its manufacturing capacity for export, putting a cap on technology transfers to Japan and compelling Japan to open up its market to US industrial and agricultural products and to increase its military purchases. Thus were conditions generated for bursting the Japanese economic bubble at the beginning of the next decade. The Japanese banks had created the bubble by excessively generating credit on the basis of overvalued corporate and land assets, for expanding production and speculation.

On Third World Countries

Q22. And in the Third World countries you visited, what did you observe?

I saw India in 1987 being put under pressure to undertake "economic reforms" and open up its economy to foreign direct investments and loans. The IMF and the World Bank were pushing the Rajiv Gandhi government to adopt such measures as liberalization, privatization and deregulation.

I saw China's economy overheating, in the rush to build office and residential towers and put in more resources into special economic zones for low value-added export-oriented manufacturing. The comprador big bourgeoisie was reemerging and was combining with imperialist firms and overseas Chinese big compradors. The people's communes had long been dismantled and fragmented into small plots and privatized under the guise of leasehold. The rural industries had also been privatized under the guise of management leases.

I saw North Korea in 1987 and 1988 with the Korean Workers Party and the Korean people firmly standing up against US imperialism, pursuing socialist revolution and construction and seeking the peaceful reunification of Korea.

I saw Nicaragua in 1988 as a country that had succeeded in an anti-authoritarian uprising but had not succeeded in carrying out a social revolution. The US was doing everything to bleed the extremely poor country by engaging it in a war of attrition, through the armed Contras based in Honduras.

I saw Cuba in 1988 upholding national independence and the socialist aspirations of the people and courageously overcoming the embargo and military threats of the US. I also sensed the Soviet Union adding to US pressure on Cuba by demanding hard currency for its oil deliveries.

Q23. The CPP was optimistic about the revolutionary linkage of socialism and national liberation movements against US imperialism in 1987 and 1988. Did you share this view?

What I observed during my travels led me to think that had it not been for the revisionist betrayal of socialism, China and the Soviet bloc countries would have been able to take full advantage of the deep-going crisis, defeats and weaknesses of US imperialism from the 1970s onward.

By the second half of the 1970s, in the Soviet Union, the revisionist betrayal of socialism since 1956 had plunged the economy into grave stagnation despite highly increased Soviet military prowess. In China Deng Xiaoping had reversed the socialist line of Mao, without doubt since 1978. While I was aware of the dark side of those countries that continued to call themselves socialist, I thought that they could be approached to support revolutionary movements if only for a shared purpose of confronting a common imperialist enemy.

At that time, the Chinese and Soviet parties were no longer locked in ideological dispute and they avoided references to proletarian internationalism. But each party could still be heard making anti-imperialist remarks on certain issues. In 1986 and 1987, I was still optimistic that the combined movements for socialism and national liberation could fight US imperialism effectively. But by 1988, I began to see more clearly than ever before the signs of the oncoming turmoil in the Soviet Union and China.

On the Crisis of China and the Soviet Bloc

Q24. What was your reaction to such events in 1989-1991 as the turmoil in China, the fall of the regimes in Eastern Europe and the disintegration of the Soviet Union? Were you surprised or were you prepared for them?

I was not surprised. I had an acute sense of how terrible is modern revisionism as a betrayal of socialism and I had expected its consequences. Such an acute sense came from the anti-revisionist foundation of the CPP and from my previous studies on how the revisionists took power in the Soviet Union and proceeded to restore capitalism.

In 1988, I gained an inkling of a big upheaval brewing within the Soviet bloc countries when I learned that Party cells in government offices, army, economic enterprises and cultural institutions were being dissolved.

The Soviet Academy of Social Sciences started to publish blatantly anti-Marxist and counter-revolutionary articles. In an anti-imperialist conference I attended in Sheffield University in the United Kingdom in 1988, the official Soviet representative, a Gorbachovite, stood out of place with his obsequious pro-US imperialist statements.

In 1987 and 1988, I saw in China a construction frenzy overheating the urban economy. This later necessitated a 20 per cent cutback on construction, increasing unemployment, inflation, corruption and the inadequate study and boarding facilities in universities. I anticipated that turmoil could soon arise from the situation.

Q25. Your words imply that what you term revisionist policies were set into motion deliberately and with malice aforethought. Is it not possible that these downhill policies arose out of the situation—economic, political, etc.—of, say, China and the Soviet Union and these men and women in power had no choice but to follow the logic of the situation?

I do not think that revisionist policies arose as a matter of malice aforethought by a few conspirators. Neither do I think that they arose inevitably from objective conditions.

In both the Soviet Union and China at different times, Rightist and revisionist currents emerged even as socialist revolution and construction made great advances. The proletarian revolutionaries asserted that these advances must be the basis for further class struggle and socialist advances. But Right opportunists would refer to the same advances as reasons for laying aside the class struggle and whipping up selfish motives by stressing purely economic incentives.

Right opportunism evolved into full-blown revisionism when the Right opportunists gained ascendance and adopted the policy of prematurely liquidating the class struggle in terms of ideology and policy. In the Soviet Union, the revisionists from Khrushchov through Brezhnev to Gorbachov falsely asserted, "the proletariat had accomplished its historic mission of building socialism". In China, the revisionists pontificated that the "class struggle was dying out".

The modern revisionists sprang mainly from a new generation of bureaucrats and intellectuals who, under initial conditions of prosperity, gained some privileges, alienated themselves from the general mass of workers and peasants and became petty bourgeois in mentality. Further, they began disdaining the proletariat and the class struggle and generated revisionist notions and attitudes. The favorite breeding ground of the petty bourgeoisie is the superstructure, which they use to reinterpret the socialist advances, revive backward ideas and habits and bring in the influence of the international bourgeoisie.

Socioeconomic progress gave rise to both socialist and antisocialist currents. It seemed adequate that Stalin paid attention to those that could be construed as enemies of socialism and agents of imperialism. But one year before his death, he realized that unhealthy petty bourgeois currents were running rampant. Someone in his midst like Khrushchov would surface to represent the revisionist current, reverse the line of Stalin and make revisionism prevail at the highest level.

Mao's line of combating modern revisionism and his theory of continuing revolution under proletarian dictatorship appeared to be adequate in consolidating socialism. The Great Proletarian Cultural Revolution prevented the revisionists from taking power for one decade. But the revisionists headed by Deng Xiaoping would still be able to use and manipulate a resurgent petty bourgeois base. They had enough power and influence to undermine and reverse the line of Mao and rapidly unleash the forces of capitalist restoration.

When a revisionist ruling clique takes power, as in the Soviet Union after the death of Stalin and in China after the death of Mao, a bureaucrat big bourgeoisie overthrows the proletarian dictatorship and imposes its own class dictatorship over the proletariat and the people in both the economic base and the superstructure of society.

Q26. Please explain what you mean by the word "superstructure."

The superstructure consists of the politics and culture that are based on, reflect and interact with the economic base of society. Having provided for the maintenance and reproduction of the economic base, a certain form of class society can appropriate a part of the surplus product to support a group of people devoted to philosophical work, politics, scientific studies and cultural activities in the superstructure.

The exploiting class that extracts from the exploited class the surplus material values above subsistence uses such surplus not only for economic reproduction but also for building a superstructure that legitimizes, puts into order and prettifies the class rule of the exploiting class.

In a socialist society, the proletariat uses the surplus from production for economic growth and building a superstructure that upholds the proletarian class dictatorship and proletarian culture in the transition from capitalism to communism through socialism.

Q27. The disintegration of the Soviet Union and rise of capitalism in China have led people to say that the socialist experiment had failed, the socialist cause is hopeless and that the end of history is capitalism and liberal democracy. What is your response to this?

Indeed, the revisionists in the Soviet Union betrayed socialism and reversed the socialist line soon after the death of Stalin. The same thing occurred in China soon after the death of Mao. But we must recognize that before the revisionists could prevail and begin to destroy socialism, several decades of socialist revolution and construction had achieved great successes in the economy, politics and culture.

The revisionists used the succeeding decades to undermine, breach and destroy socialism in the Soviet Union and China. And since the turmoil in China, the disintegration of the Soviet Union and the full restoration of capitalism in the revisionist-ruled countries in the 1989-91 period, we have witnessed the grievous economic, political, social, cultural and moral degradation suffered by the people in all countries where the new bourgeoisie defeats the proletariat and the people and destroys socialism.

But it is complete nonsense for anyone to believe that the socialist cause is hopeless and that history has ended with capitalism and liberal democracy. As long as the monopoly bourgeoisie exploits and oppresses them, the proletariat and the people will continue to fight for socialism.

Right now, the struggle for socialism is rising because of intensifying oppression and exploitation. Amidst conditions of crisis, the proletariat and people are reinvigorating themselves with the legacy of the great communists and learning lessons from the theoretical and practical achievements of proletarian revolutionaries in the past as they rise up to confront the oppressors and exploiters.

For the socialist cause to advance again, more has to be done than merely hanker or even to fight for it in quick response to the calamities that imperialism wreaks on humanity. We need to analyze the previous positive and negative experiences in building socialism and learn all the major lessons to guide us in the current and prospective rounds of struggle for socialism against imperialism.

Q28. What are the lessons to be drawn from the long experience of socialism leading to the events of 1989-1991?

The most important lesson for communists is to keep firmly the proletarian revolutionary stand, grasp class struggle as the key link in carrying out socialist revolution and construction, and pursue the proletarian cultural revolution to be able to carry the socialist revolution through to the end.

It is necessary but not enough to overthrow the class dictatorship of the bourgeoisie and establish the class dictatorship of the proletariat, socialize the means of production and further develop the socialist economy, educate and train professionals and technicians and push further the technological and scientific revolution. It is necessary to persevere in the proletarian class struggle against the bourgeoisie.

It is necessary to carry out a proletarian cultural revolution to combat revisionism, prevent the restoration of capitalism and consolidate socialism for an entire historical epoch until socialism defeats imperialism on a global scale and creates the conditions for communism.

Before then, the communist party should lead the proletarian cultural revolution as a mass undertaking of an educational character and with guarantees of the right to due process.

To give up class struggle prematurely, as the Soviet revisionists did by declaring that there were no more exploiting classes and therefore no more class struggle in the Soviet Union and as the Chinese revisionists likewise did by declaring that class struggle was already dying out, is to take the road of overthrowing the proletariat and restoring capitalism.

The events of 1989-1991, which completely exposed the bankruptcy of revisionism and the full restoration of capitalism, vindicates Lenin's line against revisionism and liquidationism, and Mao's theory of continuing revolution under proletarian dictatorship through the Great Proletarian Cultural Revolution.

On Revisionism and the CPP

Q29. Following the events of 1989-1991, what was the most significant act of the CPP vis-à-vis the new international situation?

The most significant act of the CPP was to launch and carry out the Second Great Rectification Movement in early 1992. This movement would strengthen the CPP ideologically, politically and organizationally and keep it Marxist-Leninist, against revisionism and for socialism.

For its own guidance and for sharing with all communist and workers' parties abroad, the CPP issued and distributed widely the document *Stand for Socialism Against Modern Revisionism*. This document clarified the history and outcome of modern revisionism and called for the study of Mao's critique of modern revisionism and his theory and practice of continuing revolution under proletarian dictatorship.

Q30. Your view on the Great Proletarian Revolution goes very much against the grain of current political thought. Some say that the excesses of the GPCR indeed eased the return to power of the Deng Xiaoping faction by weakening and in some instances, ousting the anti-revisionists within the Chinese Communist Party.

"Left" opportunist or ultra-Left errors were indeed committed in the course of the Great Proletarian Cultural Revolution. These errors were the result of honest inexperience and excessive enthusiasm. But there were also the obviously ultra-Left acts committed with deliberate malice by the Rightists who masqueraded as "Left" in order to sabotage and discredit the cultural revolution and cause a Rightist backlash that would create the conditions for Deng Xiaoping to return to power.

A major error was to let loose factional groups fighting each other and dividing the masses. The factionalism fouled up the alliance between the Left and the Middle against the few Rightists, the revisionists in power. The Left was also split. After Mao died, the Right coalesced with the Middle to isolate, further split and defeat the Left.

Nevertheless, a comprehensive view of the GPCR as a historical phenomenon should recognize its 10-year course and achievements from

1966 to 1976 and, of course, its subsequent defeat. Without the GPCR and Mao's previous struggles against the Rightists and revisionists, the Chinese revisionists would have defeated socialism much earlier. We need to understand the basic principles and methods of the GPCR, which, for 10 years, kept the Red flag flying, and China Red.

We need to understand the "Left" and Right opportunist currents that created conditions for the defeat of the GPCR and the victory of the Chinese revisionists headed by Deng Xiaoping. The diehard Rightists and revisionists were the principal enemies of the GPCR. They undermined and redirected the GPCR until they could reverse Mao, especially after his death.

We draw lessons from the positive and negative experiences in the GPCR in the same way that Marx drew lessons from the short-lived Paris Commune of 1871, in order to sharpen our understanding of the proletarian socialist revolution and illuminate the road for further advance.

Q31. *Did the disintegration of the so-called socialist bloc lead to a stronger capitalist system?*

The world capitalist system appears stronger because of the complete restoration of capitalism in Russia, China and elsewhere. But even before the 1989-1991 period, such countries had already come under the rule of revisionists who liquidated socialism and took the road of capitalist restoration.

They had a mixed up or schizophrenic economy of state capitalism and private capitalism and they became a weak part of the world capitalist system. They came under the crushing blows of the crisis that hit the entire world capitalist system and brought about recessions in the global centers of capitalism, the bursting of the Japanese economic bubble and stagnation of the German economy in the same 1989-1991 period.

The complete integration of these former socialist countries into the world capitalist system appears to have strengthened the latter. But the crisis has devastated and impoverished these countries. They tend to become "compradorized" and take on the character of backward third world countries at the mercy of the traditional imperialists.

But let us say for the sake of argument that Russia, China and some other countries overcome their current economic and financial crisis and become strong industrial capitalist countries. The global capitalist crisis of overproduction is bound to worsen and the tendency of the world capitalist system to implode will grow stronger. The system cannot allow too many competing industrial capitalist countries. There is the rub. In fact, the crisis of the world capitalist system has been worsening without let-up for nearly all countries since 1991.

Q32. *Although rife with crises, the world capitalist system appears to be going strong under the thrust of "free market" globalization. How do you see this current phase of expansion by world capitalism?*

The US and its imperialist allies have worsened the crisis of the world capitalist system as they push "free market" globalization. The neo-liberal reforms (liberalization, privatization and deregulation) have only served to accelerate the accumulation and concentration of capital in the hands of the monopoly bourgeoisie.

All types of goods, raw materials, basic industrial products and high-tech goods, have been overproduced. Most victimized are the overwhelming majority of countries that have only raw materials to offer to the global market. They suffer from chronic economic depression, widening trade deficits and crushing debt burdens.

Economies like those of South Korea, Taiwan, Hong Kong, Malaysia and Thailand having an overproduction of some basic industrial products and low value-added semi-manufactures for export have also suffered from the bankruptcies of major firms and have plunged into recurrent and more prolonged recessions.

In most of the 1990s, the US under the Clinton regime could appear to enjoy growth and prosperity by taking the lead in high-tech production and by attracting funds from Japan and Western Europe and raking in super-profits from the global hinterlands.

But the US economy itself has taken a plunge since the year 2000. The stock market has been in a prolonged state of collapse since its March 2000 peak and industrial production has rapidly declined since October 2000. The high tech bubble has burst and the "new economy" of "economic growth without wage inflation" has collapsed.

Q33. *I'm glad you mentioned high-tech. Have you spent time looking at the role of high technology in present world capitalism?*

Yes, I have done so.

As the monopoly bourgeoisie adopts higher technology, the social character of the forces of production rises. Commensurately, the contradiction between the social character of production and the private character of appropriation intensifies, especially because the monopoly bourgeoisie is pushing the laissez faire spirit of unbridled self-interest or greed.

To maximize profits and prevail in the competition, the monopolies must increase constant capital (plant, equipment and raw materials) and press down variable capital (wages). The crisis of overproduction ensues, as the rising level of productivity runs against the dwindling capacity of the wage earners to buy products.

The use of finance capital to stimulate production, consumption, and speculation and thereby to accelerate the concentration of capital in the hands of the monopoly bourgeoisie also goes out of control when the crisis of overproduction intensifies. The financial overhang crashes down on the real economy as bankruptcies ensue from corporate and personal failure to pay debt.

I am describing what is now dramatically taking place in the world capitalist system. But I wish to make one more point. Although high technology is available, the monopoly bourgeoisie uses it essentially for profit making and not for serving the people. Thus, it is adopted only up to a certain point, in the futile attempt of the monopoly bourgeoisie to maintain or increase profitability, prevent or solve the crisis of overproduction.

There is the view that the economic crisis is a kind of creative destruction, because winners in the competition are supposed to move on to higher levels of technology, productivity and efficiency. This is a one-sided view that ignores or disregards the horrendous human cost that such crisis imposes. Consider the magnitude of productive forces destroyed, the prolonged stagnation, the growing trend of chauvinism, racism and fascism and the threats and outbreaks of aggressive war. These brutal inefficiencies of an exploitative and wasteful capitalism urge us to replace monopoly capitalism with socialism.

Q34. *The former US president, Bush Sr., claimed that a "new world order" was coming or had come into existence. What was he referring to, in your view?*

When Bush Senior blabbered about the "new world order," he was gloating over the quick sequence of US victory in the Cold War, the disintegration of the Soviet bloc and the successful US-led war of aggression against Iraq.

In fact, he was using a euphemism for what was in fact a "new world disorder," characterized by boundless arrogance and aggressiveness of the US as the sole superpower. It could opt to use the UN Security Council and the NATO, build a war coalition as in the 1991 war of aggression against Iraq, or act unilaterally to wage wars of aggression.

Since the slogan of the "new world order" came into currency, the US has tightened its control over oil resources in the Middle East. It has required even its own allies among the oil producing countries, especially Saudi Arabia and the United Arab Emirates to foot the bill for US military bases, troops and equipment. This has caused grave social and economic problems for these client states. The US has been able to push its own and Israeli interests at the expense of the Palestinian and Arab peoples.

Subsequent to the successful aggression against Iraq, the US and its imperialist allies pushed for the fragmentation of former Yugoslavia and whipped up the Balkan wars in order to justify the expansion of US and NATO military forces along the borders of Russia. This was to ensure US control of the flow of oil to the Mediterranean from Central Asia and the Caspian Sea via Turkey and to build pipelines to preempt pipelines planned along more direct routes to Germany (via Chechnya or via Danube-Rhine river) as well as to China (via Siberia or border states in Central Asia).

The US has been openly categorizing as rogue states those assertive of their independence, pressuring them with economic blockade and threatening them with acts of military intervention and aggression. These countries include the Democratic People's Republic of Korea, Cuba, Iraq, Iran, Libya and so on. It continues to block the return of Taiwan to China and has gone so far as to bomb the Chinese embassy in Belgrade with a cruise missile to teach China a lesson for aiding the government of Yugoslavia.

In the decade of the 1990s, we have seen not only the wars of aggression launched by US imperialism but also the massacres occurring in countries (especially in Africa) crushed by the impositions of the IMF and made vulnerable to regimes of open terror and to internecine conflicts incited by rival reactionary forces that use ethnocentrism, religious bigotry, racism and other backward ideas to rally a following.

Post-September 11

Q35. The younger Bush, the current president, appears to be very much at the center of the world stage. Following the September 11 attacks, he seems to be enjoying some kind of popularity. He has even managed to get US troops back to the Philippines. What do you think of Bush's moves, thus far?

Bush Junior is emphatic about his ultra-Right position. Like Reagan, he wants to step up military production as a way of reviving the sick US economy. He also wants to provide giant corporations with extra resources through huge tax cuts, purchase contracts, subsidies and so on.

The US trade deficit keeps on growing and the foreign debt is mounting. The US budgetary surplus under the Clinton administration has evaporated. The budgetary deficit is huge. And now Bush intends to raid the Social Security funds to engage in deficit spending in favor of the military and at the expense of the American people.

The September 11 attacks have come in handy for the Bush regime. It has used these to consolidate the judicial appointment of Bush as president, whip up jingoism, launch the wars of aggression against Afghanistan and Iraq, deploy combat troops to the Philippines, threaten the countries it calls the "axis of evil" (Iraq, Iran and North Korea), push repressive measures in the US and abroad and justify accelerated military spending.

Bush is propelling racism, fascism and aggressive war. The US is grabbing for itself the spoils from launching aggression against Afghanistan and Iraq. It has secured control over more oil resources in Central Asia and has practically secured the oil route over Afghanistan and Pakistan, down to the Arabian coast and the Indian Ocean. It is laying the groundwork for a struggle for a re-division of the world among the imperialist powers.

Q36. Were the September 11 attacks acts of terrorism? How could any group believe that such attacks against the US would be acceptable?

Whichever group was responsible, the September 11 attacks on the World Trade Center were clearly acts of terrorism. They involved the massacre of civilians, whether in the hijacked airplanes or in the office towers of the World Trade Center. However, they were provoked by prior and far bigger US acts of terrorism in the form of wars of aggression and continuous acts of imperialist exploitation and oppression.

Because of worldwide monopoly control of media and communication, the grievances of the people affected by such US acts have been actively suppressed, or just simply ignored. The voices of the poor and the powerless have been drowned out by imperialist propaganda and entertainment.

Thus among non-Marxist-Leninist forces, some are driven to desperate acts of terror (including acts of self-destruction) to call attention to and draw support for their cause. They differ completely from Marxist-Leninist revolutionaries who launch all forms of mass-based struggle, including armed offensives, against state terrorism.

Note that the cultistic and fanatical religious groups the US Bush administration now accuse of being terrorist have leaders previously connected to the US Central Intelligence Agency for carrying out acts of terrorism. Thus, quite a number of people believe that Bush must have somehow engineered the September 11 attacks.

The US is making bloodcurdling cries for wars of aggression and fascist repression. It is using the September 11 attacks as a pretext for terrorizing the proletariat, oppressed peoples and nations and the countries assertive of independence.

Q37. *Some people would characterize your view as blaming the victim in the wake of September 11. Please explain further.*

I do not blame the victims, those who died and were maimed as well as the American people who were somehow deeply hurt. They are different from the US monopoly bourgeoisie and US government that wreak havoc on the lives of the people of the world and sow hatred in the whole world.

The American people must consider the fact that the September 11 attacks were in retaliation for far bigger acts of terrorism done by the US against other peoples. They cannot protect themselves by supporting wars of aggression. The best way for the people in the US to protect themselves is to fight US imperialism in its home ground and prevent its acts of terror overseas.

The US has certainly been guilty of far bigger kinds of terrorism than the September 11 attacks. In fact, the US is the world's number one terrorist for launching imperialist wars of aggression and perpetuating the daily violence of exploitation.

The 3000 victims of the September 11 attacks are far smaller in number than the 1.5 million Filipinos killed by the US military forces in the course of the US conquest and pacification of the people of the Philippines from 1899 to 1913.

Even when Japan was already offering to surrender in 1945, the US dropped two atomic bombs in succession over Hiroshima (August 6) and Nagasaki (August 9) and massacred more than 100,000 civilians in a matter of seconds, rising to moe than 210,000 by year-end. The US did this to outrace the Soviet Union in the occupation of Japan.

US military forces killed more than 10 million people directly in its wars of aggression in Korea, Indochina and elsewhere, as well as indirectly through puppet regimes of open terror like those of General Videla of Argentina, Syngman Rhee and Park Chung Hee of Korea, Ngo Dinh Diem and Nguyen van Thieu of Vietnam, Lon Nol of Cambodia, Suharto of Indonesia, the Shah of Iran, Marcos of the Philippines, Pinochet of Chile, Fujimori of Peru, Mobutu of the Congo and so on.

And let us take the case of Iraq in the Gulf war of 1991 and its aftermath. The US forces killed half a million Iraqis in the war itself and subsequently caused the death of another 1.5 million Iraqi people and 750 thousand Iraqi children below the age of five, as a result of economic sanctions.

Q38. *Can any help be expected from Russia and/or China, to break this US power monopoly? How have people fared in these two countries?*

We have to understand the economic, social and political changes that have occurred in Russia and China in order to consider what can be expected of them in relation to your question of breaking US power monopoly. So far, the leaders of these two countries have maintained friendly relations with te US. Later we might be able to see their increasing contradictions with the US or their increasing ability to take advantage of the contradictions among the three strongest global centers of capitalism.

In Russia and China, a small percentage, around two per cent of the population, has benefited the most from the bourgeois freedom to exploit the rest of the population. The big bourgeoisie in these countries consists of the bureaucrat capitalists and their business and family relations in the private sector. They have basically a big comprador character, subordinated to the foreign monopoly firms.

Those who have become big bourgeois have a history of being bureaucrat capitalists or being connected to them through several decades of revisionist rule. They have enriched themselves by having access to or by privatizing public funds, lands, energy, equipment and other resources from the state and by going into joint ventures with foreign monopoly firms.

In China and the former Soviet bloc countries, the big bourgeois parasites and criminals have taken advantage of the state sector of the economy, siphoned off resources and privatized state enterprises entirely or partially. In certain cases, privatization is deliberately left partial so as to allow the racketeers to continue to siphon off funds from the state.

Following the historical pattern of the Soviet Union, the Chinese bureaucrat capitalists have debated on how much and how fast the privatization of public assets should proceed. The dominant political heirs of Deng Xiaoping, who are frankly big comprador in character, think that the time has come to liquidate the Communist Party openly and completely by letting the private capitalists join the Party ranks in full force and to privatize the state sector of the economy at an accelerated pace.

The bureaucrat capitalists who take a bourgeois nationalist posture and wish to delay the decomposition of state enterprises are losing out to the big compradors in the drive to integrate China into the World Trade Organization (WTO). Having already dismantled the socialist economy, China is being pushed by the global crisis of capitalism to further come under the sway of imperialism and big comprador capitalism.

On Party Relations

Q39. Going back to the Communist Party of the Philippines, in a world minus the big socialist countries of the past, how much of its relations are on a Marxist-Leninist basis—i.e., with other communist parties—and how much on an anti-imperialist basis—i.e., solidarity with various parties and organizations? What are the guiding principles of these relations?

It is well known that the CPP has relations with scores of communist and workers' parties and groups and national liberation movements and hundreds of progressive mass organizations all over the world. It does not limit its relations to parties it deems Marxist-Leninist. Anti-imperialist solidarity suffices as the basis for friendly relations.

The CPP has publicly acknowledged that it has far more relations based on broad anti-imperialist solidarity than those based on Marxism-Leninism. That is but natural because the anti-imperialist formations will always outnumber the Marxist-Leninist parties. Furthermore, relations with other parties on the basis of Marxism-Leninism also involve an anti-imperialist basis.

The CPP presumes that in the course of the revolutionary struggle, revolutionary parties prove themselves to be Marxist-Leninist or simply anti-imperialist. It is keen about promoting the unity of the international communist movement as well as the broad anti-imperialist solidarity of all progressive forces.

In its relations with other parties, the CPP adheres to the principles of independence, equality, non-interference, mutual support, mutual benefit and cooperation.

Q40. Does the CPP have relations with the ruling parties of China, North Korea, Cuba, Vietnam, Laos and Cambodia? What about communist and workers' parties in the former Soviet Union and in Eastern Europe?

It is a matter of public knowledge that the CPP has had relations with the ruling parties in China, North Korea, Cuba, Vietnam, Laos and Cambodia since a long time ago. However, relations with ruling parties in a few of these countries have obviously become dormant.

I am aware that the CPP currently has relations with several communist or workers' parties in the former Soviet Union and Eastern Europe. It gives priority to parties that are critical of revisionism and are determined to overthrow the ruling new bourgeoisie.

It manages to have extensive relations because it avoids the sectarian policy of cooperating only with Marxist-Leninist-Maoist parties. It regards friendly, anti-imperialist relations with all possible forces as useful and necessary for advancing the revolution in the Philippines and the whole world.

It takes the position that communist and workers' parties sharpen their revolutionary line and raise the level of their revolutionary consciousness and practice when they have the opportunity to cooperate and discuss with Maoist parties. Such opportunity can easily arise, especially at this time when the big revisionist ruling parties are either gone, weakened or discredited.

International Work

Q41. The CPP participated in the Third Conference of the International Conference of Marxist-Leninist Parties and Organizations (ICMLPO) in 1992 and then chaired the ICMLPO until its Fourth Conference in 1994. For the CPP, what are the significance, implications and consequences of such international activities? What is the role of the CPP in the ICMLPO?

By participating in the International Conference of Marxist-Leninist Parties and Organizations, the CPP gains the opportunity to exchange ideas and experiences and seek common understanding and cooperation with parties and organizations that adhere to Marxism-Leninism-Mao Zedong Thought, have a positive attitude to Mao and Stalin and oppose revisionism.

The CPP joined and helped to prepare the Third Conference of the

ICMLPO. It put forward the rules of organization that would stabilize the conference and attract more participants. At that conference, the Party was elected to chair the Joint Coordinating Group that would prepare and hold the Fourth Conference.

The Third and Fourth Conferences of the ICMLPO were significant because they drew up the resolutions to combat the ideological and political offensive of imperialism, which was gloating then over the so-called fall of socialism.

From 1992 onward, the CPP was able to promote the document *Stand for Socialism Against Modern Revisionism* through the IMCLPO. This served as a weapon against the imperialist ideological and political offensive.

The ICMLPO continues to be an important ideological and political forum for debating, clarifying and resolving issues pertaining to the world situation, the revolutionary forces and the tasks in the international communist movement.

Q42. You chaired the International Seminar on Mao Zedong Thought in 1993. What are the significance and consequences of this international gathering?

The International Seminar on Mao Zedong Thought on December 26, 1993 was held both to honor the great Mao Zedong on his 100th birth anniversary and to recall to the revolutionary parties of the proletariat his great contributions to the development of Marxism-Leninism, up to the critique and repudiation of modern revisionism and to the theory and practice of continuing revolution through the proletarian cultural revolution.

Many known followers of Mao contributed papers to the seminar on various questions of history, objective conditions and burning issues. The delegates participated enthusiastically in the debates. They approved the General Declaration on Mao Zedong Thought to serve as a beacon for the revolutionary forces.

The seminar was significant for reminding communists and the people in general that Mao posed the problem of modern revisionism as the destroyer of socialism and offered the solution. The seminar reinforced the revolutionary conviction of the Marxist-Leninist-Maoists and demonstrated that there is a way for combating revisionism, preventing the restoration of capitalism and consolidating socialism.

I am very happy to have chaired the seminar. We had a key role in inviting the delegations from various countries and drafting the General

Declaration on Mao Zedong Thought. The seminar and declaration constituted a major event for upholding Marxism-Leninism-Maoism against the ideological and political offensive of imperialism in the wake of the 1989-91 events.

Q43. *I am aware of quite a number of definitive speeches on important issues that you delivered at the Brussels seminar. What is this seminar and since when have you been participating in it? How do you compare this seminar to the ICMLPO?*

The Brussels seminar is sponsored and hosted annually by the Workers' Party of Belgium. It has a wider range of participants than the ICMLPO because it includes communist and workers parties and organizations that belong to various ideological currents. Also among the participants are the ruling parties of North Korea and Cuba as well as communist and workers' parties that have recently arisen in the former Soviet Union and Eastern Europe.

I believe that through the seminar the CPP is able to exchange views and experiences with more parties from more countries than those in the ICMLPO and develop relations on a Marxist-Leninist basis as well as on a broad anti-imperialist basis. The annual seminar is a good venue for various parties to air their ideological and political positions. It addresses the need for promoting the Marxist-Leninist and anti-imperialist position on a wide scale through the papers contributed and the resolutions adopted.

Although it hosts the seminar, the Workers' Party of Belgium consults with the participants on how to conduct it and gives them the leeway whether or not to sign resolutions proposed by any delegation. I am deeply pleased to have been a speaker on major issues in almost all years of the Brussels seminar.

Q44. *The CPP chaired the International Seminar on People's War in 1998. What were the achievements of the seminar?*

The published papers of the seminar show that for the first time Marxist-Leninist parties waging, preparing and supporting people's war came together and approved a general declaration on people's war. The declaration stresses the point that wherever the line of new-democratic revolution through protracted people's war is possible and necessary, Marxist-Leninist parties must lead such a revolution.

The strategic line of protracted people's war in chronically crisis-stricken agrarian countries is put forward as of crucial importance because it can realize revolution on a wide scale at any time. Protracted people's war does not depend on one or two or a few uprisings, or on the occurrence of inter-imperialist wars. It takes advantage of the chronic crisis in economically and socially backward countries.

It relies on the people as the inexhaustible source of revolutionary strength. The people's army accumulates strength by launching tactical offensives over a long period of time and encircles the city from the countryside. Eventually, it becomes possible to seize the cities and thus achieve revolutionary victory nationwide.

As you can see from the Vanguard magazine and its website, the parties waging people's war and other participants of the seminar have tried to keep in close touch with each other. It is obvious that they have been increasing their common understanding and practical cooperation.

Q45. You initiated and chaired the founding of the International League of People's Struggles (ILPS) in May 2001. And now you are its general consultant. What is the significance of this international formation?

I chaired the International Initiative Committee that prepared and founded the ILPS. I consider the ILPS an important weapon of the broad masses of the people of the world for opposing imperialism. It is resolutely and militantly against "free market" globalization and the new world disorder due to imperialist oppression and aggression. Now, the international united front against imperialism has a new militant force.

The ILPS aims to unite the truly progressive organizations and the broad masses of the people in their fight against imperialism in as many as 18 fields of concern. It seeks to assert the role of truly progressive forces and differentiate their militant stand from the reformism of so-called nongovernmental organizations (NGOs) financed by the imperialists and managed by petty-bourgeois racketeers, including anarchists and Trotskyites.

The ILPS can adopt and apply the policy and tactics of the broad united front against imperialism and all reaction. The Left can win over the Middle and take advantage of the splits among those on the Right. The progressive forces of the Left should use every possible way to increase the mass organizations and masses under the ILPS flag.

Q46. There is a noticeable lack of party-led, party-guided mass and

people's organizations in the West. What, in your view, is the reason for this?

There are some communist and workers' parties in North America, Japan and Europe that lead mass organizations, including trade unions, organizations of youth and women, solidarity organizations, in support of peoples' struggles abroad.

But many parties have weakened or disintegrated due to revisionism and opportunism and the inability to overcome the tremendous odds posed by the monopoly bourgeoisie and by its special agents in the economic, social, political and cultural fields.

As the crisis of the world capitalist system worsens, we can expect proletarian revolutionaries to emerge as spontaneous mass protests and strikes independent of the yellow trade union bureaucracy increase in frequency, become more organized and necessitate firm Marxist-Leninist leadership. Sustained revolutionary practice through the mass movement will give rise to and develop more revolutionaries that are proletarian.

Q47. You are also the chief political consultant of the National Democratic Front of the Philippines (NDFP) in its peace negotiations with the Government of the Republic of the Philippines (GRP). What political gains has the NDFP made in carrying out the peace negotiations in a neutral venue abroad or in other words on an international plane?

The Dutch government facilitated the GRP-NDFP peace negotiations from 1992 onwards. So did the Belgian government in 1995, particularly the opening of formal negotiations. The Norwegian government has facilitated the resumption of peace negotiations since 2001 after Estrada terminated these in 1999. Third party facilitation by a foreign government raises the level of seriousness of the GRP-NDFP negotiations as well as the international or diplomatic political standing of the NDFP.

The NDFP and the revolutionary forces and people it represents can no longer be regarded as a mere domestic police problem of the GRP. They are on an equal footing with the GRP as co-belligerents in a civil war and as negotiating parties in a neutral venue abroad.

In the first place, they have acquired the status of belligerency by dint of revolutionary struggle. They are not a mere rebellious or insurgent force. They have a system of government, a leading party, a disciplined army with a structure of command and a significant portion of the Philippine population and territory.

Towards the international or diplomatic recognition of its status of belligerency, the NDFP has deposited with the Swiss Federal Council the Unilateral Undertaking to Apply the Geneva Convention and its Protocols, in accordance with Article 96, paragraph 3 of Protocol I.

Under the GRP-NDFP Comprehensive Agreement on Respect for Human Rights and International Humanitarian Law, the GRP has also agreed that the armed conflict between the armies of the GRP and the NDFP is governed by international humanitarian law and that the NDFP is a co-equal of the GRP as an authority that can arrest suspected violators of human rights and international humanitarian law, and subject them to investigation and, if evidence warrants, to trial.

Q48. Both the CPP and you as its founding chair enjoy a good reputation and international prestige among communists and anti-imperialists. Is the CPP using this prestige to promote revolution in the world? Is the CPP initiating or helping initiate a center for the international communist movement?

The CPP stands out as a revolutionary party of the proletariat because it has been able to fight, preserve itself and advance in a country that has long been in the iron grip of US imperialism and the local reactionaries.

The CPP stands out also because it rises at that time in which big ruling communist parties and socialist states are gone. It seeks to make good use of its high international prestige to promote the resurgence of the socialist and anti-imperialist movements.

I do not think that the CPP is bent on initiating or helping initiate a new center of the international communist movement. Even the ruling communist or workers' parties in the countries which continue to call themselves socialist have not initiated the formation of such a center.

An initiator or a group of initiators for such a center would have to take on very heavy responsibilities. Apart from the problem of attending to tasks at home and uniting various parties abroad, such a group would have to contend with threats and counter-actions from the imperialists.

A number of parties are talking about the need to build a new International. Representatives from such parties have been attending international conferences and seminars. From year to year, let us see to what extent they can come to a common level of understanding through resolutions, how they conduct themselves towards each other and what kind of preparations they are willing to undertake.

THE GIANT OAK

(*Tribute to Comrade Mao Zedong*)
By Jose Maria Sison

In the bitterness of winter
The giant oak stands erect,
A hundred years old,
A tower of countless seasons.
The mayflies of summer
Are no match to the oak
And the merciless cold.

He who has departed
But whose spirit lives on
And cannot be exorcised
By all sorts of sorcerers
Is sometimes carved out
From a branch of the oak
In the image of his foes
For rituals to steal
The magic of his name.
There are the kisses of betrayal
On the parchment,
Droning incantations of sacrilege
And myths of infamy
Against his great memory.

When foes are haunted
By his thoughts and deeds
They are in mortal fear
Of the living force inspired
For the bigger battles ahead,
As the light and darkness
Clash in the horizon
And as the best and the worst
Are driven to define themselves.

26 December 1993

Professor Sison with Senator Legarda in Utrecht, Netherlands. As majority floor leader of the Philippine Senate, Senator Legarda has visited Professor Sison several times to work for the release of prisoners of war held by the New People's Army. (NDF International Office photo collection)

Lecturing at youth camp, June 2003. (Sison family photo collection)

At the initialling of the Comprehensive Agreement of Respect of Human Rights and International Humanitarian Law at The Hague in March 1998. (Sison family photo collection)

Chapter Five

Trends and Prospects

Q1. Whereto is neo-liberalism or "free market" globalization taking the world?

It is pushing the world downward from one level of economic, social and political disaster to another. It is intensifying major contradictions in the world and bringing about social and political turmoil on a wide scale.

It has hastened the accumulation and concentration of capital in the No. 1 imperialist country at a far faster pace than under the Keynesian policy bias. Investments have flowed into the US from Japan and Europe and super-profits from elsewhere. However, the US economy has plunged since the year 2000 and is aggravating the global depression.

The crisis of overproduction in all types of goods—agricultural, mineral, basic industrial and high-tech products—and the ensuing bankruptcies and financial meltdowns cause terrible hardship and suffering for the working people in the US and other imperialist countries and so many times more in the third world and former Soviet-bloc countries.

The imperialists headed by the US have manifested their gross incapacity to solve the economic crisis. They are using all sorts of monetary and fiscal incentives for the monopoly firms in an attempt to revive the economy. But such incentives have failed to stimulate consumer demand.

The market continues to shrink as mass unemployment increases, as incomes of the working people are eroded and many firms fall into bankruptcy. Financial resources flow to the biggest monopoly firms, assuring mammoth profits for big investors and high executives.

Q2. Are we therefore to expect more violence—coups and countercoups, religious and ethnic conflicts, wars of aggression and armed revolutions?

The worsening economic and social crisis will certainly lead to more violence. Currently, there is far more counterrevolutionary violence than revolutionary violence. In a little over a decade, the US and its allies have already launched three wars of aggression (on Iraq, former Yugoslavia and Afghanistan).

The propensity of the imperialists to carry out aggression rises as they increase their war budgets and step up war production in an effort to reverse the worsening crisis and to stop people's resistance and as they compete among themselves.

The US and other imperialists will also continue to foment armed religious and ethnic conflicts as well as coups and countercoups in client states to further weaken them for imperialist domination. Driven to desperation by the socioeconomic crisis, the propensity of the local reactionaries for repression, violent rivalries, coups and civil wars will continue.

In a situation of increasing counterrevolutionary violence, the revolutionary forces and people can take the initiative of carrying out armed revolution. Several armed revolutionary movements in the third world, especially those of India, Nepal, Peru, Turkey, Philippines and Colombia, are showing the way.

Q3. Can a terrorist group launching attacks like those of September 11, 2001, damage US power significantly? Can we expect more such groups to operate against the US? How will the US stepping up war production in the name of a worldwide so-called war against terrorism affect the world?

A terrorist group such as the one that carried out the September 11 attacks cannot go far towards bringing down the biggest terrorist of all, US imperialism. The attacks on civilians aboard the planes and in the twin towers of the WTC have outraged the people of the world in general and provided the US with the pretext to undertake a far bigger kind of terrorism all over the world.

The US war of aggression against Afghanistan has killed many Afghan civilians, several times more than those killed in the September 11 attacks. The US is poised to launch more wars of aggression and is pushing the adoption of repressive laws both in the US and in the world at large.

The utter cruelty of the US and its worst puppets will continue to foment the rise of small terrorist groups seeking vengeance for prior grievances and making wild attacks on vulnerable points of the US, including nonmilitary targets. It is a case of small groups driven to desperate terrorist acts against the gigantic terrorism of the US imperialists.

It is worthwhile to consider that 15 of the 19 individuals involved in the September 11 attacks came from Saudi Arabia and expressed certain strong motivations for their sense of self-sacrifice. They have been so outraged by US and Israeli barbarism in attacking the Palestinians and by the US permanently deploying military forces in the "holy land" of Saudi Arabia and making this client state foot the bill for US personnel and equipment to the extent of drastically bringing down the living standard of the people.

The US is now hell-bent on increasing war production and deploying military forces under the pretext of a global "war on terrorism". It is systematically misrepresenting as "terrorists" people waging revolution, nations fighting for liberation and countries asserting independence. What will ultimately defeat US imperialism will not be the terrorism of some anarchists or religious fanatics but the armed revolution of broad masses of the people and their organized forces.

Contradictions

Q4. Can you definitely state what the main contradiction is in the world today?

The main contradiction today is between the imperialist powers and the oppressed peoples and nations. It is so in two respects: first, because imperialist oppression and exploitation are most intensive and extensive among the oppressed peoples and nations; and second, because armed revolutions led by revolutionary parties of the proletariat are today taking place in Asia, Africa and Latin America and will probably increase and intensify before a global war can break out among the imperialists or before the proletariat can seize power from the monopoly bourgeoisie in any imperialist country.

Nowhere other than in Asia, Africa, and Latin America are there armed revolutionary movements led by the proletariat and actively fighting imperialism and seeking to seize political power in the process. No matter how few these armed revolutionary movements still are, they have the potential of increasing rapidly amidst the grave crisis of the world capitalist system.

Q5. *Is the contradiction between imperialists and countries or states assertive of national independence a distinct development of a major contradiction or is it simply a ramification of the main contradiction?*

The contradiction between imperialists and countries or states assertive of national independence is distinctly a major contradiction in the world. It may be described as an outgrowth or ramification of the basic contradiction between the imperialists and oppressed peoples and nations, as well as an offshoot of contradictions among imperialist powers.

The US has already waged wars of aggression against such countries as Iraq, Yugoslavia, and Afghanistan that have invoked their national independence against US impositions. It has also blacklisted some eleven countries as targets of US military intervention supposedly for harboring terrorist cells but in fact for asserting their independence and national interests against US imperialist impositions.

In the wake of the aggression against Afghanistan, Bush has called North Korea, Iran and Iraq the "axis of evil". The US continues to be wary of China and Russia, which even though no longer socialist can be assertive of their national interest and national independence.

The contradiction between imperialists and countries or states assertive of national independence is of distinct importance, as evidenced by the accomplished wars of aggression against Iraq, Yugoslavia and Afghanistan and by the continuing ravings and threats of the US against "rogue states" and "terrorist-harboring" states.

The US has gone as far as to announce that it is ready to commit aggression unilaterally against any country in Asia, Africa and Latin America when collective action under the name of NATO or the UN Security Council is not possible or is undesirable to the US.

Q6. Historically, the last time socialism and national liberation movements made significant advances was in connection with WWII. The US response was to launch the Cold War and head the imperialist alliance. This alliance seems to be holding. Even Russia is happy to be a "partner." What are the prospects of inter-imperialist contradictions flaring up and unintentionally stimulating revolutionary movements?

The imperialist countries have their contradictions over economic, trade, financial, military and other interests and policies. But so far they have managed to settle their differences amicably, for two reasons: the well-developed mechanisms for settling problems and, more importantly, a big mass of client states to which they can still shift the burden of the crisis.

For the US-led imperialist alliance to crack and give way to bitter inter-imperialist strife, the crisis of the world capitalist system must continue to worsen until class struggle in imperialist countries becomes very acute and chauvinist and fascist currents run high and one or more imperialist countries start to challenge US hegemony.

Right now, among European imperialists, there are grumblings over the fact that the US tends to act unilaterally on various issues. Also over the fact that while the US demands financial burden-sharing in undertaking acts of aggression and seeks to reduce US casualties by using multination troops, it collects most of the spoils after successful collective acts of aggression such as those against Iraq, Yugoslavia and Afghanistan.

In these aggressive wars, the US has tightened its control over the oil supply from the Middle East, the Caspian Sea and Central Asia. It is frustrating plans for more direct oil routes (alternative to those controlled by the US) from sources in the former Soviet Union to Central and Western Europe as well as to China, Japan and Korea.

The US has gone deeply into Central and South Asia. It is bound to collide against the interests of Russia and China in Central Asia or arouse fears that it is trying to outflank the two countries. It is also bound to run into trouble in trying to satisfy both India and Pakistan, whose reactionary leaders like to grandstand with nuclear weapons in their hands for rousing their people's support domestically.

Using history as a guide, one can say that inter-imperialist contradictions become fiercer when the economic crisis leads to an overt struggle for a re-division of the world, when it produces fascist rule in one or more imperialist countries and when just any one of the imperialist powers or one of their client states generates incidents to upset the balance in the whole situation.

Currently, the US under the Bush regime is taking the lead in warmongering, in launching aggression and in pushing fascist laws in its own home ground as well as in the whole world.

Q7. *Is there a possibility that nuclear weapons would come into play in an inter-imperialist war and place humankind at risk?*

There is such a possibility. Political and military strategists of the imperialist powers continue to consider nuclear weapons for blackmail, for deterrence and for actual use. We cannot write off the possibility of nuclear powers using nuclear weapons in an all-out inter-imperialist war as we confront the possession of such weapons by the imperialist powers.

So far, nuclear war has been averted because mutually assured destruction between warring nuclear powers is a deterrent. But the people and the revolutionary forces can preempt or stop nuclear war by overthrowing the counterrevolutionary state possessing nuclear weapons. They can turn the threat of nuclear war into an urgent necessity and justification for waging revolutionary civil war.

The US is still the only country in the world to use the atom bomb to annihilate entire city populations. It is also uniquely the only country waving the nuclear first-strike doctrine to ceaselessly threaten other countries. The Bush regime has made matters worse by deciding to build the US missile defense system and vociferously threatening other countries with a preemptive nuclear attack.

This insanely arrogant position of the US challenges and invites some of its enemies to circumvent the missile defense system by a resort to miniature or "luggage" nuclear bombs that can be emplaced in advance and detonated at strategic points in the US. The September 11 attackers demonstrated how the US can be attacked from within and thus how its missile defense system can be rendered superfluous or useless. As in the principle of judo, the very armed strength of the US can be turned against it.

Q8. *How is the basic contradiction in imperialist countries between labor and capital developing? What are the prospects of socialism in the imperialist countries? Or is fascism the likelier prospect?*

All the three global centers of capitalism are reeling from the crisis of overproduction and from the financial collapse and bankruptcy of an increasing number of giant corporations. Formerly inflated corporate assets are now being deflated because of huge losses and falling profits, nonpayment of bank loans and sell offs in the stock markets.

Two big waves of mass disemployment have occurred in the last decade. The earlier wave consisted of mass layoffs in the drive to raise production through the increase of constant capital (high-tech equipment, plant and raw materials) and decrease of variable capital (wage fund) in order to maximize profit. The recent and current wave consists of mass layoffs resulting from production cutbacks and bankruptcies, following the drastic drop in consumer demand, excess stock inventories and shrinkage of the market.

Under current conditions of economic crisis in the industrial capitalist countries, the class struggle between the monopoly bourgeoisie and the proletariat is bound to intensify in an all-round way. Great opportunities have been opened by these conditions for communist and workers' parties, and other subjective forces to grow in strength and effectively fight the ruling system of the monopoly bourgeoisie.

Strikes and protest actions of workers, women, youth and other people against the ruling system are surging. Even in the US, the Battle of Seattle against the WTO broke out in 1999 and was followed by similar militant protest actions in various capitals of the imperialist countries. But there is still the crying need for rebuilding communist and workers' parties based on Marxism-Leninism.

At the same time, fascist formations have already arisen in various imperialist countries. The monopoly bourgeoisie and its ideologues and propagandists have long bred the culture of anti-communism, creeping fascism, chauvinism, racism and sexism. They are an active force for deflecting the attention of the working class from the class struggle and for opposing the development of the revolutionary party of the proletariat.

Aiming for socialism in imperialist countries is not a simple matter of the workers freeing themselves from the bureaucratic control of the labor aristocrats and from the pro-imperialist ideological influence of the petty bourgeoisie and peacefully taking over the existing economy and technology. The working class must win the battle for democracy by mobilizing the entire people, seizing the initiative from all forces and institutions directed by the monopoly bourgeoisie and defeating the forces of fascism and finally the bourgeois state system of violence.

Socialism's Re-emergence

Q9. What are the odds of socialism reemerging in countries where it was established but eventually defeated? How would the revolutionary forces and the people carry the socialist cause forward? What role should they play in confronting the escalation of oppression and exploitation by the imperialists and local reactionaries?

The odds are great against the re-emergence of socialism in those countries because for several decades the revisionist renegades had misrepresented themselves as communists, and at the same time misrepresented the process of capitalist restoration as a process of strengthening socialism. The revisionist renegades have ascribed to Marxism-Leninism, socialism and the communist party the revisionist practice of oppressing and exploiting the people.

Even after fully and openly restoring capitalism, after casting away the communist and socialist signboards, the new ruling bourgeoisies have added their voices to the imperialists in heaping blame on socialism for the continuing and ever more drastic deterioration and breakdown of social conditions. Thus, the enemies of socialism strike two blows against the socialist cause. The revisionists inflict a double whammy on the proletariat and the people.

Wherever socialism has been defeated and capitalism is restored, the proletariat and the rest of the people are subjected not only to massive doses of anticommunist and antisocialist propaganda. The new bourgeoisie is always poised to use the coercive apparatuses of the bourgeois state to suppress any revolutionary movement.

But a proletarian revolutionary party can keep alive the revolutionary legacy, including the works of Marx, Engels, Lenin, Stalin and Mao and the people's collective memory of the achievements in socialist revolution and construction through constant ideological, political and organizational work.

The time will certainly come when references to the revolutionary legacy and the current revolutionary slogans will rouse the proletariat and people to clamor for revolutionary change. That will be when the crisis becomes so severe that the new bourgeoisie will no longer be able to rule a people determined to wage revolution and when a revolutionary party arises and develops to lead them.

Despite great odds, the proletarian revolutionary parties in the countries where socialism has been reversed may still have better chances of bringing about socialism than those of some countries in the third world where the socioeconomic conditions are extremely backward and where a communist or workers' party has not yet taken root.

The proletariat and the people that succeed in bringing back socialism in countries where it was defeated will certainly play a great role in the anti-imperialist struggle by reducing once more the economic territory for imperialist exploitation and by being able to contribute further to the advance of the world proletarian-socialist revolution and the broad anti-imperialist movement.

Q10. For a materialist, you lay great emphasis on subjective factors. Isn't this contradictory?

I lay great emphasis on subjective factors because we deal with social change, especially radical social change. Conditions of crisis are not enough. The old social system will not collapse on its own dead weight no matter how decadent and moribund it is. The subjective forces, *i.e.*, the conscious and organized forces, must act on the objective conditions. They must develop to bring the revolution to victory.

To be a materialist, more precisely a dialectical materialist, one must take into account the unity of opposites in things and processes, in the relationship of matter and consciousness and in the interaction of objective material conditions and subjective forces in the relative maintenance or in revolutionary transformation of society.

Revolutionary ideas can develop from fighting the oppressive and exploitative social conditions. They become a material force when they are grasped by the masses and translated into action by them. The subjective forces are the conscious and organized masses in the revolutionary party of the proletariat, the people's army, the mass organizations and organs of political power.

As Lenin taught us, there can be no revolutionary movement without a revolutionary theory. Thus, the first requisite in the building of the revolutionary party of the proletariat is ideological building in Marxism-Leninism.

Consequent to theoretical education is the mass political education in the general line of new-democratic revolution in semi-feudal and semicolonial or neocolonial countries; and the general line of socialism in the developed capitalist countries. The revolutionary consciousness of the masses must continuously be raised so that they can be mobilized for the advance and victory of the revolution.

Q11. *Is it sufficient to go back to Mao's teachings on combating revisionism and preventing the restoration of capitalism? How do you handle the past, present and future in the struggle for socialism?*

It is necessary, but not sufficient, to simply go back to Mao's most advanced teachings on consolidating socialism, combating revisionism and preventing the restoration of capitalism. There must be a good combination of upholding revolutionary principles and taking into account conditions peculiar to a country and the new conditions in the world.

The achievements of the past and positive and negative lessons learned from experience must be carried over to the present. Further, the accumulated achievements and lessons available at present must be the basis for advancing into the future. The general direction of the revolutionary process is from capitalism through socialism to communism.

In the course of establishing socialism, the revolutionary forces and people gain all-round strength by overcoming all obstacles put up by the imperialists and the local reactionaries and by making full use of favorable objective conditions.

To win the socialist revolution, the revolutionary party of the proletariat must in the first place adopt and carry forward the revolutionary principles of Marxism-Leninism from Marx to Mao, up to Mao's theory and practice of continuing revolution under proletarian dictatorship.

The advanced detachment of the proletariat must learn positive and negative lessons from the experience of the proletariat in order to develop further the winning theory and practice of the revolution. The proletarian party wields criticism and self-criticism, the rectification movement, the socialist education movement and the cultural revolution as weapons for combating opportunism and revisionism.

The new material conditions are unfavorable to the big bourgeoisie and favorable to the proletariat in the long run. Let us consider high technology, particularly microchip technology. The big bourgeoisie has used it to accelerate transactions and processes related to production, trade and finance.

One result is that the microchip technology has pushed the crisis of overproduction and the rapid concentration of capital in the hands of the big bourgeoisie. It has facilitated fantastic scales and levels of financial speculation. It has speeded up communications and the spread of disinformation and the most absurd kinds of entertainment.

Under socialism, microchip technology can be used to advance the class struggle against the opponents of socialism, gather and analyze the most accurate information for economic planning and planned production, accelerate the processes of production, respond to the immediate and long-term needs of the people, to promote the active participation of the masses in democratic processes and all kinds of social activity and to raise the level of education and culture on the widest scale.

Q12. Time and again, I have heard people of various left formations speak of the need for a New International. Is there a possibility of this becoming a reality? When and how?

All serious communist and workers' parties affirm that they are inspired by the principle of proletarian internationalism. They express the determination to wage revolution in their respective countries and thereby advance the world proletarian revolution.

A new International, with a definite organized structure is bound to arise from the resurgence of the international communist movement. It is germinating in the general development of revolutionary struggles led by the communist and workers' parties.

It is important for communists to cite the need and to call for a new International. It is fine that conferences and seminars of communist and workers' parties are being held to clarify the situation and line of revolutionary struggle. The ideological and political ground is being laid for a new International.

However, it is still difficult to say when the New International can be formally established. The most effective way to prepare its establishment is for the communist and workers parties to win great victories in the struggle against imperialism, revisionism and reaction in their respective countries. Someday the Marxist-Leninist International will be based in a strong socialist country.

On Globalization

Q13. How can the people carry forward the struggle against imperialist globalization? What are their chances of succeeding? What have you done by way of promoting this struggle?

All over the world, the proletariat and the people are struggling against imperialist "globalization". While the crisis of the world capitalist system is sharpening and deepening, they are raising their anti-imperialist consciousness and building the anti-imperialist and democratic organizations in various countries. They are waging legal mass protest actions, putting forward their demands and clamoring for fundamental changes towards a democratic, just and prosperous society free of imperialism and reaction.

The revolutionary parties of the proletariat are preparing for the seizure of political power in order to change the entire ruling system. In certain countries, such parties are leading the new democratic revolutions through protracted people's war. People's war will arise in more countries and help bring about the rise of armed revolution in the imperialist countries.

The spirit of proletarian internationalism and broad international solidarity against imperialism are energizing the proletariat and the people. An international united front of all anti-imperialist and democratic forces is developing.

I am confident that the proletariat and the people will win greater victories from year to year against imperialist globalization. The current US warmongering, wars of aggression and stepping up of war production will aggravate and deepen the crisis of the world capitalist system. The broad masses of the people will continue to raise the level of their consciousness and resistance against escalating oppression and exploitation.

To contribute my bit to the struggle, I have written articles and delivered speeches to sum up and analyze the crisis of the world capitalist system, condemn imperialist globalization and war and clarify the tasks towards defeating imperialism and reaching the goals of national liberation, democracy and socialism. I have given briefings to numerous delegations going to conferences or mass actions against the imperialist-organized conferences.

I am proud to have chaired the International Initiative Committee, which founded the International League of Peoples' Struggle. The ILPS aims to bring together and coordinate the anti-imperialist and progressive forces that have emerged against "free market" globalization and imperialist war.

Q14. *The underlying worldview of a greater part of the current anti-imperialist movement—such as the anti-WTO mobilizations, anti-sweatshop movement, debt relief coalitions, etc.—is more liberal than*

Marxist. As a matter of fact, a strong anticommunist thread runs through the various organizations which are, by and large, single-issue—i.e., environment, bread-and-butter unionism, immigrant and migrant rights, etc. While people's wars and communist parties gain from these mobilizations and movements, there is the debit side of having to contend with anticommunist thinking and the dissemination thereof within, ironically enough, an anti-imperialist front. How should Marxist-Leninist parties conduct themselves in this situation?

It is necessary for Marxist-Leninist parties to develop a broad united front with bourgeois liberals and other political forces that are to some extent reactionary or anticommunist but are relatively better than the force identified as the enemy in a given period of time.

Thus, Marxist-Leninist parties have directly or indirectly allied themselves with a broad range of political forces that oppose US imperialism, the US-led imperialist alliance, IMF, World Bank and WTO and various policies and manifestations of these inimical forces.

By being sectarian, parties of the proletariat cannot realize and advance the revolutionary movement and instead will isolate themselves from the people. They need to reach the broad masses of the people in their millions (whatever may be the given level of their political consciousness) through the broad united front. Those who profess Marxism-Leninism cannot simply demand that other political forces adopt their ideological position; they need to work at arousing, organizing and mobilizing the masses to be able to raise their political consciousness and activity to a progressive or revolutionary level.

In developing the broad united front against imperialism, Marxist-Leninist parties must maintain independence and initiative and must engage in unity and struggle. Unity means going into concerted actions with various political forces and the masses on certain common political grounds against the common enemy. Struggle means putting forward and explaining the line that serves the interest of the broad masses of the people and mobilizes them, keeping intact the revolutionary core principles of the Marxist-Leninist party, ensuring the progressive direction of the common front and countering any attempt to mislead the revolutionary mass movement.

The broad united front may or may not be formally organized. The allied forces may have conferential, coordinating or liaison organs. To maintain unity in a necessary alliance and yet engage in struggle, the

Marxist-Leninist parties must continue the common cause and common action and at the same time engage in struggle on just and reasonable grounds, with restraint and in the persuasive style.

Q15. *You said earlier that the big bourgeoisie uses petty-bourgeois ideas and concepts to deceive the people. Can you explain how this is done?*

The big bourgeoisie describes its own ruling political system as "liberal democracy" and its economic system as "free enterprise" or "free market" economy. Thereby, it conceals the reality of the class dictatorship of the bourgeoisie and the reality of monopoly capitalism.

Bourgeois constitutions use liberal language to draw a bill of rights. In the abstraction of the rights of the individual vis-à-vis the powers of the state, the big bourgeoisie and the working people are lumped together as classless individuals. The right of the big bourgeoisie to own the means of production and exploit the working class takes cover under the abstracted right of the individual to private property for their personal enjoyment and the pursuit of liberty and happiness.

The right of the big bourgeoisie to persecute and oppress its class opponents likewise takes cover under the abstracted freedoms of the individual as well as under exceptional clauses for emergency rule, suspension of the writ of habeas corpus, martial law and the like.

The term "free market" in "neoliberal" globalization is a clear case of imperialist use of petty-bourgeois concepts and language. Nowadays, the imperialists also fund so-called nongovernmental organizations run by petty-bourgeois functionaries to promote such concepts as "civil society" and "culture of peace" to deny the violent and oppressive character of the bourgeois state and denounce armed revolution.

Since a long time ago, the big bourgeoisie has used political agents recruited from the ranks of the petty bourgeois intellectuals in order to misrepresent socialism in petty-bourgeois terms. I refer to social democrats, who peddle bourgeois liberalism among the workers by giving it a socialist dress. In recent decades, the big bourgeoisie has also used pacifism and environmentalism to promote supra-class illusions in a subtle manner for undermining the revolutionary cause of the proletariat.

Bourgeois feminism has been used to draw away women from the revolutionary national and class struggle towards some kind of supraclass struggle between men and women. Chauvinism and ethno-centrism have been used to fragment in a petty bourgeois manner what is otherwise a comprehensive understanding of the class struggle and the need for partisanship to the revolutionary class.

Class Struggle

Q16. How do the monopoly bourgeoisie and the proletariat carry out the class struggle in the various aspects of the capitalist society? And how does such struggle continue in socialist society?

The bourgeoisie seeks to maintain the capitalist relations of production in order to control the forces of production (the proletariat and the means of production) and continue to extract surplus value from the proletariat. But the proletariat wages trade union struggle in order to improve wage and living conditions. It further carries out the class struggle at a higher level under the leadership of the revolutionary party of the proletariat.

The capitalist relations of production cannot be done away with, unless the workers rise to a level of revolutionary consciousness and militant activity that enable them to take advantage of the crisis of the capitalist ruling system, seize political power and establish the class dictatorship of the proletariat.

After the bourgeoisie loses political power and ownership of the means of production, the proletariat consolidates the political power that it has seized and proceeds to carry out socialist revolution and construction. Within the socialist society, however, the bourgeoisie harbors a deep resentment over its loss of ownership or control of the means of production and is driven to use the superstructure to return to a dominant class position.

Unrepentant bourgeois elements can pretend to have remolded themselves and seek to penetrate the organs of political leadership and cultural institutions in order to propagate their old ideas. New petty-bourgeois minded elements can also arise from the new crop of bureaucrats and intellectuals in the economic, political and cultural institutions.

If the revolutionary party of the proletariat relaxes vigilance and fails at maintaining and constantly developing revolutionary consciousness, the bourgeois elements in the superstructure would be able to put forward revisionist ideas and policies, which are in fact bourgeois but which they disguise as proletarian or as "classless" or "universal".

Within a socialist society, the proletariat must continue the class struggle against the bourgeoisie for a whole historical epoch until socialism defeats imperialism on a global scale and communism becomes possible. If such class struggle were not carried out, the revisionists would take power and restore capitalism.

Q17. *How do imperialists use religious bigotry and chauvinism to deceive the people? Nowadays, religious fundamentalism and ethnic conflicts run rampant in many backward countries. What is the relationship of such ultra-reactionary phenomena to imperialism?*

As a decadent and moribund type of capitalism, imperialism uses the most reactionary ideas and forces in order to preserve its political and economic power. It does so in both the industrial capitalist countries and in the backward countries.

Hitler manipulated the old Christian bias against the Jews as "Christ killers" in order to rouse the Germans to join the Nazi party. He blamed the Jews for the defeat of Germany in World War I and for the impositions made by the victors on Germany. He further whipped up the chauvinist notion of a superior Aryan race.

The US and other imperialists have long instigated and stirred up chauvinism, racism, ethnocentrism, religious bigotry and fundamentalism, and communal conflicts in order to suppress or undermine the communists and other progressive forces in the imperialist countries and abroad.

Right now, Islamic fundamentalism is so much in the news as the enemy of the West because some Islamic fundamentalist groups have turned against the US. But the US had systematically promoted the very phenomenon of Islamic fundamentalism to prepare the massacre of more than one million Indonesians in 1965 and to counter the influence of the Soviet Union in Central Asia, Middle East and Africa.

The US and other imperialists have also promoted Christian charismatic groups and Christian parties as a counterforce to the communists and progressive forces in Eastern Europe, Latin America and elsewhere. The imperialists and local reactionaries have also fielded armed pseudo-religious fanatical groups to fight the revolutionaries.

But communists and other revolutionaries have successfully worked to arouse, organize and mobilize the broad masses of the people on social problems and on the revolutionary solution, to avoid religious controversies and to expose and frustrate the imperialist use of the most reactionary ideas and forces.

In the Philippines, communists and other revolutionaries have had a fine record in avoiding religious controversies, in frustrating the imperialists and local reactionaries in using religion against the revolutionary movement and in proactively cooperating with the Christians for National Liberation and the Moro Revolutionary Organization as allies within the NDFP. The NDFP has also forged an alliance with the Moro Islamic Liberation Front. It has promoted mutual understanding and fellowship among Christians, Muslims and other people of faith as well as nonbelievers.

Q18. *In the next 10-20 years, where do you see the US and other imperialist powers taking serious blows and consequently weakening and suffering defeats and setbacks?*

Events most adverse to the US and other imperialist powers can take place in Asia, Africa, Latin America and the former revisionist-ruled countries in Eastern Europe, before the imperialist powers directly confront each other in the struggle for a re-division of the world and before any revolutionary upheaval within any major imperialist country.

The economic and social disasters and the political turmoil in the semicolonies, dependent and retrogressive countries will result in a further contraction of the global market for the imperialist powers, the rise of people's war and other armed revolutionary movements, and more intense contradictions between the imperialists and some states assertive of national independence.

The imperialists will try to avoid a break up of the alliance that they built and used against the Soviet Union during the Cold War and that they continue to use consistently against the oppressed peoples and nations. But they are prone to drastic changes of policy because of worsening economic crisis and the rise of the reactionary forces in the imperialist camp.

The US has taken advantage of its own imperialist allies in promoting "free market" globalization and has grabbed all or most of such spoils as oil resources, supply routes, military contracts and reconstruction projects from their victories in the wars of aggression against Iraq, Yugoslavia and Afghanistan. Conflicts are beginning to surface between the US and its own imperialist allies over the division of spoils in the Middle East, Balkans, Central Asia, South Asia, East Asia, Latin America and Africa.

While the crisis of the world capitalist system worsens, the people waging revolution, the nations fighting for liberation and the countries asserting national independence can induce the development of revolutionary movements of the proletariat and the rest of the people in imperialist countries.

Moribund Capitalism

Q19. The cycle of busts and booms continues even now in the US, as a process of "creative destruction" leading to fewer but bigger and stronger monopoly firms and a stronger US imperialism and a stronger US-led imperialist alliance. Are there developments affecting the balance of power among the imperialists?

Imperialism, clearly more than ever, is moribund capitalism. The concentration of high technology and finance-capital in a few imperialist countries means the long-term ruin of all other countries and the general stagnation and increasingly worse recurrence of busts in those few imperialist countries.

The crisis of overproduction now involves all types of goods, raw materials (agricultural and mineral), basic industrial goods and high-tech goods. It has caused a chain of financial collapses involving huge amounts of bad loans, unredeemable bonds and sinking stock values. The heavy overhang of fictitious or speculative capital has fallen hard on the real economy, exposing widespread bankruptcies and making it difficult for the monopoly bourgeoisie and its states to stimulate economic recovery.

The current global capitalist crisis and the drastic contraction of the global market are increasingly straining the relationship of the US with its imperialist allies as well as some puppet states. Eventually, the struggle for a re-division of the world among the imperialist powers will become conspicuous. Japan and European Union cannot be predisposed indefinitely to accept their being at the short end of relations with the US.

The crisis of the world capitalist system has brought intolerable hardships to the proletariat and the people. But at the same time, the crisis itself offers them the opportunity to develop their revolutionary strength. Imperialist crises and wars have generated the favorable conditions for new-democratic and socialist revolutions.

The Philippine Situation

Q20. Do you foresee developments in East Asia which will help advance the Philippine revolution?

The countries of Southeast Asia will continue competing with each other in producing and exporting raw materials and low value-added semi-manufactures. In turn, China's cheaper semi-manufactures will push out of the global market the semi-manufactures exported by Southeast Asia.

The aspirations of the people for national industrialization in the Philippines and the rest of Southeast Asia will be frustrated by the propensity of Japan, South Korea, Taiwan and China to overproduce basic industrial products and consumer electronics.

The Filipino people will suffer terribly from being unable to produce and export any type of goods not in oversupply in the global market. They will be unable to cover the country's trade deficits and payment for its mounting foreign debt. The export of contract workers will certainly slacken because of the global slump and the competition offered by so many other impoverished countries.

The exacerbation of the economic and social suffering of the people will make the ground even more fertile for people's war in the Philippines and the rest of Southeast Asia. It is of crucial importance for the people in one or several neighboring countries, especially Indonesia, to wage people's war.

The US has a dual policy of engagement and containment towards China. Engagement is now the principal aspect of the policy as the US is supporting the "liberalization" of Chinese economy and politics. But the US is prepared to put containment on a higher gear should China turn unwieldy in any way.

The Philippine revolution will benefit from any manifestation of anti-imperialist defiance from China and North Korea against a higher level of US aggressiveness towards them. Moreover, any grave deterioration of the Chinese social economy will result in a sustained political turmoil and the probable resurgence of the Left in China, most probably starting outside of the ruling communist party.

Q21. What is the general direction of the ruling system in the Philippines?

The ruling system of big compradors and landlords in the Philippines is rotten and doomed. Its adoption of privatization, deregulation and liberalization under the US-directed neo-liberal policy stress of "free market" globalization has aggravated and deepened its crisis.

This policy stress reduces the puppet state to being a mere tax collector and guarantor of foreign loans under conditions of prolonged depression.

The Philippines cannot offer anything to the world capitalist market except goods already in oversupply, like raw materials and low value-added semi-manufactures.

The reactionary government cannot even pretend to be for national industrialization and land reform. The ruling system has no interest in transforming the agrarian and semi-feudal economy into an industrial capitalist one.

Any reactionary ruling clique in the Philippines easily becomes the much-hated enemy of the people as it escalates exploitation and oppression. The people see it as corrupt, repressive, mendacious and as an unmitigated puppet.

Q22. How will the revolutionary movement develop? What are the chances for victory of protracted people's war?

The revolutionary movement of the people is developing steadily under the leadership of the CPP. The unwavering general line is the new-democratic revolution through protracted people's war. The chronic crisis and continuous deterioration of the domestic ruling system and the world capitalist system guarantee the continuous advance of the movement.

The protracted people's war is expanding and intensifying. It integrates the revolutionary armed struggle with genuine land reform and mass-base building. Every advance in the people's war is well founded on the expansion and consolidation of the mass base.

The more than 128 guerrilla fronts will eventually develop into stable base areas. These will arise from adjoining guerrilla fronts that expand and merge with each other. The guerrilla fronts in every region will increasingly coordinate and conjoin under the leadership of the regional Party committee and its regional NPA command. Regional strike forces of the NPA will use the guerrilla fronts as staging areas for tactical offensives and thus further strengthen and galvanize the links among the guerrilla fronts in every region. In turn, the stable base areas will develop, expand and conjoin to become liberated areas. Ultimately, the entire nation will be liberated.

Through tactical offensives, the NPA will advance from its current stage of strategic defensive to the strategic stalemate and finally to the strategic offensive. The armed strength of the revolution is accumulated in the countryside over a long period until it becomes capable of defeating the enemy in the cities and on a nationwide scale.

The revolutionary forces and people in the Philippines expect that armed revolutionary movements abroad and the overextension of the US on a global scale would help the new-democratic revolution in the Philippines before, during and after its victory.

Q23. How do you weigh the costs of waging armed revolution against the costs of keeping the current ruling system?

The costs of keeping the reactionary ruling system are far higher than the costs of waging armed revolution. Exploitation and oppression exact a terrible toll on the people and are precisely what drive the people to wage armed revolution.

We should be able to see the high cost of the violence of daily exploitation to recognize the necessity and lower cost of armed revolution. The people decide to wage armed revolution when they are already fed up with the unjust and rotten ruling system. In waging the armed revolution, they stand a chance of winning and instituting a just and progressive social order.

War Technology

Q24. Is it not possible for the Indonesian solution—i.e., large-scale massacres, thoroughly wiping out communists, their families and organizations, to the millions if necessary—to be applied to the Philippine revolutionary movement?

That evil kind of solution is not possible because the CPP has been underground for a long, long time and has avoided exposing its membership. To kill all or most communists, the reactionaries would have to engage in large-scale massacres, kill too many non-communists on mere suspicion and make a lot of big mistakes in a trice.

You know how reckless anticommunists are even in propaganda. They denounce as communists all patriots and progressives in the national-democratic movement. Any regime trying to destroy the CPP through massacres would be overthrown by a broad anti-fascist united front because such a regime would indiscriminately target a huge part of the population.

The imperialists and reactionaries have continuously unleashed anticommunist campaigns of suppression since 1969. But they have failed to destroy the revolutionary forces. They used the Marcos fascist dictatorship for 14 years to try to destroy the revolutionary movement. Instead, the movement grew in strength. It is difficult for the reactionary military forces to kill communists who are at the core of a growing armed revolutionary movement.

The Indonesian communists in 1965 were vulnerable to mass arrests and massacres because their party had been very much exposed in open mass activities and they had no people's army carrying out a people's war. The PKI had no definite line to wage a protracted people's war in the face of the US-Suharto scheme of military fascism and wide-scale massacres.

Q25. In the wake of the September 11 attacks and US aggression in Afghanistan, US military forces have entered the Philippines for combat. The US and the Manila government say that those forces are deployed merely to train the puppet troops and yet boast that they are there for combat as part of the "global assault on terrorism". Is there a legal basis for the foreign troops to participate in combat operations? Do they have targets and objectives, apart from the Abu Sayyaf and so-called terrorist groups?

Even under the legal system of the reactionary government, there is no basis for the US military forces to participate in combat operations in the Philippines. The GRP constitution prohibits foreign military bases, foreign combat troops and foreign military facilities, unless by treaty. The US has no treaty with the Philippines allowing it to deploy US troops for military operations against Filipinos in combat zones.

The US-RP Mutual Defense Treaty allows the US troops to come to the Philippines and help Philippine troops only in case of an attack on the Philippines by an external aggressor. The Abu Sayyaf is a tiny local bandit gang engaged chiefly in kidnap-for-ransom operations.

The Visiting Forces Agreement allows only joint US-RP annual training exercises in non-combat zones and only for a four-week duration. It does not allow US troops to carry live ammunition. Neither does it allow them to be in combat zones for combat operations for as long as six months to one year.

By engaging in military intervention, with the agreement of the Macapagal-Arroyo regime, the US is establishing military bases and facilities and is preparing the ground for fighting the New People's Army, which it has blacklisted as a terrorist organization.

The US wants to entrench itself militarily in Mindanao in order to tighten its control over the oil and other natural resources in the Philippines,

Indonesia, Brunei and Malaysia as well as the trade routes linking these countries. In this connection, the US has been using a divide-and-rule policy by stirring up and manipulating religious and ethnic conflicts, and in the process has weakened its own puppet governments. The US has conjured the specter of an expansionist China to instill fear among its puppets and justify the "protective" presence of US military bases and facilities in the region.

Q26. Considering the recent devastating attack on Afghanistan, aren't you concerned about the war technology the US can bring to bear upon a peasant army? Do you think Filipinos will not only endure but also prevail over the unimaginable suffering a high-tech attack will bring? How will the NPA fare in such a confrontation?

The patriotism of the Filipino people should not be underestimated. They fought long and hard for the removal of the US military bases. They succeeded in removing these in 1991. Rallying to the revolutionary forces, they are ceaselessly asserting national sovereignty and territorial integrity against the intervention of the US military forces.

The patriotic and progressive forces constantly remind the people that US military forces killed 1.5 million Filipinos from 1899 to 1913. Any US bombing that would kill Filipino civilians is bound to ignite a powerful and sustained storm of popular outrage and revolutionary offensives.

Asserting national sovereignty, the Filipino people have the will to fight US military intervention and aggression. They are capable of waging a protracted people's war for national liberation and democracy against the US and the local exploiting classes. For a long period of time, they can use both guerrilla warfare and regular mobile warfare. They can draw plenty of lessons from their own rich experience and from the experience of the Vietnamese people in their war against US aggression.

The social and physical terrain in the Philippines is favorable for people's war. The people's army can inflict casualties on US ground troops and capture US prisoners and weapons. Night-vision goggles, electronic trackers or sensors and other sophisticated gadgets in the hands of US and puppet troops can eventually fall into the hands of the NPA fighters.

The US cannot effectively use the satellites, cruise missiles and other high-tech weapons against a highly mobile people's army, with inexhaustible mass support. Such weapons can be effective only against governments defending fixed and exposed physical structures, whose monetary value is higher than that of the missiles and bombs used in their destruction. It would be self-defeating for the US imperialists to use cruise missiles against the improvised nipa huts of the people's army.

Of course, the time will come when the revolutionary government takes over the national capital region and becomes responsible for the defense of the fixed and exposed structures there. But by then, there shall have been significant changes in the international environment as to render US use of cruise missiles and other high-tech weapons pointless or useless against the Philippines. For instance, would the US overexert itself in the Philippines while incurring more losses elsewhere?

Q27. Those in the women's movement are understandably angered by the return of US troops in the Philippines. The origins of large-scale prostitution and sex trafficking can be traced to the US military bases. Would the New People's Army act to discourage US troops from patronizing brothels?

I presume that the NPA will act in many ways to discourage US troops from patronizing brothels in the Philippines.

The opposition of the women's movement to the encroachment of US troops on Philippine territory as a violation of national sovereignty and of womanhood is correct. It is outrageous that the presence of US military troops in the Philippines and elsewhere has promoted prostitution and sex trafficking on a wide scale.

Peace Talk Gains

Q28. If the revolutionary forces are so determined to win the new-democratic revolution through protracted people's war, why should the National Democratic Front of the Philippines engage in the peace negotiations with the Government of the Republic of the Philippines? How do peace negotiations jive with people's war?

The GRP has negotiated with the NDFP because it recognizes the growing strength of the revolutionary movement and no longer believes that purely military means can destroy the people's army. It seeks to use the peace negotiations as a complement to its offensive military campaigns. Its scheme is to use peace negotiations to try to deceive the people and to confuse the revolutionary forces.

However, The NDFP has its own objectives in agreeing to carry on peace negotiations with the GRP. A minimum objective is to frustrate the attempt of the reactionary government to present itself as the exponent of a just and lasting peace.

From the current negotiations, the NDFP has gained experience that will be useful for negotiating the surrender of enemy forces on the eve of the complete defeat of the reactionary ruling system. This is the complete opposite of the GRP attempt to use the peace negotiations for inducing the revolutionary movement to split or to capitulate.

Short of ending the armed revolution, certain agreements beneficial to the people and the revolutionary forces can be gained from the current negotiations. To cite one, there is the GRP-NDFP Comprehensive Agreement on Respect for Human Rights and International Humanitarian Law.

The NDFP has gained more opportunities to put forward the national and democratic demands of the people on a national and international scale. If the GRP does not satisfy the just and reasonable demands of the NDFP, then the justness and reasonableness of the armed revolution would be underscored.

The NDFP will continue to gain international or diplomatic recognition for the people's democratic government, first as a co-belligerent in the ongoing civil war and ultimately as the sole government of the Philippines. In this regard, the NDFP has deposited with the Swiss Federal Council its Declaration of Undertaking to Apply the Geneva Convention and Protocol I.

The NDFP can use the peace negotiations to keep open the possibility of a truce and of an alliance with the reactionary government to cooperate in confronting a bigger enemy. In the experience of China, the Chinese Communist Party and the Kuomintang agreed on a truce and alliance in order to fight the Japanese invaders in World War II.

The NDFP line of the peace negotiations is no different from that of the new-democratic revolution through protracted people's war. It is to seek the completion of the revolutionary struggle for national liberation and democracy. As a form of legal struggle, the peace negotiations are secondary to the daily legal mass struggles of the mass organizations. In turn, the legal forms of struggle are secondary to the revolutionary armed struggle, which is the overall main form of struggle.

However, if properly conducted, as it is now being properly conducted, the peace negotiations can put the NDFP on an equal footing with the GRP in the eyes of international law and the international community.

They can open the way for the NDFP or the people's democratic government to gain diplomatic recognition for its status of belligerency and to enter into agreements with foreign governments without these becoming liable for interference.

Q29. Why negotiate abroad? Is this for seeking diplomatic recognition for the NDFP status of belligerency? Why has GRP agreed to negotiate in a neutral venue abroad?

The NDFP and the GRP have agreed to negotiate in a neutral venue abroad because the NDFP has learned bitter lessons in negotiating with the GRP in Manila in 1986. NDFP personnel and friends were put under military surveillance; and later, information gained from such surveillance was used in lethal operations against the NDFP.

It is possible to negotiate in the territory controlled by the NDFP in the Philippines. But the GRP does not wish to recognize such territory of the NDFP. Thus, it would rather go to the neutral venue abroad. The NDFP also sees a disadvantage in exposing to the enemy the territory that it controls.

Seeking diplomatic recognition for the NDFP or the people's democratic government is a perfectly legitimate purpose for a revolutionary movement that has already acquired the status of belligerency by dint of hard struggle and has compelled the enemy to negotiate.

In representation of the revolutionary forces and people, the NDFP has come to a highly dignified position by negotiating with the GRP on an equal footing in the light of international law. The GRP-NDFP peace negotiations have enjoyed the endorsement and support of the European parliament by virtue of its resolutions in 1997 and 1999. They have benefited from the facilitation by the Dutch, Belgian and Norwegian governments.

Ensuring the Correct Path

Q30. In case you win, what guarantees do you have that mistakes and crimes, which have occurred, do not recur? What are the guarantees against such a phenomenon as modern revisionism?

Our victory in the new-democratic revolution would mean that we have gained a wealth of experience in dealing with problems, and that we have developed the principles, policies, processes and measures for dealing with them. The timely evaluation of work and criticism and self-criticism will continue to be an effective way of preventing the recurrence of previous mistakes. When serious mistakes become deeply rooted and gain wide influence, then a thoroughgoing rectification movement will have to be undertaken.

For dealing with crimes committed, the judicial system guarantees due process. The constitution of the people's democratic republic, under its bill of rights, guarantees that the accused is presumed innocent until proven guilty, that guilt is proven based on evidence and justice is properly meted out. We can distinguish political mistakes from criminal offenses even when these are interconnected.

To prevent the possible recurrence of modern revisionism, the CPP benefits from the study of the history of how Lenin and Mao defeated revisionism and also how revisionism destroyed socialism in several countries and from the CPP's own study and practice of combating revisionist and opportunist ideas within its own ranks.

Lessons learned from previous events serve as guide for preventing or combating the recurrence of mistakes, crimes and the phenomenon of modern revisionism. But these problems will have to be confronted under new concrete circumstances. This process requires a mastery of dialectical and historical materialism. There are no ready-made or bottled remedies for automatic application in the future.

Looking to the Future

Q31. After the seizure of political power in the Philippines, how do you think the CPP will manage the relationship between the working class and the peasantry?

The CPP will have to develop an even stronger basic alliance between the working class and the peasantry. This alliance is the political foundation of the new-democratic revolution. It also constitutes the foundation for building socialism, which requires the completion of land reform, the collectivization and mechanization of agriculture in stages and so on. Without the support of the peasantry, the working class cannot seize and consolidate political power.

The working class is the leading force while the peasantry is the main force in the new-democratic revolution and in the early stage of socialist revolution when the peasantry is still the largest class. The political combination of the working class and the peasantry is necessary for defeating imperialism and the local exploiting classes before and during the socialist revolution and construction.

In the socialist economy, industrialization is the leading factor and agriculture is the foundation. The peasants produce the food and raw materials for the workers in industry. In exchange, they get from the workers the manufactured consumer and producer goods.

The revolutionary party of the proletariat shall ensure a good balance among heavy industry, light industry and agriculture in order to avoid imposing a heavy burden on any part of the working people, to accelerate all-round economic development and to hasten their enjoyment of the benefits of socialism.

Eventually, the pre-socialist peasantry will disappear due to the collectivization and mechanization of agriculture and the absorption of the surplus labor in the rural areas by both rural and urban industries. Ultimately, the percentage of the working people devoted to agriculture will diminish upon the advance of socialist industrialization and urbanization.

Q32. What will be the future of women in socialist society in the Philippines?

Lenin has taught us that the proletariat cannot liberate itself without liberating women. Mao has also made the observation that women hold up half of heaven. I have always believed that participation in the revolution is a liberating process for women and is a measure of the advance of the revolution. Male comrades have a responsibility to fight against the oppression of women so as to encourage and advance this liberating process.

In the 1960s, we were very happy whenever we observed that women comprised at least 10 percent of the leadership and participation in meetings and mass actions. Now, we are getting far more than that, variably between 25 percent and 60 percent. The women's organizations and movement are necessary for the current and future struggles to assert women's economic, social, political and cultural rights as equal to those of men.

In the course of the new-democratic revolution, the women advance their struggle for gender equality by participating and assuming positions of responsibility as well as performing various other tasks traditionally reserved for or monopolized by males in feudal and semi-feudal society. In socialist society, women will find fulfillment and assume responsibilities on an equal footing with men. By their own struggle, they will achieve complete gender equality under socialism. By liberating themselves, the women help the men to liberate themselves from prejudices and material conditions that imprison and stifle them.

Q33. *How will the CPP maintain revolutionary consciousness among the youth from generation to generation?*

To win the new-democratic revolution, the CPP must be able to arouse, organize and mobilize the youth for revolutionary service to the people. It must be able to do likewise in socialist society. Otherwise, the youth would start to adopt all sorts of unhealthy notions and activities and stray away from the revolutionary road.

Under the leadership of the communist youth league, the youth can imbibe the revolutionary spirit in a national, scientific and mass culture and learn the theory and practice of Marxism-Leninism. The youth must actively contribute to the substance and style of revolutionary education and culture. Only thus can these be interesting to the youth.

The youth must engage in a proletarian cultural revolution to combat revisionism, degeneration among the bureaucrats and the antinational, antidemocratic and anti-people aspects of old habits, ideas and customs and to keep the great red banner of socialism flying high.

Q34. *To maintain a high level of dedication may have been easier in the immediate post-WWII period when there were socialist countries, which seemed to prove that socialism was possible. What would be the principal motivation for young men and women, a new generation, to hold on to the idea of first, the eventual victory of socialism; and second, that socialism can be sustained?*

It is true that because of the rise of several socialist countries and the great wave of national liberation movements in the period immediately after World War II, there was a high level of confidence in the victory of socialism and consequently a high level of dedication to the socialist cause among young men and women.

But let us not forget that the revolutionary youth then and afterwards recognized that the proletariat and the people harvested great victories by taking up the challenge and confronting the terrible assaults of the fascists before and during the war and resolutely and vigorously fighting them.

It is not true that dedication rises only with the assurance of current victories or with the hope of further victories. Suffering from the intolerable oppression and exploitation by the imperialists and local reactionaries can incite the youth of today to look for the revolutionary solution and to fight selflessly for the revolutionary cause.

In the early 1960s, we young Filipino revolutionaries were in the first place challenged to fight the enemy because of the Filipino people's suffering and only in the second place encouraged by the existence of socialist countries and the national liberation movements.

At that time, we had to revive the revolutionary movement from more than a decade of destruction by the enemy and the Right opportunism of the Jesus Lava clique. The most talented among us gave up self-gratifying opportunities in the ruling system in order to serve the people and their revolutionary cause.

The principal motivation of the young Filipino revolutionaries today is to do what is morally just, scientifically correct and politically effective for the Filipino proletariat and people to win national liberation and democracy. They wage the new-democratic revolution and look forward to a socialist future.

They are inspired by the proven all-round success of socialism during the time of Lenin, Stalin and Mao, and by Mao's theory and practice of continuing revolution under proletarian dictatorship to consolidate socialism, combat revisionism and prevent the restoration of capitalism.

They feel fortunate to be armed with the ideological weapons for socialist revolution and construction in the future, even as they feel challenged by the enemy to fight according to given circumstances at every stage of the Philippine revolution.

Q35. How will the CPP handle the national minorities in the Philippines? What about the Bangsamoro who are seeking secession or regional autonomy?

The CPP and the people's democratic republic respect the right of the Bangsamoro and other national minorities to self-determination. The socialist constitution is certain to guarantee their rights. Policies and measures shall be adopted to correct the historical and current wrongs against them in every social aspect.

It is alright for the Bangsamoro or Moro nation now to fight for secession from an oppressive state. The right to secede is encompassed by the right to self-determination. When a non-oppressive state guarantees their fundamental rights, regional autonomy and their legitimate interests, the exercise of the right to secede would not be necessary.

Nevertheless, the right to secede will continue to be guaranteed. It remains an inalienable right for them to invoke and exercise against any attempt of any part of the state or the population or an entire retrogressive state to oppress them.

Q36. *Nearly 10 percent of the population has left the Philippines to become migrant workers or permanent residents or even citizens of other countries. What is the policy towards them before and after the victory of the Philippine revolution?*

Before the victory of the new-democratic revolution, the policy is to call on them to support the revolution in any way they can, wherever they are. When they return to the Philippines, they can take roles and functions more actively in the revolution.

After the victory of the new-democratic revolution, the policy is to attract them back to the Philippines to help the motherland in any capacity. They can return permanently to participate continuously in socialist revolution and construction. Whether young or old, they as patriots can make their contributions.

They can continue living and working abroad if they wish to do so. But they can come for vacation and they can also retire in the Philippines. When they are in the Philippines, their profession, expertise, technical training and means can be mustered for the all-round social progress of their motherland.

Q37. *Do you think that the new-democratic revolution can win and the socialist revolution can begin in the Philippines within your lifetime?*

It is probable, but it is not certain. It is probable because of the continuing revolutionary efforts of the people in the Philippines and elsewhere. But I do not know exactly how long I shall live, one, two or three decades more, I do not know.

It does not matter to me whether or not I see the great victory of the new-democratic revolution in my lifetime. What matters to me is my striving to contribute the most and the best that I am capable of. I hope the successors to the revolutionary cause can benefit from the contributions of their predecessors and make greater strides in the revolutionary struggle.

Some Personal Considerations

Q38. The US has revived the CIA mission to undertake covert operations to assassinate anti-US leaders. Does this threat worry you?

Such a threat does not worry me. I exercise more caution than before but I enjoy my work and whatever leisure time I get. Comrades and I try to make it difficult for the CIA and its hired foreign assets to hit me; and ensure that even if I get hit, it would be difficult for the assassins to conceal themselves.

No longer do I take public rides alone nor move around without companions, without photographic and cell-phone coverage. We may not be able to stop my assassination. But we can make it so difficult as to make it demonstrable that only the US CIA can do it.

Q39. Are you not bored by having to be in exile for a very long time? When will you return to the Philippines? Under what conditions will you return?

I am not bored. As I told you before, I feel at home anywhere in the world because, after all, I am an internationalist. At any rate, I also manage to keep in close touch with our compatriots in the motherland through their visits and by e-mail and other electronic means.

Lenin and Ho Chi Minh were not bored at all during their exile despite far slower trains to and from Russia or the steamships to and from Indochina because they had more than enough work to do while waiting for the next mail from home.

I shall return to the Philippines when the NDFP decides to let me do so. My return should allow me to be helpful to the people's movement for national liberation and democracy.

Q40. We have spoken of possible developments over large scales of time and place, involving large forces. How do you see your own life developing within this framework? You were also deeply affected by the death of Comrade Antonio Zumel. Did it seem that such a fate could be in store for you? Does it still seem to you that dying in a land far from the people and country on which you have invested so much commitment, work, time and affection, is preferable to prison and/or death by enemy hands?

While abroad, Comrade Zumel was able to work and accomplish much for the Philippine revolution. That he died abroad does not diminish his contributions.

I may also die abroad. Or I might be able to return home alive and rejoin the revolutionary struggle. But the important thing is that I do my best wherever I am.

Some may think that I could do more work for the revolution had I not left the Philippines in 1986. But probably Oplan God Save the Queen could have finished me off also in 1986. In 1987 and 1988, I could have been either imprisoned or killed during the spates of arrests and assassinations. There was Oplan Jericho designed in 1989 to kill suspected communists, with the killing made to appear as done by their fellow communists.

Against those dark possibilities, I feel content that while abroad since 1986 I have been able to write and speak so much on a wide range of issues in order to promote the Philippine revolution and serve the Filipino people.

Q41. As of now, what do you think is your legacy to the Filipino people?

As I pointed out earlier, I have tried to integrate Marxism-Leninism with the concrete conditions and practice of the Philippine revolution. I have clarified the semi-colonial and semi-feudal character of Philippine society, the character of the current Philippine revolution as national-democratic of a new type, the friends and enemies of the revolution, the main tasks of the revolution and the socialist future of the Philippine revolution.

My legacy consists of my writings and my political and organizational accomplishments. I consider also as part of my legacy the narration of my experience in confronting grave dangers to life, limb and liberty, having been imprisoned for a very long time and having endured exile even longer. I hope that my legacy will inspire the later generations of the Filipino people and help to ultimately free them from imperialist and reactionary rule and to bring them to socialism.

Q42. Are you satisfied with this legacy? Or is there something you wish you could have done or done more of?

I am basically satisfied with what I have so far contributed to the Philippine revolution. But I still hope to be able to do more in the remaining years of my life. At any rate, the important thing is that I always try to do my best. I have no regrets in devoting my life to revolutionary work. The only regret that I have is not being able to do more work for the revolutionary cause.

Q43. What is your message to the Filipino people?

Persevere in the struggle to complete the new-democratic revolution against US imperialism and the local exploiting classes. Then begin the socialist revolution. Again, persevere in this until imperialism is defeated on a global scale and communism becomes possible.

Q44. What is your message to the people of the world?

Persevere in the broad anti-imperialist movement. This is the democratic base of the world proletarian revolution. Monopoly capitalism has become more rapacious and violent. We must combat imperialism until its global defeat, build socialism and aim at the attainment of communism.

Q45. You have expressed nothing of personal desires and wishes. Do you think you are still capable of narrowing your focus enough to consider what Jose Maria Sison, independent of the movement, of organizations, of responsibilities and obligations, might want for himself alone? If so, what could such a wish be?

I have no desire independent of the class struggle and the revolutionary movement, if by desire you mean that which carries a modicum of thought and which is not spontaneous or trivial. Still in the service of the people and the revolution, I can only desire writing more poetry than either polemical or theoretical prose.

SOMETIMES, THE HEART YEARNS FOR MANGOES

Sometimes, the heart yearns
For mangoes where there are apples,
For orchids where there are tulips,
For warmth, where it is cold,
For mountainous islands,
Where there is flatland.
Far less than the home,
And the flow of kith and kin,
Unfamiliar and now familiar
Things and places trigger
The pain of sundered relations,
Of losses by delays and default.
Direct dialing, fax machines,
Computer discs and video casettes
And visitors on supersonic jets,
Fail to close the gap
Between rehearsed appearances
And the unrehearsed life at home.
There are colleagues and friends
That make a strange land loveable.
But they have their routines,
Their own lives to live,
Beyond the comprehension
And pertinence of the stranger.
Those who seek to rob the exile
Of home, kith and kin,
Of life, limb and liberty
Are the loudest to mock at him
Who is helplessly at sea,
Uprooted from his soil.
The well-purposed exile continues
To fight for his motherland
Against those who banished him,
The unwelcomed exploiters of his people,
And is certain that he is at home
In his own country and the world.

March 30, 1994

Workers from the Kilusang Mayo Uno (May First Movement) expose real terrorists, including Bush, Powell, Macapagal-Arroyo and General Angelo Reyes. (NDF International Office photo collection)

POSTSCRIPT: REVOLUTION VERSUS TERRORISM

Q1. When we started this book project, we were on the way to the peace negotiations between the Government of the Republic of the Philippines (GRP) and the National Democratic Front of the Philippines (NDFP) in Oslo, Norway in June 2001. You said then that you wanted to relax. Thus, instead of taking the plane, you decided that we take the long train ride from Utrecht to Copenhagen and then the boat ride to Oslo. What were you unwinding from?

I wanted to relax after putting in so much work before, during and after the First International Assembly of the International League of Peoples' Struggle (ILPS) in Zutphen. I felt relieved of some two years of work as Chairman of the International Initiative Committee.

My work for preparing, organizing and founding the ILPS overlapped with other types of preoccupation. I was involved in encouraging and promoting a broad united front to arouse and mobilize large numbers of people in the Philippines in the effort to isolate, weaken and ultimately topple the corrupt and repressive Estrada regime.

A flurry of activities to prepare the resumption of the GRP-NDFP peace negotiations followed the fall of former President Joseph Estrada. A series of GRP officials came to Utrecht in February and March 2001 in order to discuss preparations for a conference on solidarity for peace in Manila and for the resumption of the peace negotiations in April. Norwegian officials also came to pave the way for the Norwegian government to serve as facilitator in the peace negotiations.

I also paid attention to issues with regard to the May elections in the Philippines, in which three congressional candidates of Bayan Muna (The People First) would win. Before the elections, many candidates from the major parties came to see me or telephoned me, asking for advice and support.

During the trip, I was happy about many successes, including the complete frustration of the plot of Estrada and certain elements to assassinate me. Since then, I had looked forward to taking a leisurely ride on a passenger boat.

Q2. You stopped your cigarette-smoking habit of more than thirty years in early May 2001 at the peak of preparations for the founding assembly of the ILPS. It seemed odd to do away with nearly a lifelong habit at a time of intense activity and excitement. How did you decide to give up smoking so abruptly?

Over the years my son Jasm had been the most insistent that I stop smoking for my own good and for others who inhaled the secondhand smoke. Of course, many immediate and close relatives and friends had repeatedly advised me to stop, especially since the early 1990s. So you might say that many people whose good advice I did not follow encircled me for a long time.

But I started to consider doing away with cigarettes in 2000 when I began to experience shortness of breath in running after a bus or climbing the stairs. A series of doctor-friends examined and told me that I had chronic bronchitis. They advised me to stop smoking. Still I did not follow their advice.

In December 2000 a doctor-friend noticed my shortness of breath after I ran a short distance to take a ride in her car. During the car ride, she scolded me for not following medical advice and not looking after my own health for the sake of serving the Filipino people. Later on, when I visited her clinic on May 4, 2001 on the way home from the Brussels communist seminar, she gave a final blow to my stubbornness by subjecting me to a spirometer test. This showed my lung capacity at a dangerously low level. This test result finally convinced me to stop smoking.

I was then with some Filipino friends, including a lawyer and a doctor, who suggested to me to take a written oath of no smoking. I readily accepted the suggestion both for the fun of doing it and for the serious purpose of firming up my resolve. I improvised the oath and signed it, together with three doctors, one lawyer, one accountant and one driver as witnesses. Since then, I have never lighted nor puffed on a cigarette.

Q3. You were never tempted to smoke or take the littlest puff? Did this become some kind of character test? What difficulties did you undergo? Knowing some of the attacks made against you since we left Oslo in June 2001, after the breakdown of the GRP-NDFP peace negotiations, I am sure you were agitated enough to be tempted to smoke.

Indeed, resisting the urge to smoke became a test of character, a test of will. The temptation to smoke was recurrent. But I did not yield even to the suggestion of gradually reducing my smoking.

The urge to smoke was strongest whenever I wrote an article or speech. But I did not give in. Oftentimes, I dozed off to avoid smoking, after I decided to stop taking candies to fight off the urge to smoke. I was taking too many naps, especially when staying at home to work.

I had difficulties kicking the habit. For the first few months, I experienced profuse salivation, restlessness and drowsiness from nicotine withdrawal. I noticed myself gaining weight, whether I took or abstained from taking candies but took too many naps.

The family doctor prescribed one type of lung dilator after another in order to deal with my chronic bronchitis and continuing shortness of breath. Each type of lung dilator gave me some bad side effects, like skin rashes and localized muscle spasms. After some six months, I stopped using the lung dilator and took regular doses of Vitamin C and did breathing, walking and singing exercises.

Attacks directed against me annoyed me a number of times. For instance, the GRP cited the killing of Col. Rodolfo Aguinaldo, a notorious human rights violator since the time of Marcos and an armed combatant, to declare the indefinite recess of the GRP-NDFP peace negotiations in

June 2001. Then the reactionary military spread the lie in the press that I was the one who ordered the killing. Later on, former Senate President Salonga attacked me in August 2001 by rehashing his old charge that I was responsible for the Plaza Miranda bombing. But such annoyances did not drive me back to smoking.

Q4. You were still not tempted to smoke when the September 11 attacks occurred in the US? Didn't you anticipate that this event would somehow and in some manner impact on your existence?

I consciously viewed the September 11 with calm and much reflection. This did not agitate me enough to make me smoke. Without any difficulty, I was able to write my article dated September 18, expressing condolences and sympathies to the American people and urging them to reflect on the role of US imperialism in perpetrating the biggest kinds of terrorism and in generating hatred for the US monopoly establishment and causing the terrorist attacks of 9/11.

I assumed then that the US government would react strongly to 9/11. I estimated that the US would rage after the suspects it named, like Osama bin Laden and the Al Qaeda, and that the Bush regime would use the attacks as pretext for extending its "war on terrorism" to all the anti-imperialist forces. But I did not expect that so soon after 9/11 the US would scheme to put me on its list of "terrorists" for target by itself and by its imperialist allies.

On November 22, 2001, I received a warning from a high Manila government official, Speaker Jose de Venecia, that the US would list the Communist Party of the Philippines, the New People's Army and me as "terrorists" and demonize us in the US and globally. He said that the US is so powerful and no other force on earth could stop it from undertaking "punitive" measures. He suggested that the only way out was to convince the NDFP to sign a "final peace agreement" prepared by the Manila government.

The threat from the direction of the US served to rouse my fighting spirit but did not drive me back to smoking. I issued a series of statements against the US scheme to further tighten its military hold on the Philippines through a Mutual Logistical Support Agreement with the puppet government and to bring into the Philippines US combat troops under the pretext of fighting in a "second front" in the so-called war on terrorism. At the time, the "first front" was supposed to be in Afghanistan, where the

US-led coalition had already overthrown the Taliban regime but failed to locate Osama bin Laden and destroy Al Qaeda.

Q5. *It seems strange that a high official of the Philippine government, Speaker Jose de Venecia, would warn you about the impending "terrorist" label. Was it a warning or was it a threat? Please explain the circumstances and provide details of what he said.*

It could either be a warning or a threat or both. Macapagal-Arroyo and de Venecia were in Washington on November 18 to 20, 2001 and then they proceeded to attend the international conference of Christian democrats in Mexico on November 20. From Mexico, Speaker de Venecia called me up on November 22 and told me that soon the US would label the CPP, NPA and myself as terrorists and would subject me to punitive measures.

He said that after such listing, even he would find it difficult to phone me or meet me personally lest he himself be tagged a terrorist. He said further that the best way for the NDFP to counter the plan of the US is to sign a "final peace agreement" with the GRP soon enough. I asked him to come to Utrecht to explain further what the matter was all about.

So, he came with retired general Eduardo Ermita, presidential adviser for the peace process, Silvestre Bello III, GRP negotiating panel chairman, and Silvestre Afable III. He handed to NDFP negotiating chairman Luis Jalandoni and me a copy of the GRP-drafted "final peace agreement" and a copy of a Central Bank letter informing him (de Venecia) of measures being prepared for the freezing of assets in suspect bank accounts.

Q6. *Were those papers discussed? What else did you do or not do?*

We discussed neither one of those papers. What the GRP and the NDFP negotiating panel chairmen discussed and prepared was the draft of a document of understanding to accelerate the peace negotiations in accordance with The Hague Joint Declaration and other agreements. The plan was to reach agreement on the document and sign it in the presence of Kjell Bondevik, the newly elected Prime Minister of Norway.

We flew to Oslo Norway for an audience with Prime Minister Bondevik on December 1, 2001. But before we could meet him, the GRP negotiating panel chairman told the NDFP negotiating panel chairman that they could not sign the document of understanding because Defense Secretary Angelo Reyes objected to it and wanted it to be brought to Manila for further study. At any rate, we had the audience with the Norwegian prime minister. He graciously received both the GRP and NDFP delegations at the same time.

Q7. *Whose bright idea was it to pressure the NDFP with the threat of criminalizing or demonizing as "terrorist" the CPP, NPA and you? The Manila government or the US government?*

Various sources within the Macapagal-Arroyo regime informed me that the advance team for Macapagal-Arroyo's Washington visit pushed the idea of intimidating the NDFP with the terrorist tag within the framework of US-Philippine cooperation in the so-called war on terrorism.

The advance team sat with operatives of the Departments of State, Treasury and Defense to plot the criminalization of the CPP, NPA and myself as "terrorists". When Macapagal Arroyo arrived in Washington, the dirty plot was ready for bilateral approval by her and Bush. After approval, Speaker de Venecia communicated the warning or threat to me.

The US and the GRP can easily agree on a scheme to threaten the NDFP, with the objective of pushing it towards capitulation. That is the content of the "final peace agreement". But the US has its own objective. It can go along with the GRP in pressing for the capitulation of the NDFP. But it knows that the NDFP will not capitulate. It wants to scuttle or at least paralyze the GRP-NDFP peace negotiations, stir up further troubles and pave the way for direct US military intervention in the Philippines.

Q8. *It is strange that despite there being no criminal charge against you in the Philippines, the US accuses you of terrorism. Don't you also find it absurd that the US charges the CPP, NPA and you with a criminal offense that is non-existent in the penal code of the GRP, thereby assuming jurisdiction over acts of rebellion in the Philippines?*

You are correct. Since 1998, after the GRP certified that there is no pending criminal charge against me, no criminal charge has ever been formally brought against me in the Philippines or anywhere else in the world. It is only belatedly that the GRP authorities are trying to rig a murder charge against me for the killing of Col. Rodolfo Aquinaldo.

You are also correct in pointing out that terrorism does not exist in the penal code of the GRP. The penal code regards as acts of rebellion those acts of the revolutionary forces and people that are aimed at overthrowing the GRP. Under the Hernandez doctrine of political offense, the killing of

Col. Aguinaldo is an act of rebellion by the NPA and not a common crime of murder. It is wrong for the US to usurp jurisdiction over such acts in the Philippines and superimpose on them the term "terrorism".

Q9. As chief political consultant of the NDFP in peace negotiations with the GRP, you are supposed to be protected by the Joint Agreement on Safety and Immunity Guarantees (JASIG). You are also protected by the Comprehensive Agreement on Respect for Human Rights and International Humanitarian Law (CARHRIHL). Doesn't the accusation of terrorism violate these agreements?

Yes, indeed, the agreements you mentioned are violated. The GRP has violated them by conniving with the US in criminalizing and punishing me as "terrorist" for the purpose of intimidating and pressuring the NDFP to capitulate.

The JASIG prohibits the GRP from trumping up any criminal charge against me and attempting to use as evidence my statements and actions made in the exercise of my democratic rights and in connection with the peace negotiations.

The CARHRIHL requires the GRP to follow the Hernandez doctrine in charging revolutionaries. The GRP cannot supplant the charge of simple rebellion, clearly a political offense, with the common crime of murder or worse "terrorism" which does not exist at all in the penal code of the GRP.

The GRP also violates the national sovereignty provision of The Hague Joint Declaration by allowing the US to usurp jurisdiction over the actions of the revolutionary forces in the Philippines and to charge them with terrorism abroad. The GRP is shameless in failing to uphold Philippine jurisdiction over criminal acts of US military personnel in the Philippines and in allowing US jurisdiction over alleged acts of the NPA.

Q10. The "terrorist" label seems to have angered you exceedingly. What dire consequences can arise from it?

Anyone in my position would be outraged. It is clearly unjust for an imperialist power like the US, the biggest terrorist in the world, to label me a terrorist. I do not deserve that calumny, the campaign of slander and the punitive measures that come with it.

The Dutch authorities, following the signal of the US, have frozen my joint bank account with my wife and have terminated the social benefits that are due to me as a recognized political refugee and as one entitled to protection under Article 3 and to the right to private and family life under Article 8 of the European Convention for the Protection of Human Rights and Fundamental Freedoms (ECHR). I am deprived of basic necessities such as food, housing and medical care and I am liable to suffer a chain of losses and liabilities arising from failure to comply with obligations.

I am treated as if I were already convicted of a heinous crime called terrorism. In violation of the right to due process guaranteed by Article 6 of the ECHR, I am punished for being a "terrorist" without due process. Also in violation of Article 1 of Protocol 1 of the same Convention, I am deprived of property that legitimately belongs to me. If I do not fight back juridically and politically, the US, Dutch and European authorities will proceed to further violate my rights.

An order has been issued to the border police and customs authorities to interdict and detain me should I travel outside of the Netherlands. This is aimed at harassing me. The US can have me arrested and detained under conditions more severe than those of other prisoners. These include solitary confinement, sensory deprivation and prevention of access to legal counsel, documentary evidence and witnesses for an indefinite period of time.

The worst legal threat so far publicly made against me is the threat of extradition to the US under the US-Dutch extradition treaty. But my Philippine counsel Atty. Romeo T. Capulong and my Dutch counsel Victor Koppe, who is an expert on extradition law, have pointed out that the US will have difficulties inventing an extradition case against me.

Lawyers and friends have advised me to be careful with my personal security because the US might opt for assassination rather than extradition. Bush has publicly announced that assassination of anti-US political leaders is in the agenda of covert operatives of the US Central Intelligence Agency. Under the guise of anti-terrorism, the US is practically promoting fascism all over the world, in collaboration with imperialist allies and puppets.

Q11. Speaker de Venecia warned you in November 2001; but you, the CPP and the NPA were placed on the terrorist list in August 2002. To be precise, the US State Department placed you on the list on August 9, 2002 and the US Treasury Department on August 12. Why did it take a while for the threat to become a reality?

I think that the US had to concentrate first on the propaganda and the motions of going after Osama bin Laden and Al Qaeda in Afghanistan and also going after the Abu Sayyaf, which it accused of being linked to Al Qaeda. It had to ride first on the popular outrage over the September 11 attacks.

Had the US put the CPP, NPA and me on the terrorist list so soon, for instance in December 2001, it would have become too clear to so many people that it was using the September 11 attacks as a license to defame and destroy a national liberation movement. US officials might have also wanted the NDFP to mull over the threat of having its main allied organizations, the CPP and the NPA, and the NDFP chief political consultant on the terrorist list.

Rather than the US, the Filipino puppets, like Defense Secretary Angelo Reyes, were the ones who asserted loudly as early as December 2001 and January 2002 that the US intended to destroy the Philippine revolutionary movement and that the US combat troops would operate against the NPA after the destruction of the Abu Sayyaf. It is the style of the US to use its puppets according to circumstances and according to its plan.

Q12. How did the Philippine government respond to the US's usurpation of its jurisdiction when the US State Department listed the CPP and the NPA as "foreign terrorist organizations" and the US Treasury Department targeted them and you for a "freezing of assets?" And what about when other governments—like the Netherlands, Britain, Canada, Australia, and the entire European Council—obeyed the US State Department?

Gloria Macapagal-Arroyo and her Defense Secretary General Angelo Reyes and National Security Adviser Roilo Golez were jubilant. They were beside themselves with glee. Reyes and Golez said that I had no more place to hide and the latter declared publicly that the GRP would have no objection if the US extradited me from the Netherlands.

These Filipino puppets knew in advance exactly on which date the US would put me on the so-called the terrorist list. Remember that US Secretary of State Colin Powell was in Manila on August 3, 2002 to mark the end of six months of US combat troops in the military campaign against Abu Sayyaf. Then on August 5, Macapagal-Arroyo made her declaration of all-out war against the NPA. The August 9 and 12 actions of the US State Department and US Treasury Department against the CPP, NPA and me flowed directly from the Powell-Arroyo consultations.

On August 13, 2002, the Dutch government followed the lead of the US by issuing "sanction regulations against terrorism", listed the CPP, NPA and me as "terrorists" and immediately requested the European Council to likewise include all three in their list of terrorists and apply punitive measures on them.

Again, the highest officials of the Macapagal-Arroyo regime were overjoyed that governments other than the US were listing the CPP, NPA and me as "terrorists" and applying punitive measures against me. They shamelessly accepted the usurpation of jurisdiction by the US and other foreign governments over alleged actions of the NPA in the Philippines and were happy over the immediate freezing of my personal bank account and the termination of social welfare benefits due to me in the Netherlands.

Not satisfied with the action of the Dutch government, a delegation of cabinet members, headed by long-time Filipino CIA asset Blas Ople (a former errand boy of the Eleuterio "Terry" Adevoso gang of CIA assets), visited several European countries in a campaign to have the CPP, NPA and me listed as "terrorists" by the European Council.

Q13. Western Europe is supposed to be more democratic and liberal than the US. How come they followed this rather crude persecution of your person?

As in the US, the monopoly bourgeoisie basically rules the governments represented in the European Council. The US and the European monopoly bourgeoisie have their North Atlantic alliance. They cohere in policy and action to preserve common monopoly bourgeois interests against the proletariat and oppressed peoples. Thus, the European governments would easily yield to special requests of the US, like my being denied admission as political refugee and residence permit in the Netherlands and being listed as a "terrorist".

The Dutch government, in violation of the Refugee Convention, has openly and consistently argued that it cannot grant me political asylum because this would be against the credibility of the Dutch state to its US ally. Following the political baton of the US, the Dutch government and entire European Council have flagrantly violated my human rights by their action of criminalizing me as a "terrorist" without due process and of imposing punitive measures on me.

The US and the European Union have some differences over certain material interests and these are reflected by some policy differences. These differences are manifested in the positions taken by the US, Britain, Spain, Italy and the Netherlands on the one hand and by France, Germany and Russia on the other hand over the question of whether or not to unleash war against Iraq. However, they have no such differences with regard to me.

Following the example of the US, the European Council keeps secret or does not allow access to the dossiers supplied by intelligence agencies of the US and other countries. Then on the basis of such pieces of mendacity, which are at the most raw intelligence reports, they make judgements. Even ahead of legislation, they define and set the penalties for terrorism. They usurp both legislative and judicial functions.

Q14. *Can you say some more about what impact this label "terrorist" has had on you personally?*

With officials of various governments having me listed as a "terrorist" in official documents and attacked as such, I suffer defamation and demonization. In such documents, these governments have convicted and criminalized me as a "terrorist" and subjected me to punitive measures without any due process.

My democratic rights to be presumed innocent until proven guilty in a court of law, to be informed of the charge, to scrutinize and challenge evidence and witnesses and to have a fair trial before I am convicted and punished have all been violated. The heinous crime of terrorism is attributed to me and then my small bank account is frozen, and my meager means, measly social welfare benefits, are terminated.

Despite the insistence of a Dutch foundation to employ me, the Dutch immigration and judicial authorities have denied me the right to work. Their argument is that I am a "terrorist". Injustice is done to me despite the supposed jurisprudence that someone like me who is protected by Article 3 of the European Convention for the Protection of Human Rights and Fundamental Freedoms is protected by the entirety of such convention.

For more than 10 years, I was required to report only once a month to the aliens' police. Now I am required to report every week. I presume that I am now under closer surveillance than before. The customs and border police are under orders to be on the lookout for me and to treat me as a dangerous criminal.

I have to be more careful with my physical movement because I am now vulnerable to physical attacks from the covert operatives and assets of the US Central Intelligence Agency and from ultra-reactionary elements now emboldened by the post-9/11 fascist trend.

Q15. *What moral and material damages have been inflicted on you?*

The moral and material damages inflicted on me are tremendous. In fact, the moral damage due to my being demonized as a "terrorist" is incalculable. I have seen other people crack under the mental stress of being falsely accused. I also suffer a great deal of material damage.

I am prevented from getting employment on the false charge of being a terrorist. Institutions are discouraged from hiring me as a lecturer or consultant, lest they be accused of helping or facilitating terrorism. Publishers can be discouraged from publishing my writings.

My family budget is now terribly upset because my bank account has remained frozen since August. On October 28, 2002 the European Council extended what the Dutch government had started in Europe on August 13, 2002—freezing my bank account and stopping the payment of social benefits to me.

You will recall that we won the human rights litigation against Marcos in the US. If the order to freeze my assets and stop banks and insurance companies from providing financial services to me continues indefinitely, then even the stipulated judgment in the US judicial system, awarding me so much for the moral and material damage inflicted on me during the Marcos fascist dictatorship, would be jeopardized.

Q16. *Can things worse than what you have just cited happen to you?*

At any time, the Dutch government can arrest and detain me on the basis of a request from the US for my provisional detention prior to extradition. The US can also request my outright extradition to the US.

However, since the US has no factual basis for any criminal charge that would allow it to request my extradition from the Netherlands, a snatch-and-kill operation or an arranged fatal "accident" against me is more likely than the fabrication of evidence for the purpose of complying with some legal process in cooperation with the Dutch government.

I have already mentioned to you that Bush has given approval to the CIA's conduct of "wet operations" against anti-imperialist leaders and has given plenty of leeway for the CIA to carry out such covert operations.

The worst can happen to me if I do not fight back. The trial by publicity and the character assassination, being done by the US and its European imperialist partners, are preparations for possible worse actions against my life, physical integrity and liberty. My fighting back may not stop the covert operations of the CIA but it underscores the justness of my cause and exposes the evil character of the imperialists on both sides of the Atlantic.

Q17. ***How are you preparing to deal or dealing with this new persecution?***

I have filed before the European Court of Justice in Luxembourg an application for the annulment of the decision of the European Council to list me as a "terrorist" and impose punitive measures on me. Outstanding lawyers from Belgium, Netherlands, Germany, France, Sweden and the Philippines are representing me. Philippine lawyers of the Public Interest Law Center are assisting them.

Another battery of Dutch lawyers is in charge of my complaint against the Dutch state for having violated my rights by issuing the sanction regulations against me. This case has the potential of going up to the European Court of Human Rights in Strasbourg after we exhaust the legal remedies in the Netherlands.

Still another set of European, Filipino and American lawyers is preparing for the eventuality that the US requests the Dutch government for my provisional detention or extradition. In the Philippines, a panel of five women lawyers is countering the attempts of the Macapagal-Arroyo regime to trump up murder charges against me for the death of Colonel Rodolfo Aguinaldo and the equally notorious GRP military asset Romulo Kintanar.

In waging the juridical struggle, I can clearly demonstrate how the common position and decision of the European Council have violated my democratic rights and how the European Council has usurped jurisdiction over matters that belong to the European parliament and the European Court of Justice. In the process, I can expose the danger of fascism as an outgrowth of the crisis of monopoly capitalism and the witchhunt being whipped up by the US on a global scale.

Q18. ***And politically, what kind of preparations have you undertaken? How are these linked to your juridical struggle?***

I have written articles, issued press statements, held press conferences, appeared on television, spoken in public meetings and participated in meetings to organize committees to defend me and other Filipinos. My most important articles and speeches appear on the websites of Committee DEFEND and the International Network for Philippine Studies: www.defendsison.be and www.inps-sison.freewebspace.com.

The Committee DEFEND defends my democratic rights and promotes the GRP-NDFP peace negotiations. It consists of representatives of a broad range of mass organizations, starting in August 2002 with only 15 Filipino, Dutch, Belgian and Turkish organizations. It has been replicated in several countries. It has mobilized hundreds of organizations of various types all over the world to participate in the mass campaign to defend me.

The mass campaign has taken the form of information meetings, protest rallies, signature collection and fundraising through film shows and sale of literature, buttons, pins, t-shirts and so on. Our campaigners have joined conferences and big mass actions against imperialist globalization and US wars of aggression in order to gather support for the defense of my democratic rights.

Lobbying has been done in important political institutions. So, we have been able to get the support of European and national parliamentarians. We have also solicited the support of the officials and members of political parties, trade unions, other mass organizations, issue-based organizations, professional organizations churches and so on.

The juridical and political struggles interact and reinforce each other. The legal arguments used in the juridical struggle reinforce the presentation of issues in the political struggle. At the same time, the mass actions in the political struggle expose the rotten prejudices that are likely to influence the courts. I rely on the funds raised through the mass campaign to sustain my legal defense.

Q19. Considering the litany of what can happen to you—from assassination to possible imprisonment in Guantanamo—the dangers of smoking seem light in comparison. I'm being facetious, by way of relieving my own unspeakable outrage at this continuing persecution. But do you have hopes that your counter-measures will have an effect?

It is necessary to fight back in every possible way in order to gain abundant support. To be prepared against the worst is to be able to hope for the best.

The grave charge of terrorism made by the US and other imperialist governments against me are very threatening and could be agitating enough to drive me back to smoking. But I remain convinced that I need not complicate my situation by jeopardizing my lungs and my overall physical health.

Q20. It is being claimed in the mass media by the US and other government authorities that the listing of the CPP, NPA and you as "terrorists" has effectively frozen the assets of the CPP and NPA in foreign banks and has cut off foreign financial funding for them. How true is such claim?

The claim is pure hogwash. You can verify that until this late date not one of the governments listing the CPP and NPA as "terrorist" has claimed to come upon and freeze any bank account or any other asset abroad belonging to the CPP and NPA.

It is well known that the CPP and NPA are self-reliant revolutionary organizations. They do not depend on foreign funding and do not keep bank accounts and other assets abroad. They are not like the corrupt bureaucrats and the families of big compradors and landlords in the Philippines that stash away wealth abroad.

Q21. Came New Year's Day 2003, banner headlines in Manila newspapers proclaimed Speaker Jose de Venecia proposing and President Macapagal-Arroyo approving a government of "national unity", with you among the most prominent national leaders included. I noticed yours was the handsomest picture alongside those of Speaker de Venecia, the big comprador Eduardo Cojuangco, Laban ng Demokratikong Pilipino president Sen. Ed Angara and Moro Islamic Liberation Front chairman Salamat Hashim. How come those in power in Manila call you a terrorist one moment and the next, ask you to join their ranks?

The proposal for a "national unity" government has something to do directly with the earlier announcement of Ms. Macapagal-Arroyo on December 30, 2002 that she was no longer running for the presidency in May 2004. The announcement was a roundabout way of her admitting defeat at the hands of the broad united front, which had been steadfast and effective in exposing the puppet, corrupt, mendacious and brutal character of her regime.

Being a lame duck president, Macapagal-Arroyo has to harp on the slogan of "national unity" in order to place herself above her political rivals amidst intensifying competition within and outside the ruling coalition and in order to dampen the opposition to her. This maneuver is calculated to eventually allow her to get back to the presidential race at her choosing or, if a constituent assembly could be convened, allow her to become a French-style president in a parliamentary system to be created by constitutional amendment.

The "invitation" made through the media for me to join the so-called national unity government was mere gimmickry. I responded immediately by expressing my disinterest in joining such a government that did not differ at all from the existing government. I pointed out the difficulty of putting together the representatives of reactionary and revolutionary forces.

Instead, I proposed the resumption of the GRP-NDFP peace negotiations in accordance with The Hague Joint Declaration of 1992 and subsequent agreements. The peace negotiations are the process within which the GRP and the NDFP could discuss and agree on what should be the basis of a national unity government.

Q22. *Explain please why Gloria Macapagal Arroyo is a "lame duck" president.*

In Philippine reactionary politics, a "lame duck" president is one who can no longer be expected to retain power after a year or so and can no longer command loyalty and obedience from political colleagues and followers, as much as before.

When a president is on the way out, political colleagues and followers start looking up to the most likely presidential successor to whom to give their support. The incumbent president becomes more ineffective and is thus seen as a lame duck.

Q23. *You must have felt as if you were on a roller coaster. As soon as Romulo Kintanar, former NPA commander-in-chief, was killed in an ambush on January 23, 2003, the highest GRP officials accused you of being a "terrorist" and being responsible for the killing of Kintanar and that of Col. Rodolfo Aguinaldo on June 12, 2001. What is your opinion on the murder charges reportedly being prepared against you by the Philippine National Police in cooperation with the Department of Justice?*

Those charges are pure hogwash. I have nothing to do with them in the first place. Until now, I have not been served a subpoena to any preliminary investigation. The GRP authorities will mess up their own investigation and ruin their cases if they insist on implicating me in murder charges and connecting me to suspects that I do not know from Adam.

Nevertheless, let me point out that the revolutionary forces have long considered both Aguinaldo and Kintanar as armed combatants of the reactionary armed forces. They were armed and accompanied by armed bodyguards when they were killed.

Aguinaldo was a notorious human rights violator under the Marcos fascist dictatorship. As governor and later as congressman, he participated in military operations against revolutionary forces. Kintanar had been a "security consultant" and intelligence operative of the AFP and the PNP for more than a decade.

The NPA has admitted the killing of Aguinaldo and Kintanar as enemy combatants. In accordance with the Hernandez political offense doctrine and the CARHRIHL, the GRP can file the charge of rebellion against the suspected killers and not murder charges.

The GRP is unjustly and maliciously implicating me in the killing of Aguinaldo and Kintanar just to give a semblance of truth to the false charge of terrorism. But anyone who knows the jurisprudence of the GRP will find ludicrous the way the GRP juggles and jumbles the charges of rebellion, murder and terrorism in the mass media.

Q24. Under what circumstances will the NDFP agree to the resumption of peace talks with the Manila government?

The terms of the NDFP for resuming the peace negotiations with the GRP are clear. The negotiations must be conducted according to the framework set by The Hague Joint Declaration. In accordance with the Joint Agreement on Safety and Immunity Guarantees (JASIG), the negotiators, consultants, staffers and supporters must not be listed or threatened with being listed as "terrorists".

The GRP has to ask the US and other imperialist powers to remove the CPP, NPA and the NDFP chief political consultant from their lists of "terrorists". It must desist from trying to intimidate the NDFP and demanding its capitulation. The GRP must respect the national sovereignty and noncapitulation provisions and the substantive agenda stipulated in The Hague Joint Declaration.

The GRP must ask the US and other foreign governments to stop usurping jurisdiction over actions of the New People's Army in the Philippines and must remind them that the armed conflict between the armed forces of the GRP and the NDFP is governed by international humanitarian law, as clearly established by the CARHRIHL, which also requires the GRP to respect the Hernandez doctrine in its own jurisprudence.

The GRP must remind the European Union and all its four pillars (Council, Commission, Parliament and Court of Justice) to respect the 1997 and 1999 resolutions of the European Parliament supporting the GRP-NDFP peace negotiations and to follow the Council Framework Decision excluding from its compass the actions of armed forces in an armed conflict governed by international humanitarian law.

Q25. Will we see the resumption of the peace negotiations before the Macapagal-Arroyo regime ends? Will the GRP-NDFP Comprehensive Agreement on Respect for Human Rights and International Humanitarian Law be implemented?

The NDFP is always ready to resume the peace negotiations with the GRP so long as this is in accordance with The Hague Joint Declaration and other agreements. From its own viewpoint and needs, it makes sense for the GRP to resume the peace negotiations.

Among the first things to be done upon the resumption of the GRP-NDFP peace negotiations is the formation of the Joint Monitoring Committee (JMC) as a channel for exchanging complaints, requests and proposals concerning respect for human rights and international humanitarian law in the ongoing civil war.

The Joint Monitoring Committee is to be formed in order to enhance the joint and separate implementation of CARHRIHL. It aims to prevent and reduce violations of the agreement and punish the violators. The success of the JMC would improve tremendously the climate for the peace negotiations.

Q26. Would the Manila government agree with the NDFP on social and economic reforms, run against imperialist and feudal exploitation, carry out national industrialization and land reform and discard "free trade globalization"?

The GRP has to heed the demands of the NDFP and the Filipino people for social and economic reforms if any degree of progress is to be reached in the quest for a just and lasting peace. The GRP must agree to drop its anti-national and anti-democratic policies and agree to the upholding of national sovereignty and territorial integrity and the defense of economic sovereignty, conservation of the national patrimony, national industrialization, land reform, better working and living conditions, and other socioeconomic reforms. As a matter of fact, its current economic policies are already making the regime sink further in crisis.

The NDFP has laid on the table the draft of the comprehensive agreement on social and economic reforms. I cannot say what social and economic reforms the GRP is willing to agree on with the NDFP.

The negotiations are held precisely to explore and determine what reforms are mutually acceptable to the two sides. The worsening social and economic crisis is helping to clarify the problems and possible solutions even while there are no peace negotiations.

Q27. *What about political and constitutional reforms which the NDFP might want to see implemented in the Philippines? Will such reforms require the creation of a new constitution? Would new political organs and processes be needed for the empowerment of workers and peasants? What happens to all these treaties and laws, which subordinate the country to imperialism? Can the Manila government accept such changes?*

Indeed, there will have to be new organs and processes for empowering the workers and peasants. There will have to be a new constitution. The unequal treaties and laws servile to the US and other imperialist powers and to the foreign monopoly capitalists will have to be invalidated, abrogated or repealed.

The comprehensive agreement on political and constitutional reforms will have to put into effect the comprehensive agreement on social and economic reforms. The two agreements must reinforce each other or be interactive for reforms to become feasible.

To say the least, it is not certain whether the GRP will agree to the political and constitutional reforms I have mentioned. It is the GRP's own lookout if it does not heed or it opposes the national and democratic demands of the people.

Q28. *What do you think of the proposal to hold a constituent assembly or constitutional convention to amend the GRP constitution in order to shift to a parliamentary form of government soon? Can you relate this to the agenda of the GRP-NDFP peace negotiations, particularly political and constitutional reforms?*

There are those who wish to hold a constituent assembly or constitutional convention soon under the pretext of aiming for a constitutional amendment to change the form of the GRP from the presidential to the parliamentary.

They want to eliminate the provisions inspired by the Miranda doctrine from the bill of rights and those provisions restricting the declaration of martial law. They want to introduce the repressive Marcosian terms of the USA PATRIOT Act and to adopt an extremely draconian "anti-terrorism" law.

They want to remove all the national restrictions on foreign ownership in all businesses and the exploitation of natural resources and completely subordinate the Philippine economy to "free market" globalization.

They want to remove the constitutional ban on foreign military bases and foreign troops in the Philippines and allow these to be re-established. They want to be able to stockpile and transit US nuclear, biological, chemical and other weapons of mass destruction in Philippine territory.

The proposal of the pro-US reactionaries in power to amend the GRP constitution is instigated by the US. It is intended to make way for the US imperialists and their puppets to engage in unbridled plunder and state terrorism with impunity. It is a malevolent scheme being pushed far ahead of the GRP-NDFP peace negotiations. The broad masses of the people must oppose it.

Q29. Can an end to hostilities be reached during the time of Ms. Macapagal-Arroyo? What is your idea of the disposition of forces?

The Macapagal-Arroyo regime has rendered difficult or impossible any further substantial progress in the GRP-NDFP peace negotiations. First, it declared an indefinite recess. Then, it unilaterally drafted a "final peace agreement", whose content seeks the capitulation of the NDFP. Finally, Secretary Silvestre Afable and GRP negotiating panel chairman Silvestre Bello III came to tell the NDFP negotiating panel that negotiations cannot resume unless the NDFP accepts the "final peace agreement".

Little time is left before the end of the regime. There is too little time for negotiating the comprehensive agreement on social and economic reforms. It is impossible to start the negotiations on political and constitutional reforms before the end of the regime. The NDFP has already declared that it would rather wait for the next regime to consider resumption of the negotiations. Macapagal-Arroyo can no longer negotiate because the US and her defense secretary Angelo Reyes prohibit her from doing so.

It is premature to discuss now what will be the disposition of forces on both sides. A truce is more likely than a surrender of arms by one side to the other. Should there be a truce, its terms would include the disposition of the armed forces of both parties. But the GRP-NDFP peace negotiations might never resume as the US continues to prohibit the GRP from engaging in them. The NDFP might also come to the conclusion that there is no more point in negotiating with the GRP.

Q30. *Do you really believe that a just and lasting peace can be achieved through peace negotiations with the GRP? Can the peace negotiations replace the armed revolution of the people?*

There are peace negotiations because there is an armed struggle between the revolutionary forces of the people and the counterrevolutionary forces of the ruling classes. The contending sides have agreed to negotiate in order to address the roots of the armed conflict, make reforms beneficial to the people and thus pave the way for a just and lasting peace.

The Filipino people and the NDFP know what they want to achieve from the peace negotiations. They have no illusions that genuine peace can be achieved through negotiations alone. It is clear that the line of struggle for a just and lasting peace is the same as the line of struggle for national liberation and democracy.

The revolutionary armed struggle is the sure process of empowering the people and satisfying their demands. The peace negotiations conducted by the most competent negotiators cannot go beyond what the people's armed revolution can achieve and therefore cannot replace it.

Q31. *Can one counterpoise revolution to terrorism? How can you achieve a just and lasting peace when the US can terrorize the whole world?*

Certainly, you can and should counterpoise revolution to terrorism, whether this is the state terrorism of the imperialist powers and the puppet states or the nongovernmental terrorism of the likes of Al Qaeda or the Abu Sayyaf. The US has practised the most reprehensible kinds of terrorism: wars of aggression, production of weapons of mass destruction, the atom bombing of civilian populations, the use of chemical warfare and instigation of puppet regimes of open terror that engage in massacres and all kinds of human rights violations.

The US stands in the way of the people achieving a just and lasting peace. It continues to generate a new world of disorder, to terrorize the world's people with weapons of mass destruction, unleash wars of aggression, whip up fascism and repression and push puppet states to go for the rule of open terror.

The US has become very active in paralysing and sabotaging the GRP-NDFP peace negotiations. It has put the CPP, NPA and the NDFP chief political consultant on the "terrorist" list and is hell-bent on engaging in military intervention and re-establishing military bases in the Philippines.

The Macapagal-Arroyo regime believes that it can depend on the US for intimidating and pressuring the NDFP to capitulate. But the main interest of the US is to scuttle the peace negotiations and rationalize US military intervention and aggression in the Philippines.

In the face of the growing terrorism of the US and the puppet government, the revolutionary forces and people in the Philippines have no choice but to fight for a just and lasting peace through a people's war along the line of the new democratic revolution. They can establish an independent, democratic, just, progressive and peace-loving government in the areas where the reactionary puppet government can no longer rule.

Q32. Mr. Bush has capitalized on the 9/11 attacks, particularly the global sympathy this generated for the American people, in order to pursue his imperialist agenda under the guise of a permanent and borderless war on terrorism. But in a single shining moment for the people of the world on February 15, 2003 and thereabouts, millions over millions of people marched against the warmongering of the Bush administration. What is your estimate of the US position and the current mass upsurge?

Mr. Bush has misused, abused and squandered the sympathy gained by the American people from the people all over the world for the tragedy resulting from the 9/11 attacks. His arrogant ravings for war, for the barbarous doctrine of pre-emptive strike and for a permanent and borderless sham war on terrorism have isolated him and his imperialist policy.

It is indeed a shining moment for the people of the world to have risen up in millions in protest against the Bush scheme of war on Iraq on February 15. Thirty million people in 600 cities and towns worldwide, with 500,000 to 2.5 million marching in several major cities of the US, Britain, Italy, France and Spain constitute a brilliant high point in the mass movement against imperialism and war.

The anti-war protests in the first four months of 2003 are comparable to the dimensions of the anti-war mass protests against the US war of aggression against Vietnam in the late 1960s and 1970s. More and bigger mass actions are bound to arise as the US and its allies continue with their war preparations and unleash wars of aggression. The bellicosity of the US can only incite the people to wage all forms of revolutionary struggle and to convert the imperialist war into revolutionary civil wars.

Q33. What drives the US and other imperialists to go to war? Don't you think that its military successes from 1991 to the present have emboldened US imperialism to go on unleashing wars of aggression? Has it not also become stronger by getting the spoils of war?

The crisis of the world capitalist system drives the US and other imperialists to wage wars of aggression against the oppressed nations and peoples and against underdeveloped countries assertive of national independence. As the crisis worsens, the contradictions among the imperialist powers tend to sharpen. The struggles for a redivision of the world among the imperialist powers become more and more obvious.

The US imperialists are emboldened by their successes in waging wars of aggression. They are being carried away by hyper power hubris. US policy makers and strategists think that US high-tech weaponry is invincible. They openly boast they can unleash wars unilaterally at anytime. They say that the US imperialists can act in any way, unilaterally or multilaterally, in serving their hegemonic interests.

From 1991 to the present, the US has been successful both in winning wars in blitzkrieg fashion and grabbing the lion's share from the spoils of war. The US-led war of aggression against Iraq allowed the US to tighten its control over Middle East oil and politics, put the Palestinians and Arabs at a big disadvantage, capture a big part of the oil income of Saudi Arabia, Kuwait and the emirates through military contracts and occupy military bases in these countries.

Through the Balkan wars and the war against Yugoslavia, the US imperialists gained control over oil sources in the Caspian Sea and Central Asia and supply routes from there to the Mediterranean. The NATO expanded to the southern flanks of Russia and the US acquired military access and basing rights in various East European countries.

In the US imperialist war against Afghanistan, the US military gained access and basing rights in former Soviet republics in Central Asia, increased US control over the sources of oil in the Caspian Sea and Central Asia and control over oil pipeline routes across Afghanistan and Pakistan down to the Arabian sea coast and the Indian Ocean.

The second US war of aggression against Iraq has enabled the US to gain direct control over the second largest oil reserves of the world, grab the reconstruction contracts, acquire US military bases right in the middle of the Middle East, further reconfigure the Middle East politics in favor of both the US and Israel, tighten US control over oil production in the OPEC and beyond and place all oil-deficient countries, including Germany, Japan and China, under US oil blackmail.

Definitely, successes in grabbing more economic territory and more control over oil sources and supply routes have strengthened the US. That is one side of the picture. But the other side is that it is becoming ever more overextended and vulnerable to the resistance of the oppressed peoples and nations and countries assertive of national independence. Furthermore, its contradictions with the other imperialist powers are sharpening.

Q34. I have observed since 1991 that the anti-war mass movement has a tendency to slow down after the US succeeds in a war of aggression. Why? What should be done?

The anti-war mass movement has the potential to grow large because it has a just cause. The people easily respond to this cause and give it a broad character, with discernible Left, Middle and Right sections. All sections united on the slogan, "stop the war". When a war of aggression succeeds, the Right section of the anti-war movement can pull the middle towards demoralization and quiescence with slogans of imperialist triumphalism, bourgeois pacifism and religious pacifism.

The results of a successful war of aggression are as outrageous as the preparation for and conduct of that war. Take the example of the successful US war of aggression against Iraq. The US occupation of Iraq and grabbing of the oil fields are exceedingly outrageous and should be able to generate more mass protests in a continuing anti-war movement.

To make that possible, it is necessary to have proletarian revolutionaries at the core of the Left section and, in effect, at the core of the entire anti-war mass movement. As the most comprehensive and most consistent anti-imperialists, they should strive to draw up the strategy and tactics. They should be able to adjust slogans according to developments in the war and the overall situation in order to keep on raising the level of consciousness and militancy in the anti-war movement. Under all circumstances, they should keep the broad and mass character of the anti-war movement, with the Left strengthening itself, winning over the Middle and taking advantage of the splits within the Right.

The anti-war movement should be closely linked with the movement against "free market" globalization on a common anti-imperialist basis. The two movements may be distinguishable but they are necessarily connected. They involve the rights and interests of the people and they mobilize the same forces and masses. One movement helps the other and easily merges with the other, whether the stress is on the anti-war movement or on opposing neo-liberal super-exploitation.

Q35. Like its imperialist predecessors, will not the US decline or even fall abruptly from its perch? Can you give us an idea of how US hegemony can unravel?

US imperialism has been in decline since the 1970s. But as I have earlier pointed out, it has been able to cover up this fact by borrowing funds heavily from abroad for consumerism, by appearing triumphant relative to the Soviet Union upon its disintegration and by taking the lead in the production of high-tech weaponry and electronic consumer goods.

But the US is rotten to the core in an all-round way. It is now seriously afflicted by economic and financial crisis. It seeks to solve this crisis by whipping up war hysteria, promoting state terrorism on a global scale, unleashing wars of aggression, stepping up war production and grabbing oil resources abroad. It is using its high-tech weapons of mass destruction and mass deception in order to impose its will on other countries.

The US is already overextended and is still trying to overreach. It has spread too many tentacles that are vulnerable to counter-attacks by revolutionary peoples all over the world and by countries that assert national independence. The US seems extremely successful in gaining relatively new footholds in Eastern Europe, the Middle East, Central Asia and South Asia and completing the encirclement of China and Russia.

It might push its luck too far too soon by bullying Syria and Iran and by dictating on China to tell North Korea what to do under pain of suffering economic sanctions, especially oil embargo. It tends to become more and more arrogant and to overplay its hand because of its high-tech military weaponry and its control of the oil sources and supply routes.

But such overreaching and arrogance will ultimately work against the US imperialists as the oppressed peoples and nations oppose and struggle against them, as governments assert national independence, as imperialist rivals resent and begin to resist extreme US rapacity and as the proletariat and petty bourgeois in the imperialist countries rise up against the dire consequences of the crisis of monopoly capitalism, such as mass unemployment, deteriorating social conditions and the growing trends of chauvinism, racism, fascism and war.

Let us not underestimate or discount what the oppressed nations and peoples can achieve by way of armed resistance to attempts at recolonizing them. After succeeding in blitzkriegs first against Afghanistan and then Iraq, US and puppet troops are now faced with guerrilla warfare and are at the receiving end of rifle fire and rocket-propelled grenades. Driven to hold on to its big gains from aggression, the US is falling into one quagmire after another.

Q36. In an earlier essay, you wrote that it takes three to four decades for an interregnum to run between the highest peaks in the global revolutionary struggle of the proletariat. Do you think that it will take some more time before a new peak is reached?

In that essay, I refer to decades between the 1848 workers' uprisings and the 1871 Paris Commune, between the latter and the 1917 October Socialist Revolution; and again between the latter and the rise of several socialist countries and many more national liberation movements after World War II.

If we consider as the last peak of the world proletarian revolution the 1975 liberation of Indochina and the 1966-76 Great Proletarian Cultural Revolution in China, it is about time in this decade for a revolutionary mass upsurge on a global scale.

In nearly three decades, great setbacks have occurred to the socialist cause due to modern revisionism and the undisguised restoration of capitalism, and to the cause of national liberation due to neo-colonialism. Imperialism has inflicted so much suffering on the proletariat and the people.

It is high time for the broad anti-imperialist movement and the world proletarian revolution to surge forward in the face of the rapidly worsening crisis of the world capitalist system. The proletariat and the people of the world have no other recourse but to intensify their struggle for national liberation, democracy and socialism against the unprecedented rapacity and terrorism of the imperialists and their puppets. We can look forward to a better world.

Appendix One

Sympathy for the Victims and Condemnation of Terrorism

18 September 2001

By Jose Maria Sison
Founding Chairman & General Consultant, International League of Peoples' Struggle (ILPS) & Chairman, International Network for Philippine Studies (INPS)

I wish to express the deepest sympathy for the thousands of civilian victims, including a considerable number of Filipinos and Filipino-Americans, in the deadly terrorist attacks in the United States on 11 September 2001. Said victims were in the twin towers of the World Trade Center and in four hijacked planes.

I extend sincerest condolences to the families and friends of those who died in the tragic event. I am sad that ordinary civilians take the main brunt of terrorist acts done in obvious retaliation against the long history and current acts of terrorism of US imperialism.

Customary laws and international conventions set the standard for the conduct of war in a civilized world in contrast with a barbaric one. Such a standard prohibits acts of terrorism against the civilian population, condemns crimes against humanity and requires respect for human rights and humanitarian conduct towards the civilian population and hors de combat.

Terrorism may be defined as the willful and malicious infliction and threat of death and other physical harm on innocent civilians. The US no less has been a notorious perpetrator of terrorism on a scale far larger than what is now being alleged against the private group of Osama bin Laden. But the people in the US should not be targeted for mass slaughter for the terrorist crimes of the US imperialists.

In recent times, the US officialdom and mass media have dished up as acts of humanitarianism and as audio-visual entertainment the mass destruction of human lives in Iraq and Yugoslavia through the use of US high-tech air power and cruise missiles on the civilian population and their social infrastructure.

The US and Israel have practically converted Palestine into a slaughterhouse for the Palestinian people. With overweening arrogance, US President Bush has encouraged the Sharon regime to destroy Palestinian lives and property at will.

The US has a long record of terrorism. It is responsible for the massacre of hundreds of thousands or nearly 10 percent of the Filipino people in the course of the Filipino-American war. It is also responsible for the massacre of more than a hundred thousand Japanese civilians in a matter of seconds in the atom bombing of Hiroshima and Nagasaki. It is further responsible for the massacre of millions of civilians in Korea, Indonesia, Indochina and elsewhere in the course of the Cold War.

The US has practiced the evil of terrorism for so long and this is now recoiling upon the US itself. The imperialist hyperpower is now reaping the whirlwind of terrorism that it has sown all over the world. Some of the adversaries of the US now consider as fair game the killing of American and other civilians in the same malignant spirit that the US does not wince at wreaking direct or collateral damage at the expense of civilian populations abroad.

In one more sense, the US is responsible for generating terrorism as its own Frankenstein. Even Osama bin Laden, the main suspect of the US in the 11 September terrorist attacks, is a former protégé of the US in fighting the Soviet armed forces in Afghanistan in the course of the Cold War.

At any rate, no amount of terrorism perpetrated by the US imperialists can justify any avowed anti-US force in perpetrating terrorism against the American people. Justice must be rendered to the victims in the 11 September terrorist attacks just as it must be rendered to the millions of victims of US imperialist terrorism.

It is now clear that the US is vulnerable to acts of terrorism arising from the contradictions within the American Right, between the US and its puppets-turned-enemies and among the imperialist powers. Such contradictions are intensifying under conditions of the worsening crisis of the world capitalist system.

The US monopoly bourgeoisie and policy-makers are increasingly self-conscious about the vulnerability of the US but they are callously using this to rationalize the suppression of the democratic rights of the people in the US and abroad. They are becoming even more hell-bent on oppressing and exploiting the people of the world.

Since the 1950s, it has become clear that the Atlantic and the Pacific Oceans can no longer protect the US from nuclear-tipped intercontinental ballistic missiles. Now, it is also becoming clear that a national missile defense system cannot protect the US from biological weapons, "luggage bombs" (miniaturized nuclear weapons in suitcases) and from hijacked jumbo jets or explosive-laden trucks.

As a consequence of the terrorist attacks in its homeground, the entire US officialdom (the Bush regime with bipartisan support) is trying to push its own colossal kind of terrorism under the pretext of fighting terrorism. Bush has received from the US Congress war-making powers similar to those given to Lyndon B. Johnson after the US-fabricated Tonkin Gulf incident and has received an initial funding of 40 billion USD.

The US has already identified the band of Osama bin Laden as the main suspect in the 11 September terrorist attacks. And yet, US State Secretary Colin Powell has declared that the US will make a "global assault" on "terrorism in general" throughout the world. US vice president Cheney and other high officials have called for the most unbridled kind of dirty tricks, such as the unlimited hiring of human rights violators and other unsavory characters and the lifting of the ban on assassination of leaders opposed to US imperialism.

The US is now using the incident as a pretext for expanding extraterritorial powers for the benefit of its military forces abroad and for launching all sorts of terrorism against the peoples that wage revolution, nations that fight for liberation and states that assert their independence. We can therefore expect more US acts of aggression, intervention and other acts of terrorism from the US and from its most servile allies and puppets.

In abject servility to the US, the Macapagal-Arroyo regime in the Philippines has volunteered the use of the Philippines again as a base for US aggression and intervention as in the past in connection with the Korean War, the Vietnam War, the Gulf War and other armed conflicts. The Filipino people must resist such scheme of the US and the puppet regime.

The people of the world, including progressive American forces, should forewarn the American people not to be carried away by jingoism, war hysteria and the anti-Arab and anti-Muslim drumbeat. The US imperialists should not be allowed to run berserk with their own brand of terrorism and to obscure their responsibility for the worsening socioeconomic crisis, the reemergence of fascism and the growing danger of war.

By unleashing acts of terrorism in the world, the US can only generate hatred for US imperialism and rouse the just revolutionary resistance of the people of the world. At the same time, it will continue to provoke such terrorists as those responsible for the 11 September terrorist attacks to give the US a dose of its own medicine.

Terrorism from any quarter is reprehensible and must be combated and eradicated. The people will ultimately defeat US imperialism as it increasingly uses terrorism. The few avowedly anti-US elements that use terrorism will only destroy themselves on the road of nihilism.

Only the revolutionary mass movement can defeat US imperialism and the local reactionaries and sweep away terrorism from any direction. As the crisis of the world capitalist system worsens and deepens, the revolutionary mass movement of the proletariat and the people in general is rising and carrying forward the anti-imperialist and socialist cause.

Appendix Two

The Sison Way

By Ninotchka Rosca

(Partly drawn from the book *Jose Maria Sison: At Home in The World*, scheduled for release by the Open Hand Publishing House.)

It seems too absurd for words: one man at the cross-hairs of the state powers of the United States, Canada, Europe and the Philippines. A man who has been deprived of a home and a country for the past decade; whose time has been largely occupied with writing, speaking, discussing. . . But once in a rare while, someone so different from the common pale that includes you and me manages to compel governments and organizations to reveal their true character.

In this case, by labeling Jose Maria Sison a "terrorist"—sans proof, sans process—freezing his and his wife's bank account (containing $1,000), and cutting off the pathetic Dutch government subsidy intended to keep him and his family at subsistence-level existence—all these actions were so palpably unjust and unwarranted, and so grossly insulting of the Filipino people, that they unmasked those who advocated them as anti-democratic, violators of human and civil rights, and just plain fascists.

As soon as Mr. Sison's most recent troubles became public, a flood of inquiries came my way: does he need help? What kind of help? Shall we start a collection? How about a medical team? One batch of students wanted to send a monthly food-care package.

Many who offered help were non-political. Some I hadn't even met. Underlying their concern was a feeling of deep personal insult, as though they themselves had been labeled "terrorist." Mr. Sison, after all, was symbol for a people's stellar resistance against a dictatorship, against the tyrannical socio-economic system which had weighed and continues to weigh down the Philippine archipelago. He is one of the few living legends of the Philippines.

Knowing the Man

Who is he? One could list down a chronicle of his life: born February 8, 1939, same day as Claro M. Recto, so that whenever students held the C.M. Recto lecture series at the University of the Philippines, they also celebrated Sison's birthday; *cum laude*, major in English – i.e., literature (not political science, as many assume); founded the *Kabataang Makabayan*, (Patriotic Youth), thus creating both the idea and the reality of people's organizations for the Philippine archipelago; founded or co-founded a host of other organizations; inspired the founding of still more organizations; re-established the Communist Party of the Philippines in 1968 and directly led it until his capture in 1977; spent more than eight years in prison; was heavily tortured and held incommunicado. Released in 1986, he founded the Partido ng Bayan and was then forced into exile in Holland where he has spent the last decade. He is the author of the seminal books *Struggle for National Democracy* and under the nom de guerre Amado Guerrero, *Philippine Society and Revolution*, *Specific Characteristics of Our People's War*, and *Our Urgent Tasks*.

Or one could list down some personal items: he is married to Julieta de Lima; they have four children together; he likes to dance; he likes to do karaoke, Frank Sinatra's "My Way" in particular which he sings "Mao's way;" he likes to play pranks on old friends; he has a very strong sense of pride matched by an occasional disregard for his own safety; he is restless but can focus for hours on work to be done; he has strengths; he has weaknesses – he would be the first to admit both, objectively.

But a person is not reducible to a simple recitation of bio-data or an accounting of what he/she is like as an individual. A person's true measure comes from an amalgam of what he/she has done, what he/she is and the impact of his/her being and activities on the community, on humankind, as it were, plus how he is perceived by that community. One has to sum up both on the individual and collective level, summarizing both the objective (what he/she accomplished) and the subjective (how were those activities received by others) impact of his/her existence.

A Legacy to His People

Jose Maria Sison's growth and practice as a Marxist and revolutionary endowed the Philippine people's movement with characteristics unique and indelible to this day. In 1961, he led university students in overrunning the congressional witchhunt of the UP faculty members, scattering the congressmen and bringing the proceedings to a halt. Multiplied a thousand times over, this method of protest would translate itself into People Power, strong enough to overthrow two presidents, though not yet, as he himself warns, an entire political system.

The vital role that youth organizations—growing from Prof. Sison's tiny SCAUP in 1959 to the KM in 1964 to the Movement for a Democratic Philippines (MDP) in 1970 – played in the country's near-instant politicization meant that the young would always have a special place in the country's political evolution. As he himself says, a movement without young people was in trouble. By the time he went underground in 1969, the KM was 20,000 strong. It was also center and core of interlocking alliances, both formal and informal, of student and youth organizations. At its full strength in the 1970-1972 period, the youth movement could mobilize up to 150,000 for demonstrations and rallies in Manila alone. More than this, it was the young who read, wrote, debated and discussed, who went to factories and fields to organize, ignoring danger and difficulties, all on a matter of principle. Under Prof. Sison's inspiration, they created a lexicon—"the three isms," "tuta" (puppet) and even "ingat" (be careful) which replaced the feudal "sige"—instantly understandable in the 7,100 islands, despite 150 languages.

Because he was himself a voracious reader and prodigious writer, Prof. Sison conferred an almost tradition of scholarship on radical Filipinos. As in no other place in the world has a people meticulously documented their own political development. Organizations churned out statements, flyers, press releases, etc., at the first hint of an issue or controversy. For a while, every organization had a comprehensive program or vision-mission-goal document, plus a welter of explicatory materials. Where books were a luxury and where the tradition was oral, this was a new and intense thing. The educational materials created a clarity of politics and political intent, where hitherto obscurantism and obtuse language had prevailed.

Because he was a poet, Prof. Sison also left the mass movement a tradition of culture-making. The KM had its own cultural arm, starting as a Cultural Bureau which eventually metamorphosed into the Panday Sining

(Art Smithy). All basic organizations, especially those of workers, peasants, women and the youth, would have their own cultural groups. Writers and artists also self-organized to participate in the people's movement. To this day, most of the country's leading writers and artists arose out of or still belong to the national democratic movement. The drive to know one's historical self created the artistic impulse to integrate modern content with traditional art forms and music. Given that as "serfs" of imperialism, Filipinos were supposed to be consumers of culture created elsewhere, this insistence on creativity helped consolidate the people's sense of self and self-respect.

When Prof. Sison submitted a draft political report in the early 1960s evaluating the leadership of the old Communist Party of the Philippines, the act had a subtext: errors and mishaps were sources of lessons. Pride, ego and "face" could not be allowed to stop any revolutionary from learning those lessons, in the interest of advancing the movement. To date, assessment and evaluation, small and large summing-ups, remain integral to the activist life, as strengths and weaknesses are identified and methodologies refined.

The involvement of Julieta de Lima in all of his undertakings undoubtedly inspired the idea of women's formal involvement in politics and the revolution. The KM had its women's bureau, designed to recruit and train women for activism and leadership. This was both new and yet a continuance of tradition. The Philippines had a women's political movement long before anyone else and the babaylan (local priestesses) led the first resistance against Spanish colonialism and Christianity. By formally acknowledging the critical value of women to a political movement, indeed to a revolutionary movement, Sison paved the way for women's historic strength to emerge from feudal/patriarchal suppression. The KM Women's Bureau is generally acknowledged as ancestress of both the underground MAKIBAKA (Malayang Kilusan ng Bagong Kababaihan—Free Movement of New Womanhood) and GABRIELA, the largest and most militant open women's alliance in the archipelago.

By giving up a life of comfort, by electing to go underground, by involving himself not only in leading but also immersing himself in revolutionary armed struggle, Prof. Sison hammered home the ideal of praxis: as you say life should be lived, so should your own life be lived. His life and work exemplified the unity of theory and practice. Armchair or cappuccino political theorists have not been held in any kind of respect in the Philippines ever since.

By his life as well, Prof. Sison made vivid the truth that even as circumstances forged a person, so could a person forge circumstances. Among a people brainwashed into fatalism, one of whose constant phrases was bahala na (it's up to god), this lesson was profound.

These unique characteristics would evolve and become the hallmarks of Philippine militancy. The organizations he led—from the KM to the CPP to the NPA—summed up these virtues in succinct phrases (*serve the people; dare to struggle, etc.*) and spread them throughout the archipelago. Such clarity of purpose and clarity of action enabled the people to weather decades of the Marcoses as well as demoralization over succeeding Philippine regimes. They helped the revolutionary movement weather four decades of repression and suppression.

No Dutch Treats

The minute we learned that Holland was placing the squeeze on Prof. Sison and Filipino exiles in the country, we stopped buying Dutch products. So no *queso de bola* (gouda or edam) for the holidays; no flights on KLM; no Philips appliances; no Shell gasoline for cars. Heck, I wouldn't even go Dutch treat!

The subtext to labeling Jose Maria Sison a "terrorist" was that to have a modicum of relief from political persecution even in our late years, we Filipinos would have to tread the imperialist way – i.e., survive through corruption and betrayal, never being true to ourselves and our people, without dignity and self-respect, without originality and creativity. In short, we had to slave ourselves to imperialism and live on the fringe of society, turning ourselves into junior versions (which are never good enough) of our colonizers.

Otherwise, what was done to Prof. Sison could be—and will be—done to every foreign-born person in The Netherlands, or Europe, or the United States or Canada.

And how does one counter the combined threat from the governments of the US, Canada and the whole of Europe? Being a simple storyteller, a *hamak na manunulat*, I can only offer a small tale. This happened recently, in the midst of a northeast autumn, in the alienating environment of a New Jersey suburb where a group of Filipino expatriates were hanging out in one of the houses. They were just having a good time, doing karaoke in the basement, pretending to be James Morrison, Madonna, Led Zeppelin.

Then someone punched in the "My Way" number. Myself not being a Sinatra fan, I voiced objections. But someone replied: "For JMS!" Instant silence, instant focus. And the whole group sang with feeling: "the record shows, he took the blows and did it OUR way!"

The governments of Europe, US, Canada and the Philippines keep trying to bury Jose Maria Sison and only succeed in having songs sung in his praise. In the midst of whatever adversity, Joma Sison constantly gives Filipinos a reason to affirm and celebrate themselves as a people. They should continue to do so, the Sison way.

INDEX

ACT 117
Afable, Silvestre 221, 236
Aguinaldo, Emilio 9
Aguinaldo, Rodolfo 219, 222, 229, 232–33
Aguirre, Alexander 67
Albert, Carlos 44
Alejandro, Lean 54, 93
Almendral, Ariel 59
Amnesty to suspected revolutionaries 56
Anti-imperialist movement
  and anticommunist thinking 192–93
Anti-subversion Law 39, 45, 66
Anti-war mass movement 240–41
  protests against Iraq war 238
Aquino, Benigno 23, 56, 58–59, 89, 93, 117
  assassination of 27
Aquino, Corazon C. 55, 94, 115
  becomes president 29
  declares war on revolutionaries 31, 54
  runs against Marcos 28
Aquino regime 115, 119, 152
  as comprador-landlord regime 90
  economic policy of 91
  Sison's issues with 93
  vs. Marcos regime 90
Araneta, Salvador 40
Armacost formula 95
Axis of evil 184

Bagong Alyansang Makabayan. *See* BAYAN (New Patriotic Alliance)
Bagong Hukbong Bayan. *See* NPA (New People's Army)
Baker, James 155
Barros, Lorena 51
BAYAN (New Patriotic Alliance) 5, 89, 115, 116, 117
Bayan Muna (The People First) 218
Bello III, Silvestre 66, 221, 236
Berroya, Reynaldo 58
Birondo, Alex 29
Boekman, Tom 61
Bonifacio, Andres 8–9, 80
Bourgeoisie
  big using petty 194
Boycott of National Elections (1986) 114–115
Brillantes, Sixto 40
Browning, Most Rev. Edmund 155
Buscayno, Bernabe 20, 21, 43, 54, 56, 93
  capture of 26
  release of 29
Bush administration 184, 186
  war on terrorism 220
Bush, George H. W. 167
Bush, George W. 1, 168–69
  pursuit of imperialist agenda 238

Capitalism 156
  growing stronger 165
  role of high technology in 166–67
Capulong, Romeo T. 224
Catholic Church
  part in overthrowing Marcos 28, 110
China
  economy 158
  reverses socialism 159
  rise of capitalism in 160–63, 171–72
Christians for National Liberation 110, 197
Cid, Cipriano 107
Civilian Armed Force Geographical Units (CAFGU) 55

Class struggle
bourgeoisie vs. capitalist 195
Committee DEFEND 230
Committee on Anti-Filipino Activities (CAFA) 40, 106
resistance against 11
Communist Party
breaking with the old party 108
founded in 1930 80
Communist Party of Indonesia (PKI) 13
disappearance of 14
Communist Party of the Philippines (CPP) 17, 76, 96, 108, 123, 150, 178, 200
achievements of 86
call for armed struggle 140–41
due process in 126
forging alliance between working class and peasant 207–8
freezing of bank accounts 231
growth under Marcos dictatorship 24–27
ideological problems in 1990s 128–30
impact of martial law on 110
maintaining strength in new international situation 164
named as terrorists 1–2, 46–47, 220, 225–26
organizational problems of 131–33
organizational victories of 137
organizing 39
political successes of 136–37
progress from 1968-1977 109
pushes study campaign in 1990s 131
re-establishment of 20–23, 42, 77, 86, 127
rebuilding in the 1960s 106–7
refuses amnesty offer 56
relations with CPSU 153
relations with other liberation movements 172
relations with ruling parties 173
seeking Soviet support 151
survival of 201
threats from within 125–27
work post-Marcos regime 31–33
working with national minorities 210
Communist Party Soviet Union (CPSU)
support of Marcos regime 153–54
Comprehensive Agreement on Respect for Human Rights 98–99, 223
Concepcion, Roberto 24
Congress of the Filipino People 85
Constitutional convention
purpose of 235–36
Corporations
financial collapse of 186
Corpus, Victor 22, 55, 119
Costs of waging armed revolution 201
Council of the European Union
terrorist list 1
CPP Constitution 78
Crisis of overproduction 181, 186, 190, 198
Cuba
revolution in 159
Culture
and revolution 19

David, Juan T. 52
De la Cruz, Nilo 57
De Lima, Julieta 12, 19
gives birth in prison 26
release from prison 88
De Venecia, Jose 67, 220, 221
De Villa, Renato 55
Del Mundo, Faustino 43
Democratic Alliance 10
Democratic revolution
led by Bonifacio 80
Diokno, Jose W. 23
Diokno, Maris 94
Drilon, Franklin 99

Eagleburger, Lawrence 155
Economic crisis
in capitalist nations 187
Engels, Friedrich 82
Enrile, Juan Ponce 28, 31, 53, 59
Ermita, Eduardo 221
Estrada, Joseph E. 57–58, 99, 100, 218

Estrada regime 99
ousting 100, 137
Evangelista, Crisanto 8, 9, 80

Fascism
rising in imperialist countries 187
Filipino-American War 46
First Quarter Storm of 1970 17, 42
Free Jose Maria Sison Committee 88
Free market economy 194
"Free market" globalization 166, 197, 199, 241
results of 181–82

GABRIELA 19, 27, 117
Garcia, Enrique Voltaire 15, 23
Globalization 192
Golez, Roilo 225
Great Proletarian Cultural Revolution 161, 164–65
GRP (Government of the Republic of Philippines) 217
Guerrero, Amado. *See* Sison, Jose Maria
Guide for Establishing the People's Democratic Government 78, 109

Hague Joint Declaration 97
High technology
use in socialist society 190–91
Hitler, Adolf 196
HMB (People's Liberation Army) 6, 8, 10, 105
Hoffman, Paul 155
Human rights litigation against the Marcos estate 67–71, 228
Human rights violations 101, 110

Imperialism
and national independence 184
as moribund capitalism 198
use of bigotry, ethnic conflict, chauvinism 196–97
vs. oppressed peoples 183–84

Imperialist powers
redivision of world among 198, 239
settling their differences 185
India
pressured to open economy 158
International Campaign for the Asylum of the Sison Family 66
International Conference of Marxist-Leninist Parties and Organizations (ICMLPO) 173
International League of Peoples' Struggle (ILPS) 176, 192
International League of Peoples' Struggles (ILPS)
founding congress of 2
International Monetary Fund/World Bank (IMF/WB)
loans to Marcos regime 25
International Seminar on Mao Zedong Thought 174
International Seminar on People's War 175–76
Internationalism 143–44, 191
vs. national interests 144–45
Islamic fundamentalism 196

Jalandoni, Luis 31, 34, 94, 95, 97–98, 221
Japan
as economic power 158
Joint Agreement on Safety and Immunity Guarantees (JASIG) 223
Jones, Gregg 55
Justice for All (JAJA) 27
Justice for Aquino 27

Kabataang Makabayan. *See* KM (Patriotic Youth)
KADENA 117
Kampanyang Ahos (Garlic Campaign) 29, 124, 125, 126, 133
Katipunan 9
Kilusang Mayo Uno. *See* KMU (May First Movement)

Kintanar, Galileo 57
Kintanar, Romulo 57, 133, 139, 229, 232–33
KM (Patriotic Youth) 5, 14, 18, 84, 107
 cultural arm of 19
 growing membership in 1967 15–16
 Women's Bureau 19
KMP 117
KMU (May First Movement) 26, 117
Kompil. *See* Congress of the Filipino People
Koppe, Victor 224

La Tondeña workers' strike 111
Labor export
 luring workers back to Philippines 211
 policy 89
Lacaba, Emmanuel 21, 84
Lacsina, Ignacio 106
Lacson, Panfilo 58
Lagman, Filemon 57, 133
Laurel, Jr., Salvador 23
Laurel-Langley Agreement 24, 41
Lava, Jesus 10–11, 13, 17, 77, 81, 105
Lava, Jose 10, 81
Lava, Vicente 81, 152
Left opportunism 118–19
 and damage to CPP 123–24, 130
 origins of 120–22
LFS 117
Liberal Party 58
Lichauco, Alejandro 23
Liwanag, Armando 134

Macapagal, Diosdado 14
Macapagal-Arroyo, Gloria 1, 101, 221, 225, 231
Macapagal-Arroyo regime 101, 229, 236, 238
MAKIBAKA 17, 19, 51
Malayang Kilusan ng Bagong Kababaihan. *See* MAKIBAKA
Marcos, Ferdinand E. 3, 14, 15, 16, 27, 67, 68, 88–89
 and Plaza Miranda bombing 59
 becomes dictator 24
 death of 29
 imposes martial law 3, 23–27, 89
 named antifascist hero 154
 overthrow of 28
 return to Philippines 90
Marcos, Imelda 16, 29
Marcos regime
 economic policy of 88–89
 human rights violations of 111
 sham land reform program 121
 suppression campaign in the 1970s 110
 vs. post-Marcos regimes 101–2
Martial law 3, 23–27, 42, 59, 89, 110
Marx, Karl 82
Marxism-Leninism 77, 82, 145–46
 disintegration of 160
MASAKA (Free Association of Peasants) 44
Mass activism 41–42, 84, 86
 against U.S. military bases 117
 decline of 119, 130
 during Marcos regime 89
 factor in overthrowing Marcos 114
 ignited in the 1960s 106
 in the West 177
 legal 137
 urban-based 117
Mijares, Primitivo 59
Mindanao Commission 121
Moro Islamic Liberation Front 197
Moro Revolutionary Organization 197
Movement for a Democratic Philippines (MDP) 18, 23
Movement for the Advancement of Nationalism 84, 108
Movement of Concerned Citizens for Civil Liberties 23

"National unity" government 231–32
Nationalist Alliance for Justice, Freedom and Democracy 27

NDFP (National Democratic Front of the Philippines) 2, 5, 77, 94, 97, 123
- alliances with religious organizations 197
- founding of 86
- objectives in peace talks 204–5
- peace talks with Aquino government 29, 30
- pressured to sign a final peace agreement 220, 222
- refuses amnesty offer 56
- relations with CPSU 153
- status of belligerency 98, 177, 206
- suspends peace talks 31

New democratic revolution 82, 114, 145
New International 191
New Katipunan 123
New world order 167–68
Nicaragua
- revolution in 159

Noble, Alexander 94
North Korea
- revolution in 159

NPA (New People's Army) 47–51, 57, 77, 96, 116, 119, 121, 122, 123–24, 141, 200, 233
- actions against US personnel 64
- building 109
- expansion of 136
- fighting strength in 1970s 113–14
- founding of 20–23, 86
- freezing of bank accounts 231
- Macapagal-Arroyo declares war on 225
- mass base building and land reform 136
- named as terrorists 1–2, 17, 46–47, 220, 225–26
- reorganization in 1990s 131

Nuclear war
- possibility of 186

October 24th Movement 15
Olalia, Felixberto 107
Olalia, Rolando 31, 53, 92
- funeral march of 117

Olympia 125, 133
Operation Missing Link 125, 126, 133
Ople, Blas 226
Our Urgent Tasks 78, 109
Oxales, Manuel 56

Panday Sining (Art Smithy) 19
Paquiz, Samuel 59
Partido ng Bayan. *See* PnB (The People's Party)
Peace negotiations 2, 3, 56–57, 90, 94, 96, 97, 99, 177, 218, 232, 236
- and armed struggle 140–41, 204–5, 237
- "final peace agreement" 236
- NDFP terms for resumption 233–34
- recess of 3, 219
- support of European nations 206
- suspension of 31

People's Army Against Japan 10
"People's Power" uprising 116
Philippine Civic Action Group (PhilCAG) 15
Philippine Crisis and Revolution 93
Philippine Insurgency 9
Philippine Society and Revolution 78, 109
Philippine-American War 9
Philippines
- and Vietnam War 14
- becomes an American colony 9
- class demarcation 8
- economic collapse 96
- economic decline 27
- fighting against US intervention 203
- foreign debt during Marcos regime 16
- future of revolutionary movement in 200
- imposition of martial law 23–27
- Japanese invasion of 9–10
- language barriers 8
- pillage and depletion of natural resources under Marcos 25
- poverty in 12, 25, 27
- Spanish control of 8

US domination of 6, 42
US economic control of 10
US presence in 16
writes new constitution 30
Piopongco, Jaime 69, 70, 71
PKP (Communist Party of the Philippines) 8
birth of 9
fall of 17
legalization of 9
merge with PSP 9
post-World War II 10–11
Plaza Miranda bombing 55, 56, 58–60, 66, 220
PnB (People's Party) 147
Sison launches 30
Powell, Colin 1
Program for a People's Democratic Revolution 78
Prudente, Nemesio 93

Quimpo, Nathan 65

Ramos, Fidel V. 15, 28, 54, 55, 67, 95–96, 119
becomes president 56
Ramos regime 95–96
economic policy of 96
Sison's struggles against 97
Reaganism 156
Rectification movement 32–33, 71, 72, 96, 124, 125, 127, 132–33
and women 139
First Great Rectification Movement 86, 108, 127
guiding principles of 128
impact of 135–38
resistance to 133–35
Second Great Rectification Movement 4, 127, 129, 135, 164
Rectify Errors and Rebuild the Party 78
Reform the Armed Forces Movement (RAM) 28, 116
amnesty of 95
OPLAN God Save the Queen 30, 53, 55
targets Sison 30, 31
Revolutionary Guide to Land Reform 78, 109
Revolutionary movements
building 82
currently fighting imperialism 184
factor in toppling Marcos 89
importance of theory 189
in the Third World 182
international support for 92, 149
organization of 79
rebuilding in the 1960s 105
why people join 76
Reyes, Angelo 225, 236
Right opportunism 118
origins of 122–23
threat to revolution 124–25, 130
Roces, Chino 23
Rowe, James 64
Roxas, Gerry 59
Russia
capitalism in 171
post-Cold War 171

Salas, Rodolfo 113, 121
Salonga, Jovito 56, 59, 71, 72, 95
Santos, Antero 51
September 11 attacks 169–70, 182–83, 186, 225, 238
Sison response to 220
Serrano, Don Leandro 7
Siazon, Domingo 67
Sin, Cardinal Jaime 28, 55, 110
Sison, Don Gorgonio 7
Sison, Francisco 68, 69, 70
Sison, Jose Maria 5
activism in college 11–12
adopting working class position 81
as trade union activist 41, 81
assassination attempts on 42–44, 53, 54–57, 57–58
asylum in the Netherlands 60–65, 93
becoming a communist 145–46
bounty on his head 49, 56
called a communist 44–45
cancellation of passport 60, 93

capture and torture of 26, 51–52, 86–87, 112–13
charged with subversion 60
charges dropped against 66, 222
coming from landlord class 83
demands dismantling of US bases 64
denial of US visa 154–56
early schooling 7
enemy surveillance of 40–41
fight against Marcos regime 88
goes into exile 31, 54
life with NPA 47–51
loses teaching fellowship 40
named as terrorist 1–2, 46, 220, 223, 225–26
on writing poetry 83
political writings 150
recognized as political refugee 61, 66
regains title of professor 29
release from prison 29
results of terrorist label 223–24, 227–29
revives Marxist movement in 1968 20–23
threat of extradition to the US 224
threats against 212, 213, 219
work with revolutionary movement 79
writing in exile 71, 72
writing in prison 26, 52
writings 78

Socialism 77
building 82
decline of 162–63
establishing 190
in imperialist countries 187
re-emergence of 188–89
women in 208

Socialist Party of the Philippines (PSP)
merge with PKP 9

Soldiers of the Filipino People (SFP) 56

Solidarity organizations
support of CPP 151–52

Soviet Union
and Cold War with US 156
betrayal of socialism 159, 160
disintegration of 162

Spanish-American War 9

Special operations teams (SOTs) 119

Specific Characteristics of People's War in the Philippines 78, 109

Struggle for National Democracy 17, 78, 107

Student Cultural Association of the University of the Philippines (SCAUP) 5, 11, 18, 40, 106

Sukarno 14, 44

Tabara, Arturo 57, 133

Tañada, Lorenzo M. 23, 42, 94, 115

Tañada, Wigberto 94

Taruc, Luis 10

Taruc, Peregrino 11

Terrorism
not in GRP penal code 222
state 237
war on 183, 220

Thatcherism 156

Trade union movement 106

Unemployment 187

United States
agreements for air bases in Philippines 27
and Cold War with USSR 156
as imperialist power 157–58
bombing of Japan 170
breaking the US power monopoly 171–72
CIA campaign against Sison 55, 64–65
conflicts with allies 197
control over oil resources 168, 185, 197, 239–40
domination of Philippines 6, 42
economic crisis 166, 181
imperialism 46–47, 77, 101, 102, 143–44, 156, 170, 183, 239–40
decline of 241–
intervention in GRP affairs 238
mass actions against US military bases 41

military intervention in the Philippines 202, 222
policy toward China 199
practicing state terrorism 237–38
preparing for war with NPA 202–3
presence in Philippines 16
removal of military bases in Philippines 117, 203
support of Aquino regime 91
support of military rule in Philippines 102
use of military force in Middle East and Far East 170
US-RP Military Bases Agreement 94, 99
US-RP Mutual Defense Treaty 202

Van Hoof, G.J.H. 63
Vietnam War 14–16, 42
Villalobos, Joaquin 121
Visiting Forces Agreement 99, 202

Walter-McCarran Act 46, 155
Wars of aggression 237, 239
by US and allies 182, 184, 185
Weinglass, Leonard 155
Women's movement 204
in Philippines 19
role in revolutionary movement 76, 138–40
role in socialism 208
uprising after Aquino assassination 27
writings 139–40
Worker resistance
trade union strikes 26
Workers' Party 84

Xiaoping, Deng 159, 161, 164, 165

Yap, Jose V. 56, 94, 97
Youth movement 18, 76, 107
growth of 138
importance of 209–10

Zedong, Mao 45, 46, 174
Zumel, Antonio 3, 212